UNEARTHED

Storied Artifacts and Remarkable Predecessors of the Saint Joseph's College Campus

Steven L. Bridge, Ph.D.

© 2016 Steven L. Bridge

Saint Joseph's College Press
278 Whites Bridge Road
Standish, ME 04084

ISBN-13 978-0-9983467-0-0

All rights reserved. No part of this publication may be reproduced, distributed, or transmitted in any form or by any means, including photocopying, recording, or other electronic or mechanical methods, without the prior written permission of the author, except in the case of brief quotations embodied in critical reviews and certain other noncommercial uses permitted by copyright law. For permission requests, please contact the author via email sbridge@sjcme.edu or at the address below:

Dr. Steven L. Bridge
c/o Saint Joseph's College Press
278 Whites Bridge Road
Standish, ME 04084

Library of Congress Control Number: 2016959043

November, 2016

To my wife, Camilla,

and my daughters,

Heather, Erica, and Emily

because I dig them the most.

un·earth

/ənˈərth/

Verb, past tense: unearthed

> 1. To find (something) in the ground by digging.
> <u>Synonyms</u>: dig up, excavate, exhume, disinter, root out, unbury.
> *Example:* "The workers unearthed a fossil."
>
> 2. To discover (something hidden, lost, or kept secret) by investigation or searching.
> <u>Synonyms:</u> discover, uncover, find, come across, stumble upon, hit on, bring to light, expose, turn up, hunt out.
> *Example:* "I unearthed an interesting fact."[1]

---

[1] From the Oxford Dictionary: en.oxforddictionaries.com.

Table of Contents

Foreword	ix
Editor's Preface	xii
Acknowledgements	xv
A User's Guide to this Book	xx
Introductory Section	xxii

Chapter 1 - Sr. Mary George O'Toole and the History of Saint Joseph's College	1
Chapter 2 - Michial Russell and the Founding of Pearsontown (Standish), Maine	11

Part I – Storied Artifacts and Remarkable Predecessors 24

Introduction to (Some of) Our the Storied Artifacts	25
Chapter 3 – Ingalls Brothers Coke Bottle	30
Chapter 4 – Jacob Ruppert Brewer Bottle	38
Chapter 5 – Haviland Teacup	43
Chapter 6 – Johnson's American Anodyne Liniment	47
Chapter 7 – Fr. John's Medicine Bottle	52
Chapter 8 – "Edison" Light Bulb	56
Chapter 9 – Rudolph Valentino Newspaper Clipping	63
Chapter 10 – Petticoat Whale Oil Lamp	69
Chapter 11 – Chinese Calligraphy Brush Wash Bowl	79
Chapter 12 – Virgin Mary Stone Relief	83
Chapter 13 – George Washington Inaugural Button	89
Introduction to Our Remarkable Predecessors	99
Chapter 14 - Moses Pearson	101
Chapter 15 - Samuel Deane	109
Chapter 16 - Sarah Jones Bradbury	121
Chapter 17 - Theophilus Bradbury	133
Chapter 18 - George Bradbury	146
Chapter 19 - Joshua Freeman	151
Chapter 20 - John Quinby	157
Chapter 21 - Jedediah Lombard, Jr.	163
Chapter 22 – The Ebenezer Shaw Family	169

Chapter 23 – Leonard Shaw 177
Chapter 24 - Owen P. Smith 188

Conclusion to Part I 198

Part II – Site Reports and Chains of Ownership 202

Introduction to the Site Reports 203
Chapter 25 – The "Curious Deer" Site 212
Chapter 26 – The "1926 Site" 220
Chapter 27 – The "Plateau Site" 230
Chapter 28 – The "Methuselah Site" 240

Introduction to the Campus Lots 247
Chapter 29 - Lot 64 and its Previous Owners 254
Chapter 30 – Lot 64/63 and its Previous Owners 258
Chapter 31 - Lot 63 and its Previous Owners 262

Crossing the Road.... 267
Chapter 32 - Lot 51 and its Previous Owners 268
Chapter 33 - Lot 52 and its Previous Owners 280
Chapter 34 - Lot 37 and its Previous Owners 298

Conclusion to Part II 306

Appendix A: Occupants of the Leonard Shaw Cemetery 310
Appendix B: Occupants of the Blake Cemetery 311
Appendix C: An Alphabetical Listing of All Lot Owners 312

Index 318

About the Author 321

Foreword

Saint Joseph's College is a special place for many reasons. One of these is the physical space we occupy—473 acres on the eastern shore of Sebago Lake, the second largest lake in Maine.

At its center, our academic community of 1500 people hums with the daily activities of class, work, and recreation. Every day, hundreds of people walk across campus on their way to class, to the Café, to a meeting. Most of the time, they are preoccupied by the business of the moment.

But every once in a while, as a member of the community moves from the core toward the periphery, he or she notices something not quite expected. The small graveyard tucked back in the woods between the residence halls and the athletic field—one of three on campus. Or the remnants of a stone foundation and cellar of a now long-gone structure, like the one just to the south of the main entrance. Who were these people? When did they live here? And what did they do?

Our standard histories of the College, offered to visitors as part of their tours and to new students, faculty and staff as part of orientations, provide part of the story—the part closest to us. Xavier Hall, an impressive Tudor structure which contains administrative offices, was named Woldbrook Hall by the Verrill family who had it built as the center of their country estate. Other reminders of the Verrills' time at Sebago are all around us. Saint George Hall, originally Ledgewood Hall, was a guest house. Mrs. Verrill's Stone Chapel, tucked down the hill behind Mercy Hall, played a pivotal role in the story of Saint Joseph's College.
But who was here before the College and before the Verrills? And why should we care?

Professor Steven Bridge has done us a great service in helping to answer the first of these questions. His exhaustive research—which can accurately be described as both figurative and literal "digging"—makes it possible for us to know something about these chronological neighbors. But the second question remains—why should we care?

There are many reasons, of course, including things like an appropriate sense of history or intellectual curiosity. But there are also deeper, more fundamental reasons.

At Saint Joseph's College our strong sense of "stewardship" shapes how we think about and act in many areas from care for our common home (stewardship of the earth) to care for each other as expressed through our core values of respect and compassion. Our sense of stewardship also extends to those areas that are not immediately before us spatially or temporally. We care about the past, and we care about the future. Equally importantly, we recognize the connections between the past and the future and our roles in making those connections.

In a book by the name of *Ceremonial Time*, John Hansen Mitchell explains his title as "a primitive concept in which past, present, and future can all be perceived in a single moment, generally during some dance or sacred ritual." "Ceremonial time" has an application in the contemporary world—it is that moment when we recognize that we are part of something larger than ourselves, something larger than what lies immediately in front of us. These moments of recognition are, at one and the same time, gift, obligation, and challenge.

The gift of knowing more about who was here before us, brings with it that obligation and challenge. The obligation is to keep that knowledge alive, to share it with others, to work to understand how the past—our past—shapes and informs who we are today. And the challenge is—as always—to make sure that those who come after us find a world that is better because we were here.

Professor Bridge's work is a gift to the College community and to all who care about what did, does, and can happen here. We welcome this newest, recovered chapter in the history of Saint Joseph's College of Maine.

Dr. Jim Dlugos
President
Saint Joseph's College

Editor's Preface

Webster's New World Dictionary defines the word "artifact" as "any object made by human work or skill." As such, Dr. Steven Bridge has created a living and contemporary artifact in this loving study honoring Maine's Saint Joseph's College by examining its terrestrial remains and the people to whom they once belonged.

It is an honor for me, as a person who has taught history to hundreds of Saint Joe's students throughout my thirty-two year tenure here, to join together with the other editors of this work, Dr. Edward Rielly (English) and Dr. Daniel Sheridan (Theology), to congratulate Steve on what is clearly a labor of love. And I stress the word labor - since anyone who opens the pages of this book will clearly recognize the countless hours of research the author expended painstakingly reviewing hundreds of documents and carefully exploring underground.

The most common or usual meaning of artifact has to do with those physical things that we leave behind. When our time is done at Saint Joe's—and even when Steve's retirement eventually arrives (albeit much further into the future due to his relative youth)—we will all want to feel that we have left something of value behind. Most teachers, with justification, point to their many students with whom they share hours in and out of the classroom, often in multiple courses (unless we frighten them away early on). We professors have all written and edited books. But this one is different. This is a book about our place, our home for many years; indeed, some of the most important years of our lives. The contribution of *Unearthed* will live on long after all of us have departed from the College, alive merely in the memories of our students and whatever changes we may have effected through our teaching, committee work, or administration. Steve's work will tell all who read it and walk this land the stories of long ago that connect us to our shared past and inspire us for our future.

With several notable and reported exceptions, the bulk of the people who inhabited these commonly shared lands were poor farmers, scratching out a meager existence through back-breaking labor upon Maine's famously poor, rock-strewn soils. My Irish grandmother from County Galway had a colorful expression very applicable also to Maine: "When you buy meat you buy bone, and when you buy land you buy stone!" Those farmers knew this instinctively, as did Steve, I'm sure, when he started digging into our campus's rocky soil in search of the small indicators that would lead him to larger stories. It was hard work, cultivating these lands, and hard work also digging for the artifacts they left behind. There are easier ways to do each, but these short-cuts do not usually reward the practitioner as thoroughly as by doing it the right way. Our predecessor farmers did it the right way and were prolific. And so did Steve Bridge. For their efforts, they are all to be congratulated and remembered. To further add to Steve's accomplishments and accolades, we should remember that he has been working outside his primary discipline of theology; nevertheless, Steve obviously pursued his research and writing "religiously" and with great discipline.

As a historian, I was especially fascinated by the many stories of the personalities involved in this intriguing tale. As a life-long resident of Portland, I was reminded again and again of the connections between any great city and its natural hinterland. Several of the families involved in this study spent many of their years in Maine's largest city. Nonetheless, the author connects them back, literally, to their roots in Pearsonstown, Standish, Windham and the Sebago Lakes regions that we all know and love. Local historians and historical societies, many of which have done and are now doing similar archaeological digs and research, will find much inspiration in *Unearthed*. I'm sure they will recognize many similar patterns of life and artifact remains in their own specific areas. For, in essence, what Steve Bridge has created for us all is a story of connections. Over time and place, between generations, urban and rural, and in so many other ways, we are all connected.

Finally, at the very start of this work, Steve pays tribute to the Sisters of Mercy who had the Courage and Hope ("Fortitudo et Spes") to move the College from its original home on Walton Street in Portland to its current residence on these grounds in Standish. Thank you, Steve, for showing the courage to venture beyond your own discipline and the hope that the fruits of your labor would not be in vain. Your colleague editors congratulate you and wish you and your family God's speed in this and all your other future endeavors.

Dr. Michael C. Connolly
Professor of History
Saint Joseph's College

Acknowledgements

I love Saint Joseph's College. I really do. I've got the greatest job in the world. Every day, I get to share that which I am most interested in, most passionate about, and most committed to with dozens of wide-eyed undergrads—the emerging leaders of the next generation. I relish my time in the classroom and the give and take of an academic exchange that promotes critical thinking and a greater understanding of the world in which we live. The College itself is a close-knit community of congenial faculty, cheerful staff, and competent administrators. Here, I've enjoyed a flexible schedule, institutional support, and meaningful recognition of my various research, teaching, and service projects. And I've found that its Mission and Core Values align so closely with my own that the advancement and promotion of the one inevitably seems to benefit the other. I really can't imagine a better "fit."

But I've discovered that my love for Saint Joseph's College extends well beyond my relationship to the institutional organization. I also love this *place*—the environs that comprise the physical campus. I swim these waters, run these trails, bike these paths, and skate these ponds. This is where I've cheered on sports teams, listened to concerts, attended bonfires, beheld sunsets, gazed upon fireworks, and marveled at meteor showers. These grounds are home to a veritable menagerie of woodland creatures. I've encountered deer, fox, bear, mink, porcupines, opossums, skunks, groundhogs, snowshoe hares, flying squirrels, muskrats, turtles, salamanders, bullfrogs, turkeys, herons, kingfishers, bald eagles, loons, grouse, tanagers, grosbeaks, waxwings, pileated woodpeckers, bluebirds...but no moose (at least, not so far). Then there are our domestic critters. At present, they include goats, sheep, alpacas, bunnies, and pigs. These reside at the farm, adjacent to the fields where my food is grown—the freshest of lettuce, tomatoes, peas, carrots, spinach, broccoli, beets, cucumbers, squash, and zucchini. I've also harvested apples, wild blueberries, raspberries, blackberries, and grapes all within the College's boundaries. This campus sustains me spiritually and socially as well. This is where I pray. It's where I met my wife. It's where we dated, got engaged, and were married. This is where I've watched my children grow. These grounds have proven to be such a tremendous blessing to me in so many ways that I can't help but consider them sacred. Like I said, I love Saint Joseph's College.

This book, and the project it represents, is a natural outgrowth of my deep affection for this place. It is a true labor of love...and I've enjoyed every minute of it. The considerable time, effort, and energy that I've invested have yielded results that, to be honest, have exceeded even my own wildest expectations. But for reasons that will quickly become apparent, I've had to keep these findings confidential. I have been anxiously awaiting the day when I could go public with this information—but I'm especially excited about sharing it with the Saint Joseph's community at large. I like to think of this work as my gift back to this place—a token of my appreciation for the countless blessings that this institution and its campus have bestowed upon me. It is in this spirit of gratitude that I primarily dedicate this work.

Beyond that, there are certain individuals to whom I owe additional debts of thanks. Let me begin with those whose historical works frame the boarders of my own: Albert Sears, Sister Mary Raymond Higgins, and Durward Ferland, Jr. Their research has provided a firm foundation upon which I have built. It is a tremendous privilege to join their company by adding this book to theirs.

Acknowledgements

I am grateful to Sister Mary George O'Toole for her steadfast commitment to Saint Joseph's College, and for her tireless promotion of its rich history. And I want to thank Michial Russell for the small but crucial role he played in piquing my interest in this matter.

As for my wife, Camilla, she deserves a Spouse-of-the-Year level of recognition. Like Mike, she played an instrumental role in setting me on this path. But since then, she has also served as my unwavering cheerleader, technological advisor, and patient partner throughout this (at times, all-consuming) process. I can honestly say that were it not for Camilla, this book would not exist. She has proven to be my godsend in every sense of that word.

I also want to thank Jim Dlugos, the President of Saint Joseph's College, for all of his encouragement and support. It was he who first suggested that I publish my results, so I was honored when he agreed to write the Foreword. Jim's presidency will undoubtedly be defined by the innovative ways in which the College is evolving. Yet even in the midst of so many progressive developments, Jim's interest in the campus's history remains evident. For that, I am grateful.

Finally, I owe a debt of gratitude to my editorial "dream team," Professors Michael Connolly, Edward Rielly, and Daniel Sheridan. I am fortunate to be able to tap into the expertise of such highly regarded scholars, and I am grateful for the time and effort each of these men put into reading the drafts of my manuscript prior to publication. Their recommendations—both large and small—have improved this work considerably. Any errors, omissions, or oversights contained within it are mine and mine alone. I readily acknowledge my own limitations with respect to this project, and would like to echo the humble sentiments of Dr. Samuel Deane (whom you will meet later):

> Amidst the laudable efforts that are now making to promote so excellent a design as the revival of [history], the writer of the following sheets is humbly attempting to throw in his mite. He has been more prompted to engage in so arduous an undertaking, by an opinion he has long entertained of the need of a work of this kind, adapted to the state and circumstances of this [College], than by any idea of his being thoroughly qualified to undertake it.[2]

Despite whatever shortcomings one may encounter here, my hope is that this little "mite" of mine might nevertheless accomplish its principle goal: to unearth a deeply buried and long-forgotten—yet extraordinarily rich—period of this campus's history.

---

[2] Samuel Deane, *The New-England Farmer* (Worcester, Mass.; Isaiah Thomas & Company, 1790), p. 2.

A User's Guide to this Book

All good publishers advise their authors to tailor their writings according to their projected audiences. The problem is that I'm straddling two worlds here. The academic in me wants to deliver something that will be useful for scholars and researchers. (The typical template for such a work includes a literature review, explanation of methodology, copious amounts of comprehensive and detailed data, the results of one's findings, and suggested avenues for further research.) Such publications prove very helpful for the analysis and advancement of their subject, but unless one is an expert, they can also be sheer drudgery to read. Therefore, the author in me wants to produce something a bit more palatable for the average consumer—something a popular audience will find interesting, informative, and perhaps even entertaining. The question I've repeatedly found myself facing is how to simultaneously satisfy both of these audiences. Here's the compromise I've reached:

The story of Saint Joseph's College is a really good one, and fairly compelling unto itself. The same can be said of the original settlement of this region. For the sake of a popular audience, I've endeavored to relate all of this information in the reader-friendly narratives found in Chapters 1 and 2. (The academicians in the crowd should note that as I proceed through these chapters, I've also managed to weave into them a literature review of these subjects.)

Following these introductory chapters, this book is then divided into two parts. The first is geared towards a general readership and features some of this campus's most storied artifacts and remarkable predecessors. This succession of brief profiles showcases "the best of the best" of our campus's material and ancestral heritage.

The second part of this book, a compilation of fieldwork and documentary research, is intended for a more specialized crowd. The Site Reports feature comprehensive inventories of hundreds of recovered artifacts from four excavation areas. Following these are the documented Chains of Ownership for all five of the campus's 100-acre parcels—from their original distribution (ca. 1773) until the College's eventual acquisition them (as late as 2013).

Hopefully, the format and strategy I've developed for this book will satisfy both intended audiences. I'd like to believe that there's something here for just about everyone. Naturally, that includes those directly or indirectly associated with the College: alumni, faculty, staff, administrators, board members, current and prospective students, trustees, donors, friends, and neighbors. This work should also resonate with those interested in local, state, or national history; armchair and professional archaeologists; and certain hobbyists and collectors. But beyond these segments, this volume is really for anyone who just enjoys a gratifying story about quest and discovery—about the thrill of the chase and the unpredictability of the find.

Introductory Section

Chapter 1
Sister Mary George O'Toole and The History of Saint Joseph's College

When it comes to the history of Saint Joseph's College, nobody knows it better than Sister Mary George O'Toole. That's because nearly 70 years of her life have been devoted to this institution in one way or another. After transferring in 1949 to the Portland-based College of Our Lady of Mercy (as the school was briefly known from 1949 to 1956), Sister Mary George graduated in 1951. She first arrived at the present Sebago Lake campus in 1956, shortly after the Sisters of Mercy had purchased this property and moved the College to Standish. That year she taught only one course but became a full-time faculty member (teaching English and Speech) in 1957. Aside from a smattering of educational and administrative leaves, Sr. Mary George has been a permanent fixture here ever since. She has held numerous faculty, staff and administrative positions, including Director of Admissions, Professor of Sociology, Resident Director for Saint Joseph's Hall, Assistant to the President, Academic Dean for Students, Associate Dean for Academic Affairs, Vice President for Sponsorship and Mission Integration, and Archivist. In addition to these roles, Sister Mary George has also accepted various appointments at the College's top level of governance, serving 16 years on both the Board of Trustees and the Board of Overseers. Having been at the College for so long, and having served it in so many capacities, her institutional memory is unparalleled.

My first introduction to Sr. Mary George was when I arrived as a candidate for an Assistant Professor of Theology position in 2000. Sister Mary George was then serving as the Vice President for Sponsorship and Mission Integration, and it was she who first introduced me, and the rest of the new hires, to the College's past. Turns out, we weren't the first ones to benefit from her considerable experience.

Not a lot has been written about the history of Saint Joseph's College. In fact, the number of officially published works on this subject is limited to two. These two works have several things in common. Both were written in the 1990s. Both were penned by alumni of the College. And both are due, in no small part, to the encouragement and assistance of Sister Mary George O'Toole.

The first work, published in 1995, is Sister Mary Raymond Higgins's *For Love of Mercy*. This hefty, 798-page tome (in small, single-spaced font, no less!) ambitiously endeavors to chronicle the entire 100-year (1883-1993) history of the Congregation of the Sisters of Mercy in Maine and the Bahamas. Within this extensive volume, Higgins devotes Chapter 9 (pp. 345-82) specifically to Saint Joseph's College.

Higgins traces the humble origins of this institution back to 1911, when some of Sister Mary Xaveria Toohey's senior students at Saint Joseph's Academy in Portland approached her requesting a course of studies that would enable them to achieve their goal of becoming teachers. The curriculum that Sister Xaveria drew up included some postgraduate courses. These began the following year (1912), at the nearby motherhouse on Stevens Avenue. Anticipating a growing trend towards higher education and foreseeing the need for more classroom space, the Sisters purchased in 1914 a three-story brick residence adjacent to the motherhouse. The building, "Saint Joseph's Home," had formerly been used for the housing of elderly women. Following the State of Maine's approval of Sister Xaveria's charter and a three-year renovation project, "Saint Joseph's Home" became Saint Joseph's *College's* home. It served in that capacity until 1956, when ever-increasing enrollments finally compelled the Sisters to find a more suitable location for the school.

The second work pertaining to the College's history is Durward J. Ferland, Jr.'s *Fortitudo et Spes: The Courage and Hope to Move a College*. This slim (53 pages, double-spaced) monograph, commissioned by then-President David B. House, was published in 1999. It also offers descriptions of the founding of the College, the move from Portland to Standish, and the subsequent development of the Sebago Lake campus. However, the particular value of this book is its presentation of life as it was during the Verrill Era (1903-55), in the decades just prior to the College's acquisition of the property. Several chapters highlight the estate's signature buildings, including Woldbrook (Xavier Hall), Ledgewold (Saint George Hall, currently housing the Office of Admissions), and the Stone Chapel. Over two dozen Verrill family photographs and various stories about the farm, recreational activities, and famous guests (namely, Cecil B. DeMille, Howard Taft, and Percival Baxter, among others) are also featured.

At the onset of their works, Higgins and Ferland acknowledge a number of individuals to whom they owe debts of gratitude. However, only one name is repeated in both cases: Sister Mary George O'Toole. (In fact, Higgins credits O'Toole as the primary impetus for her work.) Indeed, as we listened to Sister Mary George, her content mirrored much of what is found in these books. But it's her delivery that brought it all to life.

I find Sister Mary George to be a riveting speaker. Her words are so thoughtfully and carefully chosen, and then so precisely enunciated, that whatever topic she is discussing takes on added purpose and gravity. And it was in this manner that she explained to us the history of Saint

Joseph's College. She began with Catherine McAuley (1778-1841), the foundress of the Sisters of Mercy.

Catherine was born in Dublin, Ireland, into a relatively affluent family. However, her father died when she was five, and her mother's death followed 15 years later. A devout practicing Catholic, Catherine subsequently faced harsh discrimination among her Protestant relatives. In 1803, she became the caretaker of the Callaghans, a wealthy, elderly, childless Quaker couple. Despite the religious differences, they came to respect and admire Catherine, and after they passed away (1822), she became the sole beneficiary of their sizable estate.

Catherine chose to put her inheritance to good use. In 1827, she purchased land in a fashionable district of Dublin, on the corner of Lower Baggot and Herbert Streets. There, she opened a "House of Mercy," a spacious residence dedicated to the care of destitute women and orphans and to the education of the poor. Catherine's outreach was a success, and soon friends and volunteers joined her in her efforts.

As their ministry expanded, Church authorities sought more formal oversight over it. Catherine was obliged to either enroll in religious life or relinquish the work she was doing. Reluctantly, she chose the former. Following a year of instruction, Catherine professed her final vows, and on December 12, 1831, the "Sisters of Mercy" became an officially recognized religious order. Catherine lived only ten years as a Sister of Mercy, but in that time, her order expanded to include 12 foundations in Ireland, two in England, and a thriving membership of 150 religious women.

In 1841, Catherine died of tuberculous in her home on Baggot Street. Near the end of her life, many sisters came to support her, pray, and bid her farewell. Despite her ailing

Chapter 1 – The History of Saint Joseph's College

condition, she remained concerned about them. "Be sure you have a comfortable cup of tea for them when I am gone," she instructed. From that point on, the teacup has come to symbolize Catherine's care for others. In recognition of her heroic virtues, Pope John Paul II declared her "Venerable" in 1990. This represents a crucial step towards sainthood—a status that Sister Mary George hoped that Catherine would someday attain.

Catherine McAuley herself never made it to the United States. Rather, it was Sister Frances Xavier Warde, a close friend of Catherine's, who brought the Sisters of Mercy to the Americas. At the request for assistance from Bishop Michael O'Connor of the Diocese of Pittsburgh, Sr. Frances and six of her fellow nuns bravely crossed the Atlantic in 1843, becoming the first members of the community to do so. The order quickly flourished; within a few years, two academies, an orphanage, and even a hospital had been established. As word of their courage and accomplishments spread, the Sisters of Mercy were soon being recruited by other bishops throughout the US, particularly in places where the demands for Catholic education and other social services—often in the wake of increased Irish immigration and rising anti-Catholic sentiment—were especially strong. Before long, the Sisters of Mercy were established in Providence, Rhode Island (1851); Manchester, New Hampshire (1858); Philadelphia, Pennsylvania (1861); Omaha, Nebraska (1864); and Bangor, Maine (1865).

Although Mercy Sisters had been working in southern Maine shortly after arriving in Manchester, the Portland Congregation wasn't formally established until 1883, when Bishop James Augustine Healy divided the Manchester community into two separate entities: one based in Manchester and the other in Portland. Bishop Healy charged the Portland Mercies with the primary task of teaching, and new novitiates resided at Saint Joseph's Academy until the new motherhouse was erected on its grounds in 1907. It was out of this ministry that Saint Joseph's College—now one of 16 US colleges and universities that are sponsored (or co-sponsored) by the Sisters of Mercy—eventually emerged.

During my time with Sister Mary George, I heard the inspiring stories of dedicated Sisters, Presidents, and generous benefactors, many of whose names now grace the buildings on our campus. I learned of successful capital campaigns that were instrumental in propelling the College forward, and of defining academic decisions—such as the introduction of correspondence degrees (the precursor to our online offerings), the establishment of the business and nursing programs, and the creation of the Faculty Senate—that set the course for our future. I was also introduced to several watershed moments in the life of the College. There was the resolution to go co-educational in 1970. ("Buy sturdier furniture" was the somber advice given to then-President Bernard Currier.) There was the acquisition of the "MONKS" athletic uniforms from the discontinued Assumption Preparatory School in Worcester, MA. (Saint Joseph's College is currently the only school in any NCAA division and in any college athletics association to feature this mascot.) But perhaps the most pivotal event since the creation of the College was the move from Portland to Standish. For to hear Sister Mary George (and others) describe it, the relocation of the school to this particular site was, without question, a matter of Divine Providence. It is said that the Lord works in mysterious ways. Well, this case proved no exception.

Harry M. Verrill had graduated from Yale Law School in 1891 and had become a partner at his father's legal firm in Portland, Maine. He had married Louise Brown (whose family owned the Brown Paper Company in Berlin, New Hampshire) and together they had had five children. Desiring a place where he and his family could retreat from city life, escape the summer heat, celebrate holidays, pursue their pastimes, and entertain their guests, Harry purchased (1903-10) several hundred acres of prime real estate on both sides of Whites Bridge Road in Standish, Maine. Here, he developed a veritable five-star resort. He built (and then rebuilt) a sprawling mansion that featured stunning views of Sebago Lake, Frye Island, and Mount Washington. He erected a quaint, free-standing stone meditation chapel for his wife, and a picturesque, Tudor-style summer cottage for his daughter and her family. An outdoor enthusiast, Verrill installed a bathhouse down at the waterfront with changing rooms and storage facilities and an adjoining pier from which he could dock his boat. He designed a 9-hole golf course that meandered throughout the property, skirting the baseball diamond (complete with opposing dugouts) and set of clay tennis courts that he also constructed. Beside a scenic spring-fed pond, Verrill fashioned a cozy log cabin with a central fireplace that served as a skaters warming hut and ski lodge. And across the street (opposite the lake), Verrill maintained a gentleman's farm. Those grounds included a 7-room, 2-bath farmhouse, a fieldstone Norman barn, pasturelands for his draft horses, cows, and sheep, and an orchard of 50-60 fruit trees that yielded apples, peaches, and pears. By any measure, this place was a veritable paradise!

 Given all that he had developed, it is no wonder that Verrill was so reluctant to relinquish it. By the early 1950s, however, the Verrills' use of the estate had significantly declined. Louise's health had deteriorated, their children had moved away, and even their grandchildren, now mostly grown, had little time for it. Although financial prudence dictated the sale of the property, Verrill was nevertheless hesitant to part with it. Reportedly, he did his best to discourage prospective buyers by pointing out all of the flaws and minor issues involved with the site.

Meanwhile, the Sisters of Mercy had been looking for a suitable location for their College. The leading candidate for the new campus was the former Marine Hospital that overlooked Casco Bay in Portland. They were leaning favorably in that direction, but the order, wanting to explore all of its options, decided to check out the Verrill property as well. The Superior General, Mother M. Evangelist Ward, and her Assistant, Mother M. Edwina, were sent to tour the premises. The two nuns were duly impressed with the area, but a degree of ambiguity still prevailed. Those lingering doubts quickly vanished, however, when they stepped foot into the chapel and looked up. There, at each end of the sanctuary, they were greeted by the brightly illuminated stained glass image of a saint: Saint John the Evangelist and Saint Edward—the very same patron saints of Mother Evangelist and Mother Edwina!

Chapter 1 – The History of Saint Joseph's College

The awestruck nuns took this as more than mere coincidence; this was exactly the sort of sign that they had been looking for. This was God's answer to their prayers! Accordingly, on December 10, 1954, the Trustees of the College purchased 115-acres of the Verrill estate—specifically, that on the northwestern (lake) side of Whites Bridge Road. Over the next six decades or so, the College would go on to acquire additional properties adjacent to its own, including the farm across the street. Today, Saint Joseph's Sebago Lake campus encompasses a total of 474 acres of land.

By the time she finished, I was certain that Sister Mary George had taught me everything there was to know about Saint Joseph's College. But as it turns out, I was wrong. There was a lot more to this place than Sister Mary George—or anyone else, for that matter—could ever have imagined. A remarkable, long-neglected history lay just beneath our feet. The problem was, nobody knew it was there....

Chapter 2
Michial Russell and the Founding of Pearsontown (Standish), Maine

I must confess that following Sister Mary George's presentation on the history of the College, I really didn't give the matter a second thought. Rather, for the next 14 years I was preoccupied with teaching my courses, conducting my research, publishing my scholarship, and serving the institution in a variety of capacities. I dutifully rose through the ranks, from Assistant to Associate Professor. I was granted tenure, and eventually became a Full Professor. As I was doing my best to secure my future, the College's past was the furthest thing from my mind. But in May of 2014, all of that changed. Who would have guessed that a chance conversation in the College's cafeteria would lead me down such a wild and wondrous path? Or that its inadvertent gatekeeper would be none other than our colorful Farm Manager, Michial Russell?

Graduation had come and gone, and with the advent of summer vacation, a relaxed atmosphere permeated the College. The cafeteria was largely empty as it was nearing closing time, and the staff had begun wiping down the tables and putting away the food. Having just finished a late lunch, I bused my dishes and sidled up to Mike's table where he was casually holding court with some of his summer interns. As I approached, his eyes lit up. "Dr. Bridge!" he cheerfully proclaimed. He invited me to sit down and join their conversation. They were discussing that morning's project. Mike mentioned that one of his workers, while digging a trench, had uncovered some broken bottles and a pair of old-looking eyeglasses. Mike wondered aloud what else might be buried there. My curiosity was piqued as well.

I'm naturally fascinated by exploration and discovery. There's nothing quite like that adrenaline rush that comes with finding "buried treasure." But the "buried treasure" I tended to pursue was primarily geological in nature. Shortly after moving to Maine, I became acquainted with the pegmatite formations that pepper Oxford County. Rare and unique, they give rise to a wide variety of well-formed minerals. In fact, it has been estimated that up to 30% of all known mineral species are represented in Oxford County. So for rock hounds, this region provides an especially great opportunity to build a collection. By scouring the leftover rock piles (or "dumps") of abandoned mines, I've recovered semi-precious specimens of breathtaking gem-grade rock quartz, smoky quartz, rose quartz, apatite, garnet, amethyst, aquamarine, and tourmaline. Suffice to say, I was far more interested in these millions of years old marvels of nature than the recently discarded works of man.[3] But my shift towards the latter had already begun.

For three consecutive summers between 2010 and 2012, an academic research project on Saint Paul had taken me to dozens of archaeological excavations throughout Israel, Jordan, Turkey, Greece, Malta, and Italy. I quickly discovered that my geological experience came in handy, as it enabled me to read the terrain and recognize subtle differences in the topographical landscapes and stratigraphical layers. At these dig sites I also learned some of the fundamental principles and methods of archaeology. I was introduced to the tricks and the tools of the trade, and I

---

[3] As my geological interests evolved, so did my involvements in this hobby. I learned how to facet the rough material that I found, and eventually taught others to do the same. I also became a member of the Portland-based Maine Mineralogical and Geological Society. In 2012, the club moved its Annual Gem & Mineral Show—the largest event of its type in the state—to Saint Joseph's College. Our venue proved to be so well-received that it has been held here (in April) ever since. Interested readers can check out the club's website, mainemineralclub.org, for more information.

Chapter 2 – The Founding of Pearsontown (Standish)

got to practice and refine some of my own excavation skills. I unearthed 2000-year-old potsherds and pottery pieces, marble columns and iron tools, Roman glass and mosaic flooring. I knew that rural Maine wouldn't yield artifacts nearly as ancient, but as I said, my interest was piqued. I agreed to meet up with Mike at the farm the next day.

When I arrived, Mike was in the midst of a number of different projects—as Farm Manager, Mike always has a lot on his plate—but he explained that he was interested in knowing more about the history of the property. What had it been used for? How long it had been in use? Turns out, Mike is a bit of a history buff. Case in point: when the College decided to end its food service contract with an outside vendor and bring the entire operation in-house, it was Mike who proposed the new names: Pearson's Café and Pearson's Town Farm. In his dealings with the Town of Standish, Mike had learned that this area had formerly been named "Pearsontown" in honor of Captain Moses Pearson. So these names were Mike's nod to local history. (A nod that would eventually prove quite ironic....) But that's all that Mike knew about the region; he was eager to learn more.

Unbeknownst to both of us, Albert J. Sears' book, *The Founding of Pearsontown (Standish), Maine* contains some good information about this matter.[4] The earliest history of this territory, especially as it relates to Saint Joseph's College, is worth a brief review.

******

---

[4] Sears wrote this and its companion volume, the *Early Families of Standish, Maine*, largely on the basis of Dr. Albion Meserve's extensive research in the mid to late 1800s. Although Sears died in 1983, the Standish Historical Society managed to publish both of his works posthumously in 1991.

Sears traces the settling of this district back to 1745. That's the year that a British-led colonial force captured Louisbourg, a French fortress located at the mouth of the Saint Lawrence River on Cape Breton Island, Nova Scotia. This event was part of "King George's War," the third of the four so-called "French and Indian Wars" fought in the New World provinces. At the time, Louisbourg was one of the largest and most expensive European outposts on this continent. The French had fortified it so heavily that it became known as "the Gibraltar of America." And it was from this stronghold that the French (and their Indian allies) attacked the British colonies in New England and disrupted their fishing, fur-trading, and other commercial activities. Determined to eliminate this threat, Governor William Shirley of Massachusetts sent a force of 4,200 soldiers and sailors aboard 90 ships, commanded by William Pepperell of Kittery. Pepperell's First Regiment included a company of men from Falmouth (now Portland) captained by Moses Pearson. The fleet landed on May 11, and following a successful siege, the fortress was overtaken on June 17, 1745.[5] Pearson was appointed Agent of Pepperell's regiment and Treasurer of the nine regiments employed in the siege to

---

[5] The magnitude of this event was captured by the Reverend Thomas Smith, Pastor of the First Church in Portland. In his journal entry dated February 22, 1745, he writes: "All the talk is about the expedition to Louisbourg. There is a marvelous zeal and concurrence through the whole country with respect to it; such as the like was never seen in this part of the world." On July 6, Smith reports, "We had news today that Cape Breton was taken the 27th of last month. There is great rejoicing through the country. We fired our cannon five times, and spent the afternoon at the Fort, rejoicing." According to Smith, the celebrations continued on until the 18th. (Quotations taken from William Willis's *Journals of the Rev. Thomas Smith and the Rev. Samuel Deane, pastors of the First church in Portland: with notes and biographical notices and a summary history of Portland* [Portland: Joseph S. Bailey, 1849], pp. 116, 119-20.)

Chapter 2 – The Founding of Pearsontown (Standish)

receive and distribute the spoils of victory. He remained in the garrison at Louisbourg for another eight months, superintending the construction of barracks, a hospital, and repairs to the fortifications until he and his company were released from their duties by Governor Shirley in March of 1746.

According to Sears, spoils of great value were commandeered at Louisbourg. However, nearly all of it was sent back to England. This meant that the local soldiers who had borne the brunt of the conflict and its associated hardships received relatively little remuneration for their services. Dissatisfied with this outcome, Pearson and forty of his men petitioned the General Court of Massachusetts in 1749, requesting that a township be carved out of public land in York (now Cumberland) County.[6] Around that same time, the Court received a similar request from Captain Humphrey Hobbs and his company for their successful defense of the frontier against Chief Sackett in a battle near Marlboro, Vermont. On April 20, 1750, the House of Representatives granted to these two Captains, their men, and some others who had served in the Louisbourg expedition—120 in all—an area of approximately 39,000 acres (or six square miles) that included present-day Standish, Frye's Island and the greater part of Raymond Cape. The conditions of their approval stipulated that 60 of the men and their families would be settled—with houses built and land cultivated—within three years, and that

---

[6] Note that Maine was not yet a state; it did not become one until 1820. Prior to that, this region was under the governance of the Commonwealth of Massachusetts. The text of Pearson's petition, including the list of its signers, appears in William Willis's *The History of Portland, from 1632 to 1864: With a Notice of Previous Settlements, Colonial Grants, and Changes of Government in Maine* (Portland: Bailey & Noyes, 1865), pp. 419-20.

another 60 would be settled within seven years. The Proprietors were also charged with establishing a school, building a "meeting house" (church), and recruiting a learned minister to shepherd the community. For lack of a better name, the new township was originally called "Hobbs and Pearson Town."

Following the relatively swift approval and survey process, progress subsequently stalled. Humphrey Hobbs' petition to the General Court in May 1752 explains why.[7] At the time, this territory was still considered remote and inhospitable, and hostile encounters between the colonists and the Indians were not uncommon.[8] For these reasons, Hobbs sought from the Court either an extension of time or the establishment of a protective fort—as had been built in Gorham—for the safety of prospective settlers. Since the latter option involved a considerable investment of Province resources, the Court opted to grant the Proprietors a two-year extension instead.

The drawing of the First Division of land took place at the first meeting of the Proprietors, in June of 1752. The Proprietors had mapped out 123 30-acre lots (to include the 120 grantees, plus one each for the minister, church, and school) that radiated outward from the "center" of town—or what is today the intersection of Routes 25 and 35.[9] The College campus was not included in this first disbursement of land. However, there is evidence that it may nevertheless

---

[7] For the text of the petition, see Albert Sears, *Founding*, pp. 1-2.

[8] In his *History of Gorham, Me.* (Portland: Smith & Sale, 1903), Hugh D. McLellan provides an informative treatment of the relationship between the Indians and the settlers of this region, both before the war (pp. 34-42) and during it (pp. 48-59). However, McLellan's accounts are strictly from the perspective of the settlers.

[9] A map of these properties and a listing of their original recipients can be found in Albert Sears, *Founding*, front page inset and pp. 205-7.

Chapter 2 – The Founding of Pearsontown (Standish)

have been on the Proprietors' minds. On the heels of a lackluster start to their new settlement, the Proprietors voted in February of 1753 to lay out another 60 five-acre lots between Sebago Pond and Gorham Town (presumably on Standish Neck, where the campus lies). These five-acre lots would have been much easier to reach from Gorham and would have benefitted more directly from the protection that Fort Hill would have afforded. However, there are no further indications that this plan ever came to fruition.

Instead, in April of 1753, the Proprietors agreed to erect their own fort in the center of Hobbs and Pearson Town. In January of 1754, they offered varying financial incentives to anyone who agreed to settle their property by April or August of that year. And in March, they presented opportunities for land-owners to exchange their drawn lots for more desirable ones. (Clearly, they were making their best efforts to persuade people to settle here.) Construction on the fort began in the spring of 1754. It was partially destroyed by Indians in May, but it was repaired and completed that summer. By May of 1755, 30 men, women, and children resided within its barracks. To help sustain them, the Proprietors agreed to subdivide three of the adjacent 30-acre lots into 18 five-acre lots and deeded them to the residents for the cultivation of their crops.

From 1755 until 1759, as the last of the so-called French and Indian Wars waged on, incidents of fighting and bloodshed in this area increased. In 1756, in recognition of the military importance of the Hobbs and Pearson Town Fort, the General Court armed the outpost with swivel guns and ammunition, and agreed to add its men to their payroll (ten in 1756, 16 in 1757, 15 in 1758, and 13 in 1759). Captain Hobbs died from smallpox at Fort William Henry in 1757; thereafter the fledgling settlement simply became known as "Pearsontown." (It retained this name until its incorporation in 1785 as "Standish," in honor of Captain Myles Standish, the military leader of the *Mayflower's* Plymouth Colony.) Hostilities throughout the District of Maine finally came to an end with the Fall of Quebec in 1759. Gradually, residents felt safe enough to establish their homes outside of the garrison's walls.

Now that Pearsontown was poised for proper development, the Proprietors agreed to set aside land for the establishment of a sawmill. To this end, Moses Pearson personally invited Ebenezer Shaw to leave his home in New Hampshire and relocate to this vicinity. Shaw accepted Pearson's offer, and "Shaw's Mill" was the eventual result. A steady supply of board lumber greatly facilitated the town's growth. Evidently, so did Shaw's influence. Between 1763 and 1764, at least 16 New Hampshire men (most with families) came to Pearsontown. Many of these men were connected to Shaw by blood, marriage, or friendship.[10] With the steady, successful expansion of the community, the Proprietors also approved the construction of the town's first meeting house. Built in 1766, it was served by interim pastors for a few years until the Proprietors were able to

---

[10] Thomas Shaw, a relative of Ebenezer's, wrote eloquently about the hardships these early settlers faced: "Now when people remove into the woods, they very often have a hard time of it; for in new places they have bad roads or none at all, or only a footpath or spotted trees to go by, and very often get lost in the wood for want of roads, and sometimes they have no grist mill for ten, twelve or twenty miles. I know these things by experience; and again they have no squires to do justice to the oppressed nor sheriffs to catch rogues nor no law to punish them so that people very often, when they first go into the woods, do live without law or gospel for some time to come, and very often have no blacksmith to shoe a horse and have no tailor to cut and make a garment, nor a shoemaker to make a pair of shoes. These and many more inconveniences I could mention that attend settlers in a new country" (taken from Sears, *Founding*, p. 24).

Chapter 2 – The Founding of Pearsontown (Standish)

secure the Reverend John Tompson as its first residential minister in 1768.

By May of 1768, the Proprietors decided that the time had come to disburse more of the original land grant. They carved out a fresh set of 120 100-acre lots and distributed them to those land-owners whose tax assessments were fully paid and up to date. Although the plan to allocate these lots was set forth in July of 1769, the actual drawing and recording of them—according to Sears—wasn't completed until April of 1774.[11] Nevertheless, it is this *Second* Division of lots (also sometimes referred to as the *First* Division of *100-acre* lots) that included the campus lands of Saint Joseph's College. In his book, Albert Sears provides a copy of the Proprietors' Plan of Pearsontown. The layout of what would eventually become known as Standish Neck is as follows:

---

[11] The April 1774 date is twice given by Sears (*Founding*, pp. 37, 95), but I am unsure of what it actually refers to. I know of at least three deeds involving Second Division lots (specifically, Lots 63, 52, and 37) that are dated to June 7, 1773. Furthermore, I have found an even earlier listing of 26 Second Division lots that had evidently already been assigned by March 8, 1773 (cf. Moses Pearson's profile).

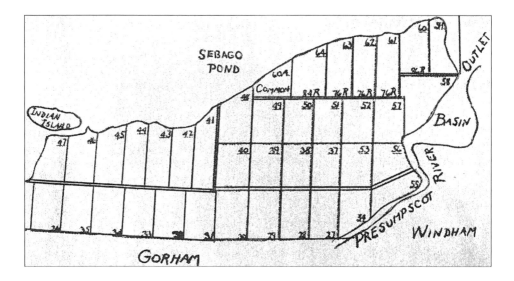

Unfortunately, unlike the First Division (and, eventually, the Third as well), the Proprietors inexplicably failed to record the names of the individuals to whom these Second Division lots were assigned. So unless later deeds happened to mention them (and usually they didn't), their original owners remain largely unidentifiable.

******

Given the ambiguity that surrounded the Second Division lots, Mike's question about the campus's prior history remained a good one—one that nobody else had really thought to ask. Moreover, it made me realize that the College actually has two distinct histories. Just as a person is composed of both spirit and flesh, so, too, our College has both a spiritual and a corporeal past. Thanks to women like Sister Mary George O' Toole and Sister Mary Raymond Higgins, we have a fairly clear picture of the College's *spiritual* heritage. But what of its *material* one? What was the history of *this* land—the physical campus of Saint Joseph's College? Albert Sears and the Standish Historical

Chapter 2 – The Founding of Pearsontown (Standish)

Society have provided valuable information about the initial settling of this area. And Durward Ferland, Jr. has contributed useful insights into our immediate predecessors, the Verrills. But what about the intervening period? What happened here between 1774 and the early 1900s? In whose footsteps are we now walking? What were their stories? Nobody knew. But I, for one, was determined to find out. I told Mike I'd do my best to get some answers.

As my quest unfolded, I eventually settled on a two-pronged approach that enabled me to dig into the campus's history both literally and figuratively. First, I sought and received permission to canvass and examine the grounds with my metal detector.[12] Of course, my arrangement with the College does not imply that others have the same permission to proceed as I have. I should be very clear about this: **any metal detecting, digging, excavating, moving or removing of natural objects or manmade artifacts (50 years or older) on College property requires the express, written permission of the College's Vice President and Chief Learning Officer. Failure to abide by this policy is**

---

[12] For the record, I proceeded under the conventional agreement that anything I discovered of significant monetary or historical value I would share equally with the College. In the metal-detecting world, this is a fairly standard way to proceed. (In England, it is actually the law of the land.) This certainly makes sense. If "finders, keepers" were the rule, land-owners would have no incentive to grant anyone access to their property. But if everything went to the land-owner, there would be no incentive for anyone to search—much less declare—their finds. The 50/50 split—a win/win for both parties—is widely considered the fairest compromise. However, I should hasten to add that if and when anything happens to me, I am inclined to relinquish my share of these finds back to the College. That is, assuming there is sufficient interest and demonstrated support for their long-term preservation, display, educational use, and safekeeping. Likewise, should anything happen to the College (God forbid), I would expect these items to be entrusted back to me.

prosecutable under the law. Once a site was located, I would survey and undertake a preliminary excavation of it, careful to document as meticulously as I could each of the items that I recovered.

My second approach involved combing through property records in the Cumberland Country Registry of Deeds. Such research enabled me to chronologically reconstruct the campus's numerous and often complicated chains of land ownership. It took me a while, but nearly all of the campus's previous titleholders have now been identified. This list, in turn, has become a valuable starting point for subsequent research which aims to bring to light the stories of our more notable predecessors.[13]

To be sure, there were probably a number of different ways that I could have undertaken this project, but this two-pronged tactic worked well. Not only were both of these approaches comfortably within my skill sets, but they also proved to be mutually informative and motivating. I found that the relics that I unearthed sparked my curiosity about their original owners. At the same time, the more I learned about the remarkable inhabitants of this land, the more determined I became to recover whatever they may have left behind. Together, the combination of field work and documentary research operated in tandem to propel this

---

[13] This is where some of my prior academic training kicked in. My graduate degree is in Biblical Theology, but the methodological emphasis that I pursued at Marquette University (and indeed, what MU is best known for) is Historical Criticism. In short, Historical Criticism seeks to make sense of a given piece of information (such as a name, an archaeological artifact, or a biblical text) in light of its original, historical context. Gathering the information necessary to fill in the backstory is not always an easy task, but it is a crucial step towards a fuller understanding of the subject/object at hand. Indeed, it is this background information that enriches our perspective and helps bring a subject/object to life.

venture forward (or rather, backward) with steady momentum. But I'm already getting ahead of myself....

Mike walked me out to the trench that his intern had recently dug. Nearby, he pointed out a small foundation—just a few wooden floorboards, really—of an old shed. I joked about finding "the mother lode" and proposed early retirement. Mike just shook his head. "Naaa," he said, "I wouldn't retire." Then he shot me a smile and sheepishly confessed, "I just love this job waaaaay too much." Truth be told, I felt exactly the same way. Mike wished me luck and headed back to the farm. I turned around and stared hard at the ground before me. In my mind's eye, I tried to perceive the deeper history beneath it. I gathered up my tools and switched on the metal detector. The display screen flickered to life. My journey of exploration had officially begun.

Part I

Storied Artifacts

and

Remarkable Predecessors

Introduction to (Some of) Our Storied Artifacts

I swept the coil of the detector in slow arcs before me as I approached the decomposing floorboards of the shed. An electronic tone pierced the silence: "Beep. Beep. BEEEEEEP." The coil hovered momentarily over an otherwise inconspicuous patch of grass. Something lay buried beneath it. My heartbeat quickened. What could it be? A silver coin? A gold ring? A strongbox full of treasure? Imagining all sorts of exciting possibilities, I set my detector aside and reached for my trowel. I made a semi-circular cut into the earth and pulled back the sod. Seeing nothing at first, I dug a little deeper. Still nothing. I grabbed my detector and checked the spot again. The signal was even stronger. Whatever it was, it was still in there. I removed my heavy gloves and started sifting through the dirt with my hands. A few inches down, I felt something hard and roundish. It was firmly buried, but after some determined effort, I worked it free. Up it came, into the light of day: one potato-sized rock. Clearly, this was not what I was looking for! I used the detector to check the hole again. Still there. I felt around some more, scooping out handfuls of loose dirt as I dug deeper. Again, I encountered something hard. But this was smoother and more cylindrical. I grew more excited until I gradually realized what it was. A thick root. I tried my best to work around it, and began clawing out the soil on either side. As I worked my way under it, something solid emerged. It was smaller, about an inch and a half long, and rust-colored. For a better look, I brushed away the grime that clung to it and cradled it into the sunlight. There it was, in all its magnificent glory: a screw. Not exactly the legendary cache I had anticipated!

My effort-to-payoff ratio clearly left a lot to be desired. However, it's true what they say: "Hope springs eternal." Besides, it was a beautiful day and I appreciated the fresh air and exercise, so I kept going. Over the next couple of hours, I found three more screws, six nails, and a bottle cap. I also encountered several shards of window glass, on which I sliced open my index finger. The cut wasn't very long, but it was deep enough to continue bleeding through my mud-caked hands for several minutes. Between the disturbed ground and the scattered drops of blood, my little excavation area was beginning to look more like a crime scene. Disappointed but undaunted, I decided to call it a day. I planned to return to widen my search and made a mental note to pack antibacterial hand sanitizer and Band-Aids for future excursions.

On Day 2, I convinced Camilla Fecteau to accompany me. Camilla is an Instructor and Lab Coordinator for the Biology Department at Saint Joseph's College. Although a bit shy and introverted, Camilla possesses keen powers of observation. They serve her well both as a scientist (in gathering research results) and as an educator (in connecting with her students). They also enable her to find just the right gift for any particular person. We were dating at the time, and it was she who had bought me my first metal detector for Christmas just a few months prior. Metal-detecting isn't exactly her "thing," but she was excited to see me get some use out of it, so we set off together. I showed her around the previous day's site before we headed towards a more remote area of the campus. Before long, we found ourselves on an abandoned forest lane. And from there, Camilla spied it first: the remains of an old foundation.

Set off back from the road, it was a U-shaped berm that blended in well with its surroundings. To be honest, had she not pointed it out, I probably would've walked right past it. As we approached, I could see some discarded junk scattered about its vicinity. A metal bucket here. An iron pipe there. The oval-shaped depression of the foundation was covered with leaves, branches, and pine needles. A few small to medium-sized trees were growing up within it. I walked into the middle and flipped on my machine. Immediately, it sounded off with a loud cacophony of tones and beeps and signals. I went back over to the edge of the foundation and dug into the thick mat of decomposing vegetation that blanketed it. As I began to peel it away, I was astonished by what I saw underneath. The entire floor of the foundation was littered with debris from the late-1800s to the mid-1920s, including dozens of beautifully embossed glass bottles. Many of them were broken, but some were still whole. I was stunned and amazed. I felt like I had just opened a long-lost time capsule. I spent the better part of that day, that week, and that month, further excavating the site. Just like that, I was hooked.

That was a little over three years ago. Since then, I have branched out and explored many other areas of the campus. To be sure, I've experienced far more Day 1's than Day 2's, and I've certainly made my share of mistakes along the way. But through trial and error, I've learned a lot as well. I've introduced new equipment and technology into the process, and with a healthy blend of persistence and good fortune, I've managed to locate 12 previously unknown, artifact-bearing sites on the College's property.[14] Collectively, these sites have yielded thousands of items that date from the late 1700s to the mid-1950s.

So herein lies the conundrum: with this many artifacts to choose from, how does one go about presenting them? My initial plan was to feature the Top Ten, in the order of their significance. But despite having a clear-cut #1, I had a very difficult time rank-ordering the rest. There are just too many

---

[14] For a more thorough treatment of these sites, see Part II.

criteria by which an object's "significance" may be determined. Are we talking monetary value? Age? Condition? Scarcity? Aesthetic appeal? Furthermore, I had a hard time limiting my picks to ten. At least 25 artifacts made my preliminary list, with another 25 "honorable mentions" waiting in the wings.

To resolve this problem, I settled on a different standard altogether. I decided to concentrate on the campus's most storied artifacts—those with the most compelling histories associated with them. Good back stories can really help bring objects to life, and the 11 that follow had some of the most interesting ones that I'd come across. These items appear in no particular order. However, I did manage to save the best for last!

Chapter 3
Straight-Sided "Coca-Cola Bottling Co." Glass Soda Bottle (Portland, ME ca. 1926)

In the spring of 2015, I found myself "in the zone." Quite by chance, I had discovered a highly concentrated area of remarkably well-preserved artifacts from the 1900s to 1930s. A few days into the excavation, I pulled out a heavy soda bottle that was embossed entirely in block script. It read "REGISTERED" near the upper shoulder, and then, in the style of an oval label across its front, "COCA COLA BOTTLING CO, PORTLAND ME" encircling "7½ OZ. INGALLS

BROS." I had never seen anything like it. It was a Coke bottle, but it looked nothing like a Coke bottle. That was because it lacked two of the most iconic elements of the brand: the cursive Spencerian logo and the classically contoured shape. Surely, this was a rare and incredible find! The only problem was that, although the bottle was in good condition, its upper neck had been broken. The mouth was completely missing. I was a bit crestfallen. But as I said, I was in a highly concentrated zone, and I reasoned that if there was one, perhaps there would be more. I kept searching. Minutes later, a second bottle emerged. It was nearly identical to the first...except this one was whole! I was SO excited! I couldn't believe my luck!

    I knew decidedly little about Coke, but, fascinated by my find, I hit the internet. Here's what I learned:[15] Coca-Cola was invented by a pharmacist (and former Civil War Confederate Colonel) named John "Doc" Pemberton. Pemberton concocted a syrup designed to be mixed with carbonated water at neighborhood soda fountains (which were, at that time, all the rage). Pemberton's tonic was first sold to the public at Jacob's Pharmacy in Atlanta on May 8, 1886. Its name, "Coca-Cola," comes from two of its original ingredients. The first is coca—not be confused with cocoa—leaf extract. Yes, this is the same source from whence cocaine is derived, and the original formula reportedly

---

[15] All of my information about Coca-Cola was gleaned from the following five websites: Collector's Weekly (www.collectorsweekly.com), the Coca-Cola Company (www.coca-colacompany.com), World of Coca-Cola (www.worldofcoca-cola.com), the University of Florida Interactive Media Lab (http://iml.jou.ufl.edu/projects/spring08/Cantwell/invention.html), and Wikipedia (https://en.wikipedia.org/wiki/Coca-Cola).

contained traces of the psychoactive alkaloid.[16] The second is the kola nut, the fruit of a tree native to the tropical rainforests of Africa. Kola nuts contain caffeine, kolanin, and theobromine—three chemicals that all function as stimulants. Accordingly, Cola-Cola was originally marketed as a "Brain Tonic" and an alcohol-free "temperance drink" with the power to cure headaches, anxiety, depression, indigestion, and addiction(!).

Pemberton's partner and bookkeeper, Frank M. Robinson, is credited with naming the beverage as well as designing the distinctive, trademarked script still used today. Following Pemberton's untimely death, Asa Griggs Candler became the sole owner of Coca-Cola in 1891. Candler was somewhat of a marketing genius, and under his leadership, sales increased significantly as the product spread throughout drug store soda fountains nationwide.

The earliest attempts at bottling Coca-Cola used heavy glass Hutchinson bottles with wired, rubber stoppers. To open the drink, one had to push the wire in, or "pop" it—which is how the term "soda pop" came to be. Candler believed this compromised the quality of the product, so when Benjamin Thomas and Joseph Whitehead approached him in 1899 with the idea of securing Coca-Cola's exclusive bottling rights, Candler literally give them away. He drew up a contract without any specified term limit and granted the pair the freedom to convey the rights to other bottling plants as they saw fit—which they did.

---

[16] Today, a Stepan laboratory in Maywood, N.J., is the nation's only legal commercial importer of coca leaves, which it obtains mainly from Peru and, to a lesser extent, Bolivia. Besides producing the coca flavoring agent for Coca-Cola, Stepan extracts cocaine from the coca leaves, which it sells to Mallinckrodt Inc., a St. Louis pharmaceutical manufacturer that is the only company in the United States licensed to purify the product for medicinal use.

Chapter 3 – Coca-Cola Bottling Co. Soda Bottle

By 1900, the newly invented crown-top bottles began to replace Hutchinson bottles. They had straight sides, but were lighter and easier for people to handle. Because they used bottle caps rather than rubber stoppers, the crown-tops had the advantage of keeping the soda fresh for longer periods of time. Consequently, the Coca-Cola bottlers were quick to adopt them. However, because each operation—some 379 by 1909—functioned independently, the shapes, sizes, and colors of their bottles varied tremendously. Nevertheless, most bottles featured the embossed "Coca-Cola" logo and a diamond-shaped paper label.

As the success of the soda grew, so did its number of imitators. Competitors tried to capitalize on Coke's popularity with slight variations on its name and logo, including Koka-Kola, Koca-Nola, Celery-Cola, and Koke—all offered in identically shaped bottles. To combat this problem, in 1912 Benjamin Thomas initiated a contest among his bottlers to design something unique for the Coca-Cola brand. The creative brief called for a bottle that could be recognized when broken on the ground or by touch in the dark. The winning entry was submitted by Alexander Samuelson and patented by the Root Glass company on November 16, 1915. Ironically, the shape of Samuelson's bottle—with its well-known parallel grooves, bulging middle, and tapered-ends—was inspired by that of the *cocoa* pod, which Samuelson had mistakenly assumed was an ingredient! Samuelson's creation was approved by the Bottlers' Association in 1916 and thus became standard issue. Known as the "Mae West" or "hobble skirt" for its resemblance to a fashionable dress of the period, the new bottle now had a uniform color as well: German green (later renamed Georgia green).

For the next 100 years, bottles of Coca-Cola changed very little.[17] And for much of that period, neither did their price. Coca-Cola remains one of the longest fixed-priced consumer items in US history. From 1886 to 1959, it cost exactly 5 cents a bottle.[18] Today, of course, Coca-Cola has practically achieved world domination. It is officially licensed in every country on the planet, except two: North Korea and Cuba.[19]

Given Coca-Cola's widespread popularity, its associated paraphernalia tends to be highly collectable. And rare bottles—particularly those that pre-date 1916—are especially prized. It is not uncommon for such "straight side" Coke bottles to fetch hundreds, if not thousands, of dollars. From all appearances, I initially figured that's what I had found. But in light of my research, some of the details just weren't adding up. For instance, while the words "Coca Cola" were present, why weren't they stylized in the trademarked logo script (which was used from 1887 on)? Why wasn't there any obvious place on the bottle for the accompanying paper label? Furthermore, a small "26 N" was embossed on the bottom. This was similar to some of the other bottles I recovered from that site, wherein the number represented the year (so in this case, 1926). But if this was a 1926 Coke

---

[17] Dating these bottles is relatively straightforward, thanks to the four-digit numbers on their base or bottom, which identifies the mold number and the year of manufacture.

[18] The fixed price of Coca-Cola from 1886 to 1959 is particularly remarkable given the events that occurred during the same time period, including the founding of Pepsi, World War I, prohibition, changing taxes, a caffeine and caramel shortage, and World War II.

[19] Ironically, Cuba was one of the first countries outside of the US to have its own bottling plant (1906). The company pulled out in the 1960s, and cannot return until the US government lifts its embargo, which prohibits US-Cuba trade except for specific agricultural and medical products. A recent thaw in diplomatic relations between the two countries has led to the lifting of the US travel ban to Cuba, so Coke's global checklist may soon be narrowed to one.

Chapter 3 – Coca-Cola Bottling Co. Soda Bottle

bottle, then why wasn't it hobble skirt-shaped? To answer these questions, I did some more research on the Ingalls Brothers and came across the following entry in an 1891 Portland-based business directory:

> INGALLS BROTHERS. Importers of Foreign Ales and Porter, Bottlers of Ales, Porters, Lager Beer, Champagne Cider, Manufacturers of Mineral and Soda Water, Proprietors of Ginger Ale and Sarsaparilla Beer, Proprietors of the Moxie Nerve Food, No. 17 Preble St., Portland, Maine.—The bottling works of Messrs. Ingalls Brothers have been well known in Portland for more than a quarter of a century. The enterprise was established in 1864 by R. Ingalls, who after carrying in on alone for a number of years associated himself with his brother, R.P. Ingalls. The business is entirely wholesale and it has now reached so great dimensions that from fifteen to twenty-five employees are needed to fill the orders. It is well known that no more refreshing or sustaining beverage can be found than Alica Beer, guaranteed to be less than one percent alcohol, large quantities of which are consumed in this country. The Messrs. Ingalls make a specialty of bottling this Alica beer and also that delicious and harmless drink, Champagne Cider. They also manufacture mineral and soda water, ginger ale, sarsaparilla and root beer. In addition to this they are the proprietors of the celebrated Moxie Nerve Food which is known and sold throughout the country, and has proved so efficacious in stimulating and strengthening over worked and tired nerves. They make a specialty of furnishing soda tanks already charged and also recharging the same. The bottling works are located at No. 17 Preble Street and consist of a three story building of 35x150 feet in dimensions. This establishment enjoys a first-class reputation and the proprietors have always maintained the most favorable relations with the trade. The Messrs. Ingalls are both natives of Shelburne NH.[20]

---

[20] George Fox Bacon, *Portland [Me.] Its Representative Business Men and Its Points of Interest* (Portland: Glenwood Publishing Company, 1891), p. 112.

Nowhere in this listing is Coca-Cola even mentioned. Obviously the Ingalls Brothers were beverage distributors; Coca-Cola was merely one of their many products. But why would they distribute it in non-logoed bottles? Turns out, they didn't. Before the Coca-Cola Company created its own line of flavored sodas, many of the independent bottlers met consumer demand by offering their own orange, root beer, strawberry, grape, and fruit-flavored drinks. They were not allowed to sell them in hobble skirt bottles or use the "Coca-Cola" script, because the drinks weren't licensed products of the Cola-Cola Company. So instead, these distributors developed their own "flavor bottles," on which they identified themselves as a "Coca-Cola bottling company" to capitalize on the brand's notoriety. While not as valuable as the bona fide Coke bottles, the flavor bottles are nevertheless collectible. As I write this, there is a bottle identical to the ones I found listed on Ebay for $50. Another similarly embossed, 1 pint, 12 oz. sized bottle is available for $800.

Secondary Sources

- "125 Years of Sharing Happiness: A Short History of The Coca-Cola Company" on *The Coca-Cola Company* website: www.coca-colacompany.com/.

- "About Us: Coca-Cola History" on the *World of Coca-Cola* website: www.worldofcoca-cola.com/about-us/coca-cola-history.

- "Antique Coca-Cola Bottles" on the *Collector's Weekly* website: www.collectorsweekly.com/coca-cola/bottles.

- "Coca-Cola" on the *Wikipedia* website: wikipedia.org/wiki/Coca-Cola.

- "The History of Coca-Cola" on the *University of Florida Interactive Media Lab* website: iml.jou.ufl.edu/projects/spring08/Cantwell/invention.html.

Chapter 4
"Jacob Ruppert Brewer" Glass Beer Bottle (ca. 1942)[21]

I found this bottle resting beside a stone wall at one of the excavation sites. I have no idea how long it had been there.

---

[21] This date comes from code information embossed on the base of the glass. The trademark indicates that it was manufactured by the Owens-Illinois Glass Company. The number 3 to the left of the trademark refers to the plant, which in this case is Fairmount, WV, which operated between 1930 and 1980. The 2 to the right refers to the date. I originally took this to indicate 1932, but Prohibition (1920-33) would have made that impossible. Rather, it must signify 1942, as confirmed by internet image searches.

Chapter 4 – Jacob Ruppert Beer Bottle

From the front, it displays well. Just below its long neck is a circular embossed imprint that reads "JACOB RUPPERT BREWER NEW YORK." Unfortunately, a long fissure curves through its posterior side, culminating in a 1½ inch-diameter moon-shaped cavity. Of course, such damage would detract from any bottle's monetary value, but in this case, the loss is fairly negligible. Even in excellent condition, such a bottle only fetches $20 to $30 anyway. No, the real value of this bottle, as I learned, is in its back story.

Jacob Ruppert, Jr. was born in New York City on August 5, 1867, to Jacob and Anna (Gillig) Ruppert—the second of their six children. From birth, Jacob seemed destined to become a brewer. Not only was his father, Jacob Sr. (1842-1915), a renowned beer maker, but so too were both of his grandfathers, Franz Ruppert (1811-83) and George Gillig (1806-62). Jacob, Jr. attended Columbia Grammar School and was accepted into Columbia College. However, the pull of his heritage proved strong, and he opted instead to follow in his father's and grandfathers' footsteps. He joined the family business in 1887 as a barrel washer, working 12 hour days for $10 a week. He steadily climbed the corporate rungs, and eventually made his way up to Vice President and General Manager. Popular and well-respected by his peers in the industry, Jacob was elected President of the United States Brewers Association, a post he held from 1911 to 1914. When his father died in 1915, he took over the reigns as President of the Jacob Ruppert Brewing Company.

It was during this same period that Ruppert became increasingly involved in civil service. He enlisted in the US National Guard (New York's seventh regiment) and was commissioned as a Private from 1886 to 1889. In 1890, he was promoted to Colonel and served on the staff of David B.

Hill, the Governor of New York. Following that, he was appointed a senior aide to Roswell P. Flower, Hill's successor, until 1895. It seems these positions sparked Jacob's interest in politics, and 1898, he launched a successful bid for the US House of Representatives. He went on to serve a total of four consecutive terms for the State of New York: two in the 15th congressional district (1899-1901, 1901-03) and two in the 16th (1903-05, 1905-07).

As remarkable as these accomplishments are, they are not what Jacob Ruppert, Jr. is primarily remembered for. You see, with his highly lucrative Brewing Company chugging along, and his political aspirations satisfied, Ruppert was looking for his next new venture. A fan of baseball since his childhood, Jacob decided to invest in a Major League team. But not just any team. In 1915, he partnered with Tillinghast L'Hommedieu Huston and purchased the New York Yankees. The Yankees were, at that time, a perennial also-ran in the American League, posting winning records only once since 1906, and only in four of their 12 seasons since relocating to New York in 1903. But Ruppert was about to change all that.

Jacob owned the Yankees for the next 25 years, until shortly before his death in 1939. During that time, he built the club up into one of the most successful franchises in the history of sports. But success didn't happen immediately. In fact, the Yankees continued to struggle through the '15, '16, '17, '18 and '19 seasons. Their turning point came on December 26, 1919, when Ruppert signed a 24-year-old phenom from the Boston Red Sox, a pitcher/outfielder by the name of George Herman Ruth. (After this trade, the Red Sox, who had won four of the previous eight World Series championships, would not claim another until 2004. The 86-year drought attributed to this trade forever became known as the "Curse of the Bambino.")

Chapter 4 – Jacob Ruppert Beer Bottle

With Ruth in the lineup, the franchise was transformed.[22] In 1920, Babe broke the single-season record for home runs as more than 1 million fans came to watch the Yankees play—a first for any MLB team. The following year, 1921, the Yankees captured their first American League pennant, and two years later, in 1923, they won their first World Series title. Fittingly, that was also their first season playing in the Bronx, in the newly constructed Yankee Stadium which Ruppert had personally financed for his team. Under his ownership, the "Bronx Bombers" would go on to claim a total of ten American League pennants and seven World Series Championships. And while his signing of Ruth usually gets the most attention, Ruppert actually acquired 19 future Hall of Famers for his franchise, including Lou Gehrig, Joe DiMaggio, and Lefty Gomez.

After suffering from phlebitis, Jacob died on January 13, 1939, just three months after the Yankees had celebrated their third consecutive World Series victory. Between his brewery empire, major league franchise, and other real estate and business holdings, Ruppert's personal fortune was estimated to be worth between $70 and $100 million. The Ruppert Brewery Company continued operations for another 26 years, until its closure in 1965. And as for the Yankees…well, they've continued their legacy. To date, they've played in a record 40 World Series, 27 of which they've won—roughly the numbers of the next three teams combined!

---

[22] While the success of the Yankees is surely to be attributed to Ruth's presence, an oft-overlooked fact is that the rise of the franchise also coincides with the enactment of Prohibition (1920-33). The nationwide ban on the production and sale of alcohol—and the closing of those breweries associated with it—would have given Jacob Ruppert much more time on his hands, time he could now devote more exclusively to the ownership of his team.

For his integral role in the establishment of this dynasty, Ruppert was posthumously inducted into the National Baseball Hall of Fame on July 28, 2013. Perhaps it was because of the 74-year gap, or the lack of any direct descendants (Jacob was a lifelong bachelor), but for his inauguration, the Hall of Fame's curators were left without many personal artifacts to commemorate Ruppert in their archive. Among the few items featured in his display case were, fittingly enough, four empty Jacob Ruppert Brewer bottles. Bottles just like this one.

Secondary Sources

- Associated Press. "Jacob Ruppert, Famous Leader of Yanks, Dies" in the *St. Petersburg Times* (January 14, 1939), pp. 1, 12.

- "Jacob Ruppert." National Baseball Hall of Fame website: http://baseballhall.org/hof/ruppert-jacob.

- "Jacob Ruppet." Wikipedia: wikipedia.org/wiki/Jacob_Ruppert.

- Leavitt, Daniel R. "Jacob Ruppert," in the Society for American Baseball Research website: sabr.org/bioproj/person/b96b262d.

- "Ruppert, Jacob, Jr." Biographical Directory of the United States Congress, accessed online at: bioguide.congress.gov/scripts/biodisplay.pl?index=R000513.

- Sandomir, Richard. "'Finally Elected to the Hall, the Man Who Bought Babe 'Root'" in the *New York Times* (July 28, 2013), p. SP2.

Chapter 5
Haviland Teacup (ca. 1903-24)

I've encountered a lot of porcelain during these excavations. As you can imagine, the vast majority of it is in the form of small, scattered fragments and shards. On occasion, I find larger pieces broken in situ that I can reassemble. But even then, the final results are rarely complete objects. After all, these items were usually discarded precisely because they were broken and unusable. So the Haviland teacup, which I recovered in three pieces, is about as complete as one can hope to expect. It is missing just a small, moon-shaped piece slightly below and adjacent to its handle. Otherwise, it is around 90% extant.

    There is something different about this teacup. In fact, I noticed it when I first unearthed it. It's lighter, more delicate, and more ornate than most of the china I've come across. I'm no expert, but it seems to be the product of superior craftsmanship. Turns out, my research into the company confirms what my senses were detecting. This porcelain has quite a colorful history. The full story can be found on the Haviland Online website.²³ An abridged version is as follows:

> In 1839 New York, a young American named David Haviland was working as an importer of English porcelain china. One day his shop door opened and a customer came in carrying a small package that was to forever change his life. The seemingly insignificant package held a broken cup that its owner wanted replaced. As Mr. Haviland took the cup in his hands, he was immediately impressed by it. He could tell that it had come from France, but from what part of France? Which of those potteries had turned out this piece? The cup had no mark of identification, and despite his experience and expertise, it baffled him. As he continued to turn it around in his fingers the quality and beauty of the cup's translucent china struck him. He told his customer he could not replace it, but his quest had begun.
>
> Once David Haviland had seen the cup there was nothing to do but go in search of it. Crossing the Atlantic at that time was a long and tedious voyage of several weeks. Nevertheless, he was determined to go to France to find the match - and more - of this unique china. Once in France there were many leads, many blind alleys, and many disappointments. A less determined man would have given up and gone home. But Mr. Haviland persevered, and his romantic and obstinate search was rewarded. He finally came to the city of Limoges, where he found the cup's match. The unique quality of Limoges' porcelain was due to the pure white kaolin clay that was mined locally. This was the same type that had enabled Chinese artisans throughout the centuries to make their exquisite pottery. With excitement and high hopes, David Haviland arranged to export his long-sought French china to New York.
>
> Unfortunately, new difficulties soon beset his path. He encountered wide divergences between the French and American tastes and requirements. The French manufacturers whose factories were of limited capacity proved unwilling to make American shapes and decorations. So David Haviland, unwilling to accept defeat, took a bold step. He decided to move to France,

---

²³ http://www.havilandonline.com/History.htm.

build his own factory in Limoges, and there make china as he saw fit.

In Limoges, Haviland developed models of the new dinnerware services that he wanted to make. He also built his own finishing shops to transform the china from plain to decorated ware. This was a radical step because up to that time, Limoges potteries had made only plain ware; it was subsequently sent off to Paris for decoration. Such innovations were difficult for some of the French artisans to accept, and they rebelled. Accustomed to their own types of decorations, they staged demonstrations of protest when they saw apprentices being shown how to produce American styles and patterns. Havilard's craftsmen often had to go about in groups to protect themselves from attack by decorators who fought such changes. But difficulties were gradually smoothed out and David's venture was ultimately established. On a momentous day in 1842 the first shipment of Haviland china was exported to the United States. Its success was immediate and soon the factory was manufacturing larger quantities of china than had ever been produced in Limoges.

Over the years the business continued to grow and innovate. Haviland hired a painter and sculptor named Felix Bracquemond to lead his design team, and Bracquemond, in turn, drew artists as renowned as Paul Gauguin and Raoul Dufy to the firm. It wasn't long before this bone-white porcelain of flawless quality featuring breathtaking designs was a frequent guest at the White House. Presidents Abraham Lincoln, Ulysses S. Grant, Rutherford B. Hayes, and Benjamin Harrison all ate off Haviland china.[24]

David Haviland's son Theodore eventually followed in his father's steps—as would his grandson and great-grandson. Since the time David Haviland first embarked on his audacious adventure and the present day, the four-

---

[24] So Collector's Weekly: www.collectorsweekly.com/china-and-dinnerware/haviland.

generation company has produced more than 30,000 patterns of fine china. Their appeal has inspired both the creation of the Haviland Collectors International Foundation,[25] which hosts an annual conference, and a Haviland Museum (located in Saint Charles, MO).[26]

Secondary Sources

- "Haviland China" on the *Collector's Weekly* website: www.collectorsweekly.com/china-and-dinnerware/haviland.

- "Haviland Collectors International Foundation" on the *Haviland Collectors* website: http://www.havilandcollectors.com/.

- "Haviland History" on the *Haviland Online* website: www.havilandonline.com/History.htm.

- "Visitor's Guide to the Haviland Museum" on the *Great River Road* website: www.greatriverroad.com/stcharles/haviland.htm.

---

[25] Their website address is www.havilandcollectors.com.
[26] The museum lacks a dedicated website, but more information can be found here: www.greatriverroad.com/stcharles/haviland.htm.

Chapter 6
Johnson's American Anodyne Liniment (ca. 1840-55)

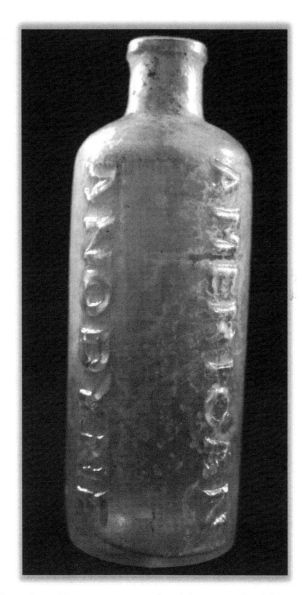

Of all the bottles I've recovered, this one holds an especially dear place in my heart. It is the only fully intact, hand-blown, open-pontiled bottle that I've managed to recover so far. The mouth has an "in rolled lip," which helps date it to ca. 1840-55. While truly avid bottle hunters may have dozens of these types of bottles in their collections, I remain quite awestruck by this little cylindrical, aqua-colored gem. Somehow it has survived the elements for 175 years or so, and even now, it continues to proclaim its original contents in boldly embossed letters: "JOHNSON'S AMERICAN ANODYNE LINIMENT."

The remedy was first prepared by Abner Johnson (1786-1847), a Maine physician who practiced in Oxford, Hancock, and Washington counties. Introduced in 1810, *Johnson's American Anodyne Liniment* contained some rather startling ingredients, compared to today's over-the-counter standards. These included alcohol (its main ingredient), acetate of morphia (i.e., morphine), and extract of hyoscyamus (a small genus of flowering plants in the nightshade family—all of which are toxic).

The liniment was formulated, bottled, and sold on a limited scale until Abner Johnson was joined in the business by his son, Isaac Samuel Johnson. Together, they manufactured and successfully marketed the remedy from their company headquarters in Bangor. In 1881, I.S. Johnson & Co. moved to Custom House Street in Boston, where it is listed in the city directories as late as 1929. However, Stephen Jennings is listed in the directories as its principal owner from 1882 onward, so it may be that I.S. Johnson retired or had died around the time the company moved from Maine.[27]

An "anodyne" simply refers to a painkilling drug or medicine, and a "liniment" is a liquid or lotion (usually oil-based) for rubbing on the body to relieve pain or discomfort. Johnson's concoction was advertised as a veritable panacea for a preponderance of maladies, such as coughs, colds,

---

[27] Christopher Hoolihan, *An Annotated Catalogue of the Atwater Collection of American Popular Medicine and Health Reform,* Vol. 3 (Rochester, New York: University of Rochester Press, 2008), p. 400.

Chapter 6 – Johnson's American Anodyne Liniment

"grippy" (influenza-related) cold, colic, asthmatic distress, bronchial (bronchitis or pneumonia-related) colds, nasal catarrh (excessive discharge), cholera morbus (acute gastroenteritis occurring seasonally and marked by cramps, diarrhea, and vomiting), cramps, diarrhea, bruises, common sore throat, burns and scalds, chaps and chafing, chilblains (itchy and/or tender red or purple bumps that occur as a reaction to cold; also known as pernio or perniosis), frost bites, muscular rheumatism, soreness, sprains and strains, bites, and any other lameness, pain, or inflammation in any part of the body. Purportedly, this cure-all could be used either internally or externally. "Generation After Generation Have Used It. Dropped on Sugar, Children Love to Take It!" proclaimed the advertisements. "Every Mother Should Have It In The House!" And evidently, many mothers did. That is, at least, into the early 1900s.[28]

The 19th century saw large numbers of "snake oil" remedies marketed and sold to unwitting consumers that were ineffective and misleading at best, but toxic, poisonous, addictive, or downright deadly at their worst. In the US, the crackdown on adulterated and misbranded drugs officially began with the passage of the Pure Food and Drugs Act in 1906. This Act paved the way for the establishment of the FDA, a federal agency specifically dedicated to consumer protection in this arena. In 1931-32, the FDA specifically

---

[28] Information collected from Smithsonian's *National Museum of American History* website, "Johnson's American Anodyne Liniment," http://americanhistory.si.edu/collections/search/object/nmah_715760; Deb Gould, "Johnson's Anodyne Liniment," http://debgould.blogspot.com/2013/04/johnsons-anodyne-liniment.html; Ferdinand Meyer V, *Peachridge Glass* website, "Abner and Isaac Samuel Johnson," http://www.peachridgeglass.com/2014/04/dr-johnsons-indian-dyspeptic-bitters-maine/.

went after Johnson's American Anodyne Liniment on a misbranding charge.

Two cases in the FDA's dockets (numbers 18676 & 19183) pertain to this matter. In both instances, samples of the product were seized and analyzed. The FDA's initial findings showed that Johnson's Liniment consisted essentially of "alcohol (14.8 per cent), a fatty oil (8 per cent), volatile oils including turpentine oil and camphor (7.8 per cent), ammonia (0.15 per cent), ether, and water." The second, subsequent analysis yielded very similar results: "alcohol (14.2 per cent by volume), a fatty oil such as olive oil (7.7 per cent), volatile oils, including turpentine oil and camphor (7.5 per cent by volume), ammonia (0.17 gram per 100 milliliters), ether, and water."

Accordingly, the FDA concluded that the product was indeed misbranded, and that "statements appearing in the labeling, regarding the curative or therapeutic effects of the article, were false and fraudulent, since it contained no ingredient or combination of ingredients capable of producing the effects claimed."[29] That judgment effectively marked the demise of Johnson's American Anodyne Liniment.

Secondary Sources

- Gould, Deb. "Johnson's Anodyne Liniment," posted Saturday, April 13, 2013 on the *Blogspot* website: http://debgould.blogspot.com/2013/04/johnsons-anodyne-liniment.html.

- "History of Medicine" on the *US National Library of Medicine* website: https://ceb.nlm.nih.gov/fdanj/handle/123456789/54476.

---

[29] FDA Notices obtained from the *US National Library of Medicine* website: https://ceb.nlm.nih.gov/fdanj/handle/123456789/54476.

Chapter 6 – Johnson's American Anodyne Liniment

- Hoolihan, Christopher. *An Annotated Catalogue of the Atwater Collection of American Popular Medicine and Health Reform,* Volume 3 (Rochester, NY: University of Rochester Press, 2008), p. 400.

- "Johnson's American Anodyne Liniment," on the Smithsonian's *National Museum of American History* website: http://americanhistory.si.edu/collections/search/object/nmah_715760.

- Meyer V, Ferdinand. "Abner and Isaac Samuel Johnson," on the *Peachridge Glass* website: http://www.peachridgeglass.com/2014/04/dr-johnsons-indian-dyspeptic-bitters-maine/.

Chapter 7
Father John's Medicine Bottle (ca. 1890-1910)

This bottle is a handsome specimen. It is composed of rich, dark amber glass, with "FATHER JOHN'S MEDICINE LOWELL, MASS." prominently embossed across the front. It is a BIM (Blown in Mold) variety with a tooled lip, which helps date it to the turn of the century. When I first unearthed it, I was immediately struck by the irony of the name. During my time at Saint Joseph's College, four different Roman Catholic priests have worked in the Office of Campus Ministry. The two chaplains who have served the longest (Tokaz and McHugh) are both named Fr. John. So it seems somehow fitting that a Fr. John's bottle has emerged here. But of course, this product is named for another Fr. John. His story is as follows.

Father John O'Brien was born in 1800 in Ballina, County Tipperary, Ireland (along the Shannon River). He was trained in Maynooth and ordained on December 24, 1828, for the Diocese of Claire. He eventually made his way to America, and served for a time in Virginia and Newburyport, Massachusetts. In 1848, Fr. John was assigned to Saint Patrick's parish in the mill city of Lowell, Massachusetts. His assignment was an especially challenging one, as Lowell was not only a bastion of anti-Catholic and anti-Irish sentiment, but deep divisions existed within the Irish Catholic community itself. Prior to Fr. John's arrival, disgruntled members of Saint Patrick's had splintered off into a second group and founded St. Peter's parish. Some of those who remained at St. Patrick's split yet again when its controversial pastor, Fr. McDermott, purchased an abandoned Methodist church just two blocks away, renamed it St. Mary's Church, and took his followers with him.

This was also a time of peak Irish immigration, with waves of newcomers fleeing the ravages of the potato famine in their motherland. Such people were caught between two worlds, wanting to retain their own identity as Irish men and women, but also hoping to integrate themselves as Americans. Fr. John understood that, especially in light of his own personal experience. His older brother, Fr. Timothy O'Brien, joined him 1851. (The "O'Brien Dynasty" would eventually come to include both Fr. John's nephew, Fr. Michael O'Brien, and his cousin, Fr. William O'Brien.) Together, they went about the work of unifying and strengthening the Irish population and meeting the needs of the wider community.

Since they were not part of earlier struggles between the Irish factions, the O'Briens found that they could move easily between the circles. They regularly attended functions at St. Peter's and St. Mary's, in addition to those hosted by their own parish of St. Patrick's. They pushed for education, and in 1852 brought five sisters of Notre Dame from Cincinnati to open a school for girls. They built a new St. Patrick's church—an imposing stone edifice of 13th century Gothic style, complete with a soaring steeple. Dedicated in 1854, St. Patrick's aesthetically transformed a previously dilapidated section of Lowell known as "the Acre," and even today, it remains one of the grandest structures in town. The O'Briens also prioritized health care for the community. They visited the sick, and as their ministry grew, they became instrumental in establishing St. John's Hospital (operated by the Daughters of Charity) in 1867.

In 1855, Fr. Timothy O'Brien died from a bout of pneumonia. That same year, Fr. John O'Brien was also taken ill. He made his way to the pharmacy of Carleton and Hovey on Merrimack Street to get something for relief. He was given a tonic that was composed of cod liver oil and had a licorice taste. Unlike many other medicines of its time, the prescription contained no alcohol. It worked so well for the priest that he began recommending folks to visit the apothecary and ask for "Father John's Medicine" – and thus, a legend was born. Soon the shop was packaging the cure for sale, and Fr. John was given a small stipend for using his name and picture. It was agreed that anyone Fr. John sent personally would not be charged for it. Although Fr. John O'Brien died in 1874, his namesake remedy long survived him. Within 50 years, it was known far and wide as pharmacies featured huge advertising displays in their windows to promote it. A factory (which still stands on Market Street) was built to handle all matters of manufacturing, bottling, packaging, and shipping.

Early literature touted that Fr. John's Medicine worked on "consumption, grip (influenza), croup, whooping cough, and other diseases of the throat" and guarantees were made by the manufacturer of its restorative powers. However, such contentions were prohibited after the passage of the 1906 Food and Drug Act. Father John's Medicine claims were subsequently downgraded to "A Nutritive Tonic and a Wholesome Medicine" for treating "coughs due to colds" and "deficiencies in vitamins A and D."

In the 1970s the company was sold. The manufacturing building was made into an elderly housing complex, and the product was no longer headquartered in

Lowell. However, this was not the end of Fr. John's Medicine. Today, it is still produced by the Oakhurst Company of Levittown, New York, and can be found on the shelves of many drugstores and pharmacies. The recipe remains essentially the same, except for one active ingredient (dextromethorphan, a cough suppressant) added in accordance with governmental regulations. It still bears the familiar portrait of the Irish priest on an old-fashioned looking label, but the beautiful, distinctive amber bottle is now—disappointingly—made of plastic.

Secondary Sources

- McKean, David. *Lowell Irish* (Charleston, SC: The History Press, 2016), throughout, but esp. pp. 44-85.

- ----------. "Lowell Irish" http://irishlowell.blogspot.com/2012/10/father-john.html.

- "Our Story: 175 Years of Service" on the *Saint Patrick's Church, Lowell* website: http://www.stpatricklowell.org/forms/175-Years-of-Service.pdf.

- *Sadliers' Catholic Directory, Almanac and Ordo* (New York: D. & J. Sadlier & Company, 1875), p. 31.

- "The True Story of Father John's Medicine" on the *UMass Lowell Libraries* website: http://library.uml.edu/clh/fath/Fath.Html

Chapter 8
"Edison" Light Bulb (ca. 1926)
(Un-Tipped Ductile Tungsten Cage Filament Lamp)

I unearthed this artifact at the very first excavation site. To this day, I am amazed that it survived in this good of condition. The glass is relatively thin, and it was completely buried. Had I stepped or kneeled in the wrong place, pressed my trowel too hard, or accidentally shifted my weight, this bulb would easily have shattered. I'm glad I didn't, because it's truly a wonder to behold.

Given its aesthetic appeal, it's easy to see why reproductions of this particular model—commonly known as "Edison light bulbs"—are so popular. They instantly create a nostalgic atmosphere wherever it is desired: in posh restaurants, bars, hotels, resorts, historic sites, movie sets, etc. In fact, their widespread popularity has been the source of growing controversy because of their notoriously high energy consumption.[30]

Just to be clear, the object that I recovered is *not* a reproduction. Technically speaking, it is an "un-tipped ductile tungsten cage filament lamp." The "tipped" (or pointed) dome was replaced by the "un-tipped" (or rounded) variety in 1919, so this particular example was manufactured some time after that. Inside the bulb is a slender central glass rod that is surrounded by radiating support hooks—five on the top and four on the bottom (known as a "5 over 4"). A long and very fine tungsten filament is threaded up and down, around the glass rod, on those hooks. Unfortunately, the original metal base of the bulb (which would allow it to screw into a socket) is missing. At the top of the dome is a small imprint which, although very faint, is nevertheless legible. This imprint, which was utilized from 1926 on, reads "MAZDA 40W 120V" encircling the "GE" monogram.

"Mazda" is the trademarked name registered by GE in 1909 for its incandescent tungsten filament light bulbs. This moniker was employed in the US by GE and Westinghouse until 1945 (and abroad by other companies thereafter). It is derived from the Avestan creator and principle God of

---

[30] For more on this, see Diane Cardwell's *New York Times* article, "When Out to Dinner, Don't Count the Watts" (June 7, 2010), available online at www.nytimes.com/2010/06/08/nyregion/08bulb.html?_r=0. The average LED bulb tends to be around six times more efficient than a regular incandescent bulb, but the average "Edison" bulb uses three times more energy than a typical incandescent. That means that the average "Edison" bulb consumes up to 18 times more energy than an equivalent LED!

Zoroastrianism, "Ahura Mazda" (lit., "Wise Lord"). "GE," of course, stands for General Electric, the company Thomas Edison founded through the 1892 merger of the Edison General Electric Company and the Thomson-Houston Electric Company. To the extent that this bulb was produced by a conglomerate that Edison (among others) helped to establish, it can technically be considered an "Edison light bulb." (But then, so too can every GE light bulb!) As it turns out, this popular designation is somewhat of a misnomer. More accurately, it should be referred to as a "Coolidge light bulb."

I suspect the average reader has never even heard of Dr. William D. Coolidge. (I sure hadn't.) Undoubtedly, this is because he toiled away in the long shadow of Edison's legendary career. Nevertheless, Coolidge proved to be a brilliant scientist in his own right. By the time he died in 1975 (he lived to be 101 and worked to the very end), Coolidge held 83 US patents and had published more than 70 scholarly papers. He was a member of nearly 40 scientific societies, won dozens of extremely prestigious medals and awards, and had received eight honorary degrees. He may have been overshadowed by Edison, but Coolidge ultimately proved capable of doing at least one thing that Edison couldn't: make an even better light bulb.

Most historians are quick to point out that Thomas Edison didn't actually invent the light bulb—despite popular opinion to the contrary. Rather, Edison's research team at Menlo Park developed the first *practical* (commercially viable) incandescent light bulb. But even this was the evolutionary result of a series of scientific contributions made by a number of other innovators, including Volta (1800), Davy (1802), de la Rue (1840), DeMoleyns (1841), Starr (1845), Staite (1848), Swan (1850), and Woodward & Evans (1874).

Chapter 8 – "Edison" Light Bulb

The principle behind incandescence is relatively simple: it's the visible light produced when a given substance is heated high enough to make it glow. (So a campfire—the burning of wood—would be incandescence in its most primitive form.) Scientists found that passing electrical currents through substances also caused them to heat up and produce light. But such a process invariably caused the substances to catch on fire and quickly break down. So designing a practical incandescent light bulb meant overcoming at least three challenges: 1) finding a way to avoid combustion/fire; 2) finding a substance that would glow brightly without breaking down too quickly; and 3) finding a way to modulate and regulate the optimum electrical current needed to pass through that substance.

Edison's predecessors had already figured out the solution to the first problem. They discovered that if the electrical current could be passed through a substance inside of a vacuum (or other oxygen-free environment), then fire could be avoided, since oxygen is required for combustion. That's essentially what a light bulb is (an oxygen-free environment) and why they are made of glass. To his credit, Edison did utilize an improved vacuum system for his bulbs.

As for the second problem, Edison realized that the ideal substance needed to have a high electrical resistance. In other words, as the current passed through it, it needed to encounter a lot of "friction." Such "friction" produced more heat (= a better glow) with less electricity. Edison and his Menlo Park researchers tested thousands of materials. They discovered that carbonized organic substances worked best, and eventually developed a filament out of Japanese bamboo that could last for up to 600 hours.

Edison also had to find the best way to generate and supply the appropriate amount of electrical current to his new filters—especially if such filters were designed to be in every home throughout the US! Indeed, that's ultimately what propelled him into the electricity business, and led to the eventual founding of GE.

As for Coolidge, he began working at the GE Research Laboratory in Schenectady, New York in 1905. Prior to that, he had earned a state scholarship to attend MIT, where he majored in electrical engineering and graduated in 1896. Coolidge continued his studies in Leipzig, Germany, where he received high marks and was awarded the doctorate summa cum laude in 1899. He returned to a research position at MIT, and had been working there when he was hired by GE.

At GE, Coolidge endeavored to find a metal alternative to replace the carbon filament that Edison had developed. Though practical, Edison's filters were not especially energy-efficient—only about three lumens per watt (lpw). European inventors had been actively searching for better filaments, and in 1904 they developed one from tungsten which produced eight lpw. Edison had known that tungsten, which has the highest melting point of any chemical element, had excellent potential as a filament. However, it was extremely brittle and required such a complex mounting structure that it was highly impractical to use. (For instance, early tungsten bulbs had to be handled delicately and couldn't be mounted upside down.) But Coolidge proved determined to overcome such issues. After years of painstaking research and experimentation on this intractable metal, he finally achieved success. He developed a process to make tungsten "ductile," or more flexible and malleable. In fact, he made tungsten *so* pliable that it could be drawn down into a wire merely one-sixth the diameter of a human hair! The result was a commercially viable filament that produced three times more light (ten lpw) than Edison's, lasted much longer, and was sturdy enough to survive being handled and mounted upside down. GE began selling the bulb under the "Mazda" name beginning in 1910, and Coolidge's ductile tungsten filament has remained the basis for incandescent lighting ever since.[31]

Secondary sources

- "Lighting a Revolution. Lamp Inventors 1880-1940: Ductile Tungsten Filament" on the Smithsonian *National Museum of American History* website: http://americanhistory.si.edu/lighting/bios/coolidge.htm.

- Suits, C. G. "William David Coolidge 1873-1975: A Biographical Memoir," National Academy of Sciences (Washington, D.C.: National Academy of Sciences, 1982), accessed online at www.nasonline.org/publications/biographical-memoirs/memoir-pdfs/coolidge-william.pdf.

- "Surprising Science: Who Invented the Light Bulb?" on *The Museum of UnNatural Mystery* website: www.unmuseum.org/lightbulb.htm.

- "Thomas Edison, Interactive modules" on the *Schenectady Museum* website: www.schenectadymuseum.org/edison/c_modules/module_identify/A30.htm.

- "William D. Coolidge" on the *Edison Tech Center* website: www.edisontechcenter.org/coolidge.html.

---

[31] This proved to be only the beginning of Coolidge's long career. His ductile tungsten proved to have a wide variety of applications, including use in x-ray and vacuum tubes, as well as in automotive ignition systems.

- "Who Invented the Light Bulb?" on the *Live Science* website: www.livescience.com/43424-who-invented-the-light-bulb.html.

Chapter 9
Rudolph Valentino Newspaper Clipping (1926)

I unearthed a small Resinol milk jar with its metal lid attached. During the cleaning process, the lid came loose, and much to my surprise, I discovered this small newspaper clipping tucked away inside. It is rare, of course, for anything made of paper to survive 90 years in the ground. Only under these types of conditions could that even be possible. (I have since recovered four more milk jars from this site with their lids still intact. I dare not break them off—but it does make me wonder what else might be hidden inside of them!)

The clipping is a photograph of Rudolph Valentino, with the following caption:

> **Favorite Photo**
> FOR THE FIRST TIME, Rudolph Valentino's favorite photo of himself is published. This picture, taken at his request by J Jack Nugent, Sunday Advertiser staff photographer, was "the most natural of all" according to the late film "sheik," who expressed the wish that it be not published during his lifetime.

Given the circumstances in which it was found, I suspect that this clipping belonged to a female admirer of Valentino. It appears to have been secreted away in this manner, perhaps to prevent her husband from knowing about it. Indeed, Valentino (nicknamed "The Latin Lover") was renowned for making the ladies swoon while provoking jealousy and spurring imitation among the male populace. Tragically, he died young and at the pinnacle of his silent-film career. His premature demise appears to have made his life all the more legendary.

Rudolph Valentino's given birth name was actually—are you ready for this?—Rodolfo Alfonso Rafaello Pierre Filibert Guglielmi di Valentina D'Antonguolla. He was born in Castellaneta (in the heel region of Italy) and first arrived in America as an 18-year-old immigrant in 1913. He worked a variety of odd jobs to support himself, including that as a "taxi dancer"—hiring himself out to wealthy socialite women who sought to "dance" with exotic-looking men. It was in this capacity that Valentino met the Chilean heiress Blanca de Saulles. (Whether these two had an affair remains a matter of debate.) When de Saulles divorced her husband, John, Valentino testified on her behalf about John's infidelities with other dancers. In retribution, John had Valentino arrested on trumped up vice charges. Valentino was eventually released, but when Blanca later shot John over a custody dispute, Rudolph fled to California to avoid involvement in another sensational trial.

Once in California, Valentino was encouraged to try acting. His brooding, swarthy image landed him a number of bit parts in silent movies—often as one of the villains. It was around this time that he first met actress Jean Acker. After a whirlwind, two-month courtship, Valentino married Acker in 1919. Unbeknownst to Valentino, however, Acker was a lesbian. Immediately, she regretted their nuptials. Shortly after their ceremony, Acker locked Valentino out of their honeymoon suite and refused to consummate their marriage. They separated, and were eventually granted a divorce in 1921.

Valentino's first real break came when screenwriter June Mathis convinced Metro executives to cast him as the lead in *The Four Horsemen of the Apocalypse* (1921). Valentino was still a relatively unknown actor, but Mathis lobbied forcefully on his behalf. The film was one of the most successful silent movies ever made. It grossed $4.5 million domestically and catapulted Valentino to fame. Shortly thereafter, Valentino landed perhaps his most famous role as *The Sheik* (1921), which further advanced his career and solidified his status as an international sex symbol.

It was around this same period that Valentino met a costume and set designer named Natasha Rambova. Despite her foreign sounding name and esoteric interests (including art, poetry, spiritualism), Rambova was actually Winifred Kimball Shaughnessy from Salt Lake City, Utah. She had changed her name as a teenager while training with the Imperial Russian Ballet Company in New York City. But regardless of her background, Valentino was smitten with her. At that time, US law required a one year wait period for remarriage following a divorce. Hoping to sidestep the law, Valentino and Rambova wed in Mexico. However, as soon as he returned to the US, Valentino was arrested and jailed on bigamy charges. June Mathis came to their rescue and posted bail. In 1923, Valentino and Rambova were officially remarried in the US.

During their marriage, Rambova proved to have considerable influence over Valentino. She encouraged him to pursue more artistic projects and demanded more creative control over his films. Because Valentino backed her, the studios had no choice but to make such concessions. Rambova's signature film was *Monsieur Beaucaire* (1924). It featured Valentino wearing white face paint, sporting a beauty mark, and dressed in lavish and frilly period costumes. Critics panned the film and many of Valentino's fans decried his effeminate portrayal. Some editorial columnists went so far as to question his masculinity and sexual orientation. Concerned about his image, Valentino felt insulted and humiliated. Since duels had recently been outlawed, Rudolph challenged his critics to settle the score in the boxing ring. None accepted, but *New York Evening Journal* boxing writer Frank O'Neil volunteered to fight in their place. Valentino, who had trained with heavyweight champion Jack Dempsey, knocked O'Neil down and won the bout.

Chapter 9 – Valentino Newspaper Clipping

As Rambova's set and costume demands grew increasingly exorbitant and Valentino's films became less popular and profitable, the studios began to fight back. United Artists offered Valentino an extremely lucrative contract—$10,000 a week plus a percentage of returns—but only on the condition that Rambova have nothing to do with the movies. The offer proved too good to refuse. Valentino signed the contract, hoping that Rambova might understand, retire from Hollywood, and decide to focus on raising a family instead. She didn't. She chose to pursue her own career, left Valentino, and filed for divorce in 1925. Valentino sought to reconcile with her, but to no avail. Subsequently, he went into a tail spin—he had a string of affairs, a series of car crashes, and at least one suicide attempt.

Gradually, however, Valentino began to get his career back on track. He starred in *The Eagle* (1925) and reprised his signature role in *The Son of the Sheik* (1926). However, it was during that film's New York premiere that Valentino became seriously ill. On August 15, Valentino collapsed at the Ambassador Hotel. (He was thought to have had appendicitis, but it was later discovered that he had perforated ulcers.) Despite having surgery, he developed peritonitis and then suffered severe pleuritis in his left lung. He languished in the hospital for a week or so, and died on August 23, 1926.

Fearful that Valentino's death might put a damper on box office receipts, his business manager decided to stage a public viewing in New York. More than 100,000 fans showed up. The mob overwhelmed the police force and the pressure from the crowd caused the large showcase window at the funeral home to shatter. In all, over 100 people were injured. However, once order was restored, visitors paid their respects to Valentino at the rate of 9,000 per hour! Following his funeral mass in New York, Valentino's body was transported back to Hollywood, and crowds gathered en route to bid their farewells. Because Valentino had no crypt of his own, June Mathis once again came to Valentino's aid. She lent him her husband's. This was only supposed to be a temporary arrangement, but when Mathis died the very next year, she was interred next to him. The two lie in state together to this day.

I haven't yet been able to determine the original source or exact date of this particular newspaper clipping. However, it evidently appeared shortly after Valentino's death. Today, it serves as a witness to "the Sheik's" iconic status and devoted following.

Secondary Sources

- "Rudolph Valentino Biography," on the *Biography* website: http://www.biography.com/people/rudolph-valentino-9514591.

- "Rudolph Valentino Biography," on the *IMDb* website: http://www.imdb.com/name/nm0884388/bio.

- "Rudolph Valentino," on the *Wikipedia* website: https://en.wikipedia.org/wiki/Rudolph_Valentino.

Chapter 10
Tin Petticoat Whale Oil Lamp (ca. 1812)

Of all the metal artifacts I've unearthed, this whale oil lamp is certainly among the oldest. It is aptly described in a 1904 *Connecticut Magazine* article, but even at that time, its features had already become unfamiliar:

> A whale oil lamp that became popular, if we are to judge from the large numbers that have come down to us as relics, was introduced about 1812, and from the peculiar flaring shape of its base was known as the "Petticoat" lamp. They were made in several sizes, but were all of the same general form—that is, egg shaped, with a larger end resting in the upper portion of the so-called petticoat. They were generally japanned tin, with a handle secured to the oil fount and the base. Beneath the so-called

petticoat, and attached to the bottom of the oil reservoir, was a round tin tube, usually about one-half inch in diameter, and in length reaching nearly to the bottom of the petticoat. We have inquired of many persons the object of this tube, and it has surprised us to see how many, even among older persons, were ignorant as to the use of this tube. This lamp, which by city users was called a "Petticoat Lamp," to people in the country it was known as the "Peg Lamp." The tube above described being used as a socket into which a stick or peg was placed, and the lower end of the stick being thrust into the ground, held the lamp in an upright position and thus afforded illumination while the farmer was employed in the cellar.[32]

The development of whale-oil lamps marked a notable improvement in the history of illumination. Prior to their use, American colonists relied primarily on homemade candles and Betty lamps. (Betty lamps resemble the oil lamps of antiquity. They consist of a shallow container for the oil with a wick lip at one end.) The earliest of the whale-oil lamps were short and made of metal, with a single wick tube protruding from the top of the reservoir. However, around 1740 Benjamin Franklin discovered that two tubes of a double burner could, if properly spaced,[33] produce three times as much light as a single tube. Franklin's spacing produced a stronger draft from the upward movement of the heated air. Because this draft fed more oxygen to the wicks, combustion was improved and more light was generated.

---

[32] C. A. Quincy Norton, "Artificial Illumination as a Factor in Civilization" in *The Connecticut Magazine*, Vol. 8, No. 4 (1904), p. 535.

[33] Franklin instructed that the two tubes of the double burner be placed so that the space between them was equal to the width of one tube. Some double-burner whale-oil lamps show this spacing, while others—such as the one that I found—do not. Technically, only the former should be classed as true "Franklin burners."

Chapter 10 – Petticoat Whale Oil Lamp

(Franklin also experimented with a third tube, but it interfered too much with the draft.)[34]

Benjamin Franklin believed his improved burner design was too important to be patented; he wanted to make this technology freely available for all. This coincided with Franklin's general interest in the US whaling industry, and in developing more sustainable practices relative to it. As the US Ambassador to France, he had helped to secure fishing and whaling rights in the Atlantic Ocean, specifically in the Grand Banks area off the coast of Newfoundland. And as overfishing began to take its toll on production numbers, he sought ways to reduce consumption rates. In addition to his burner, Franklin also advocated for a Daylight Savings Time-like approach to the workday ("early to bed, early to rise"), so as to take greater advantage of the natural sunlight.[35]

The use of whale oil benefitted the lives of many. It was far superior to animal tallow or bees wax, and its ability to produce a smokeless flame made it an incomparable fuel source. Whale oil was also used for heating, industrial lubrication, soap, candle wax, pharmaceutical compounds, cosmetics, and the processing of textiles and rope. Such a myriad of uses led to its intense demand and spurred a rapidly expanding whaling industry.[36]

---

[34] From Eugene Clute, "Flashback: Lamps and Illuminants," posted March 26. 2009 on the *Collectors Weekly* website: www.collectorsweekly.com/articles/lamps-and-illuminants/.

[35] Jerry Desmond, "Whales, Franklin and Daylight Savings Time," posted March 6, 2014 on the Birmingham History Center website: https://birminghamhistorycenter.wordpress.com/2014/03/06/whales-franklin-and-daylight-savings-time/. Franklin's essay was entitled "An Economical Project for Diminishing the Cost of Light," and it appeared in *The Journal of Paris* in 1784.

[36] George Dvorsky, "1846: The Year We Hit Peak Sperm Whale Oil," filed 7/31/12 on the *io9* website: http://io9.gizmodo.com/5930414/1846-the-year-we-hit-peak-sperm-whale-oil.

From 1680 to 1750, whalers operated from shore in boats as whales were frequent visitors to the large bays and coastal waters of New England. By 1750, however, the whales had largely disappeared from these waters, and it became necessary to use larger ships capable of traveling greater distances to pursue them. Massachusetts' seaports housed the bulk of the fleet. Early on (1700-1758), Nantucket was the busiest, but by 1840 New Bedford had emerged as the largest whaling harbor in the world.[37]

Until the beginning of the 20th century, whaling was considered an admirable occupation.

> It is only through the lens of hindsight that the whaleman's job becomes malicious or cruel. . . Oil was needed for light and lubrication; baleen was needed for skirt hoops and corset stays. That whales had to die to provide these things is a fact of seventeenth-, eighteenth-, and nineteenth-century life. . .[38]

Admirable or not, whaling was also a difficult and often dangerous occupation. The New Bedford Whaling Museum website describes the step-by-step process involved with the hunt:

> Hungry for oil, whaleships kept lookouts at the masthead every day from sunrise to sunset. Each foremast hand took a two-hour turn aloft, his eyes scanning the ocean, hoping to see the spout, a vapor plume caused by the whale's breath. Two pieces of lumber nailed to the top-gallant mast and a pair of iron hoops at breast-height were the lookout's only support as he steadied himself 100 feet above the deck....

---

[37] Norton, *Illumination*, p. 529.
[38] From "Overview of North American Whaling: Whales and Hunting" on the *New Bedford Whaling Museum* website: www.whalingmuseum.org/learn/research-topics/overview-of-north-american-whaling/whales-hunting#.

Chapter 10 – Petticoat Whale Oil Lamp

The moment when the whaleboats were launched and the chase began was filled with the frenzied excitement of a hunt. The crews raced against each other, struggling to arrive at the whale first. Even as they moved closer to danger, they could not see their prey. They faced the stern (rear) of the boat and the boatheader (a mate or the captain), who steered the boat, urged the men to row harder....

For all hands, especially the inexperienced, it was a tense moment as the small, fragile whaleboat drew up to the unpredictable and enormous mammal....The harpooneer stood at the bow (front), bracing his leg against the thighboard, weapon in hand, poised for action. "Give it to him," the boatheader shouted when the boat was within a few feet of their prey and the harpooneer plunged his barbed weapon into the whale's back. At this moment of danger, the crew backed the boat away, as the whale thrashed in pain. The jaws or tail of a 50-ton whale could smash a boat and send the crew tumbling into the water. (In rough seas or fog, losing the whaleboat was a death sentence, if the ship could not find the scattered crew.)

The whale usually dove, taking down with it the embedded harpoon. The crew allowed the line to run out to prevent the boat from being dragged down with the whale. The line was turned around a small post called a loggerhead, to slow it down as it ran out. As the whale pulled the boat, the line often played out so fast that it smoked from the friction. If the line became fouled, the boat could be dragged underwater. A seaman caught in the rushing line could be pulled from the boat. When the whale came up to breathe, it often swam on the surface, at speeds of over twenty miles per hour....The whaleboat, attached to the prey by harpoon and line, bounced along, showering the men with spray. The danger was very real that the crew might be carried so far from the ship that it could not find them again.

When the whale tired, the crew pulled on the line to draw the boat close to their prey....The harpooneer went aft (to the back) to steer, while the boatheader carried a lance forward and plunged it into a vulnerable spot, such as the heart or lungs. With each breath, the whale spouted blood. As the whaleboat backed off again, the crew observed the awesome spectacle of the death of the whale. The great beast swam violently in ever smaller circles, a pattern known as the "flurry." The end came when the whale beat the water with its tail, shuddered and turned fin out, a whaling term meaning that the whale had expired and turned over on its side.

After hours of tremendous exertion, the whaleboat crew still had work to do....The dead whale, often weighing more than 50 tons, had to be towed back to the ship by a handful of exhausted men, unless the ship could sail to it. It was important to process the whale quickly to prevent sharks from feasting on too much of the valuable carcass....The whale was made fast to the starboard (right) side of the ship with heavy chains. The crew erected the cutting stage (plank platform) above the carcass and stripped off the blubber, a thick layer of fat, with cutting spades set in 15-foot long poles. The process was very much like peeling skin from an orange, with long strips cut into "blanket pieces," weighing about a ton each. After hauling the blanket pieces up on deck, they divided them into smaller "horse pieces" and "Bible leaves," so-called because they resembled books.

Although trying out, or "boiling" (extracting oil from blubber) was carried out on shore in the early days of whaling, by the mid-nineteenth century, whaleships carried "tryworks" – big iron pots set in a brick stove. A fire was set in the stove beneath the pots; "Bible leaves" were tossed into the pots and cooked until the oil was rendered (extracted) from the blubber; the oil was cooled, placed in casks of varying sizes, and stored in the hold of the ship (the cargo space at the bottom of the ship near the water line). Onshore, it would be strained and bleached, then sold, primarily as lamp oil. The standard unit of measure, the barrel, contained 31½ gallons....

Processing a whale was nearly as dangerous as hunting one. The deck became so slick with blood and oil that a man could slip overboard to the sharks below. Others were crushed by the enormous weight of strips of blubber or wounded by cutting tools. As the blubber was being rendered in the tryworks, a wave sometimes rocked the ship and splashed scalding oil onto the crew. On rare occasions, the fire in the tryworks spread and devastated the ship.[39]

---

[39] Ibid.

Chapter 10 – Petticoat Whale Oil Lamp

The whalers targeted a variety of species. Initially, their primary objective was the Right Whale—so named because it was often found close to shore, floated after being killed, and was the source of a large supply of blubber. Consequently, it became the most endangered of all species. Eventually, however, it was discovered that the straw-colored oil from the Sperm Whale (spermaceti, or astral oil) produced a far superior glow without the disagreeable odor so characteristic of the others. Indeed, such oil is unique. It is found in the colossal heads of these creatures, primarily in a large organ called the "case." To this day, scientists debate its function, although most suspect it has something to do with either buoyancy or the whale's motion-sensing sonar. Whatever the case may be, a fully mature Sperm Whale could yield up to 500 gallons of spermaceti. And because such oil commanded higher prices in the marketplace, Sperm Whales became the ultimate prize.

The US whaling industry peaked around 1845, with five million gallons of sperm oil and ten million gallons of (other) whale oil being produced and imported annually. It's estimated that nearly 236,000 whales were killed in the 19th century alone. This had a devastating impact on the marine environment. Large populations of whales were completely decimated. Young calves would attempt to suckle on vessels that contained nothing but the rendered scents of their mothers. And some bull whales, increasingly traumatized by the attacks of their hunters, stove and rammed their boats with a distinctly calculated ferocity.[40]

It is within this context that Herman Melville's classic tale, *Moby Dick*, was written. Melville himself had at least

---

[40] Dvorsky, "1846," http://io9.gizmodo.com/5930414/1846-the-year-we-hit-peak-sperm-whale-oil.

some firsthand experience with whaling, having sailed aboard the *Acushnet* from New Bedford in January 1841. And he had undoubtedly heard the real-life story of a huge albino Sperm Whale that sailors had nicknamed "Mocha Dick," after the island of Mocha whose waters he inhabited. Mocha Dick had reportedly killed more than 30 men. He had attacked and damaged three whaling ships, 14 whaleboats, and had sunk two merchant vessels. In May of 1839, Jeremiah N. Reynolds, an American journalist and explorer, published a lengthy article about Mocha Dick in the *Knickerbocker Magazine*. Reynolds' article concluded with a detailed account of the final battle, in which this behemoth was ultimately vanquished. As the carcass was towed alongside the ship, waiting to be cut up, an eye-witness described the scene:[41]

> Mocha Dick was the longest whale I ever looked upon. He measured more than seventy feet from his noodle to the tips of his flukes; and yielded one hundred barrels of clear oil, with a proportionate quantity of 'head-matter.' It may emphatically be said, that the scars of his old wounds were near his new, for not less than twenty harpoons did we draw from his back; the rusted mementos of many a desperate encounter.

By the mid-1800s the industry began suffering the natural consequences of unrestricted harvesting. After plundering the Atlantic, Pacific, and Indian Oceans, whalers had to chase smaller whales in colder and more extreme waters, all while having to employ larger vessels over longer periods of time. This led to diminished returns and caused

---

[41] Information in the preceding paragraph and following quotation both taken from "Was Moby Dick a Real Whale" on the *About Education* website: history1800s.about.com/od/whaling/f/realmobydick.htm.

Chapter 10 – Petticoat Whale Oil Lamp

prices to soar.[42] In 1843 spermaceti had sold for 63 cents a gallon; by 1864, it had more than tripled to $1.92.[43]

Fortunately, around this same time, an alternative fuel began to emerge. In 1849, Dr. Abraham Gesner discovered a way to distill kerosene from petroleum. His method allowed for the cheap and easy production of a lamp fuel that was even more desirable than whale oil. Accordingly, the petroleum industry rapidly usurped the whaling industry. By 1876, the 735-ship fleet had shrunk to just 39. And further refinements in petroleum production resulted in even steeper price drops, from 59 cents per gallon in 1865 to just seven cents in 1895.[44]

Today, some see in the rise and fall of the whale oil industry a cautionary tale regarding our use (and abuse) of natural resources, the unintended consequences of environmental degradation, and the importance of technological advancement and innovation. Important lessons from this bygone era can still be taught through its classic literature as well as through its few remaining relics. Relics like this whale oil lamp.

Secondary Sources

- "A Brief History of Whaling" on the *About Education* website: http://history1800s.about.com/od/whaling/a/histwhaling.htm.

---

[42] Dvorsky, "1846," http://io9.gizmodo.com/5930414/1846-the-year-we-hit-peak-sperm-whale-oil.

[43] Rev. S. J. M. Eaton, *Petroleum: A History of the Oil Region of Venango County, Pennsylvania* (Philadelphia: J. P. Skelly & Co., 1866), p. 283.

[44] Dvorsky, "1846," http://io9.gizmodo.com/5930414/1846-the-year-we-hit-peak-sperm-whale-oil.

- Clute, Eugene. "Flashback: Lamps and Illuminants," posted March 26. 2009 on the *Collectors Weekly* website: www.collectorsweekly.com/articles/lamps-and-illuminants/.

- Desmond, Jerry. "Whales, Franklin and Daylight Savings Time," posted March 6, 2014 on the *Birmingham History Center* website: https://birminghamhistorycenter.wordpress.com/2014/03/06/whales-franklin-and-daylight-savings-time/.

- Eaton, Rev. S. J. M. *Petroleum: A History of the Oil Region of Venango County, Pennsylvania* (Philadelphia: J. P. Skelly & Co., 1866).

- Dvorsky, George. "1846: The Year We Hit Peak Sperm Whale Oil," filed 7/31/12 on the *io9* website: http://io9.gizmodo.com/5930414/1846-the-year-we-hit-peak-sperm-whale-oil.

- Norton, C. A. Qunicy. "Artificial Illumination as a Factor in Civilization" in *The Connecticut Magazine*, Vol. 8, No. 4 (1904), pp. 529-42.

- "Overview of North American Whaling: Whales and Hunting" on the *New Bedford Whaling Museum* website: www.whalingmuseum.org/learn/research-topics/overview-of-north-american-whaling/whales-hunting#.

- Pees, Samuel T. "Oil History," on the *Petroleum History Institute* website: www.petroleumhistory.org/OilHistory/pages/Whale/whale.html.

- "Was Moby Dick a Real Whale" on the *About Education* website: http://history1800s.about.com/od/whaling/f/realmobydick.html

Chapter 11
Carved Soapstone Calligraphy Brush Wash Bowl from China (ca. 1930-40s)

When this artifact first emerged from the ground, I had no idea what it was. Carved out of yellowish-green and reddish-purple soapstone, it appears to be tiny oval bowl (1¾ inches long, ¾ of an inch wide) flanked by a peach and associated foliage. The detail surrounding the bowl is pockmarked throughout with carpenter-ant sized holes—some impressed, some drilled straight through. Inscribed in thin lettering on the reverse, near the base of the bowl, is its country of origin: CHINA. I'd never seen anything like it. After considerable research on the internet, I finally discovered its function. This is a Chinese calligraphy brush wash bowl (and holder).

The word "calligraphy" literally means "beautiful writing." Although it has been practiced and appreciated by many different cultures throughout the world, calligraphy enjoys an unparalleled prestige in China. From as early as the Han Dynasty (206 B.C.E.-220 C.E.), calligraphy has been considered the supreme visual art form. It is more valued than painting and sculpture, and has ranked alongside poetry as a means of self-expression and cultivation.[45]

The high status accorded to calligraphy by the Chinese is probably due, in part, to the complexity and distinctiveness of their language in its written form. Unlike our own alphabetical system, each Chinese word is represented by its own unique symbol, a kind of abstract diagram known as a "character." Each word must be learned separately through a laborious process of writing and rewriting its individual character until it has been memorized. To read the average newspaper requires a knowledge of around 3,000 characters; a well-educated person is familiar with about 5,000; a professor with perhaps 8,000. More than 50,000 characters exist in all, most of which are rarely used.[46]

In the Chinese culture, *how* you write is just as important as *what* you write. For this reason, the necessary tools of the trade—the brush, the ink, the paper, and the ink stone—are collectively known as the "Four Treasures of the Study." The invention of paper is widely acknowledged to be one of China's greatest contributions to the world. But the brushes play an almost metaphysical role—they are considered to be extensions of the calligraphers themselves. They are the conduits of an individual's essence—their nature, temperament, energy, and disposition.[47]

---

[45] Charles Lachman, "Chinese Calligraphy," on the *Asia Society* website: http://asiasociety.org/education/chinese-calligraphy.

[46] Dawn Delbanco, "Chinese Calligraphy" in *Heilbrunn Timeline of Art History: The Metropolitan Museum of Art* website: http://www.metmuseum.org/toah/hd/chcl/hd_chcl.htm.

[47] Lachman, "Calligraphy," http://asiasociety.org/education/chinese-calligraphy.

Chapter 11 – Calligraphy Brush Wash Bowl

> A typical brush consists of a bundle of animal hairs (black rabbit hair, white goat hair, and yellow weasel hair were all very popular) pushed inside a tube of bamboo or wood....The hairs are not all of the same length; rather, an inner core has shorter hairs around it, which in turn are covered by an outer layer that tapers to a point. Brushes come in a wide variety of shapes and sizes that determine the type of line produced. What all such brushes have in common, however, is their flexibility. It is this feature more than any other that allows the calligraphic line to be so fluid and expressive.[48]

Given the significance of the calligraphy brush, its proper treatment and care are absolutely necessary. Brushes should be cleaned and washed immediately after use. This should be done by swishing the brush around in a jar of plain cold water. (This is where the brush wash pot comes into use.) Warm water and soap tend to dry out the natural oils in the brush hairs and may dissolve the glue that holds the hairs inside the handle. Next, excess water should be shaken from the brush, and the brush "dressed," or brought back to its original shape, with one's fingers. Finally, the brush should be allowed to air dry in this position, with all its hairs straight. (This is the purpose of the holes in the carved stone; the stems of calligraphy brushes can be inserted into them for drying.)[49]

Dating this particular brush pot is a little tricky. It is, after all, a stone-carved artifact, and calligraphy in China goes back thousands of years. Most internet listings conveniently sidestep this issue and simply refer to these objects as "vintage"—an unhelpful catchall which *really* means: "I know it's old, I just don't know *how* old." However,

---

[48] Ibid.
[49] "Oriental Brush Care" at *Daniel Smith* website: http://www.danielsmith.com/content--id-137.

the appearance of CHINA may provide something of a clue. The McKinley Tariff Act of 1890 required all foreign imports to be marked with their countries of origin. Prior to this, only more prestigious items (like fine porcelain wares, for example) were so indicated. In 1914, the law was revised and the phrase "Made in..." was required. These two laws seem to suggest that the object at hand was crafted sometime between 1890 and 1914. Unfortunately, there are too many exceptions to this later law to make it a hard and fast rule. In fact, the excavation area where this artifact emerged from has typically yielded finds from the 1930s and 40s. So for now, I'm siding with the archaeological context pending stronger evidence to the contrary.

Secondary Sources

- Delbanco, Dawn. "Chinese Calligraphy" on the *Heilbrunn Timeline of Art History: The Metropolitan Museum of Art* website: http://www.metmuseum.org/toah/hd/chcl/hd_chcl.htm.

- Lachman, Charles. "Chinese Calligraphy" on the *Asia Society* website: http://asiasociety.org/education/chinese-calligraphy.

- "Oriental Brush Care" at *Daniel Smith* website: http://www.danielsmith.com/content--id-137.

Chapter 12
Virgin Mary Stone Relief (ca. 1890-1940)

For the most part, the field work and documentary research I've conducted for this undertaking have had little to do with my professional work as a biblical scholar. I mean, both rely heavily upon the principles of historical context. But beyond that, there is decidedly little overlap between the Ancient Near Eastern milieu of Judaism and early Christianity and that of post-colonial Northern New England. However, at least one artifact that I've recovered occupies this sliver of common ground.

    I unearthed this stone relief at the base of a house foundation, around ten inches down. The site itself has typically yielded artifacts from the 1930s and 40s, but this particular object was lying slightly below a Sumner C. Davis, Jr. pharmaceutical bottle, which dates to the 1890s. Aside from its intricately carved façade, it is otherwise unmarked. It is not signed, nor does it bear any indication of its country of origin. That information could have appeared on the 15%

or so that is missing (although statistically, this is unlikely). Alternatively, this object may lack a stamp of origin either because it was crafted domestically, or it was imported prior to the McKinley Tariff Act (1890). As noted, the archaeological context is a bit ambiguous, so my rough estimate of its age (ca. 1890-1940) is about as accurate as I can be for now. I have yet to locate anything on the internet that closely resembles it.

This item is, as near as I can tell, an oval-shaped wall plaque. It is a two dimensional relief carved out of purplish soapstone. Its scene features five and a half figures—a fraction of the left side has broken off, splitting one of these figures in half. (I suspect that mislaid piece contains at least one more figure as well....) The reverse side is rough, with the natural vertical streaks and scraggly cleavages of the stone clearly visible. Just below its mid-section, a horizontal gash runs nearly the length of the piece. I assume this streak had something to do with its mounting.

The figures featured in this relief are somewhat subject to interpretation. However, the scene has unquestionably been inspired by the Infancy Narrative from the Gospel of Luke. A working knowledge of that account sheds considerable light on the identity of these characters. The young woman in the center with the flowing head scarf and ornamented blouse, her right hand resting upon her chest and her left upon an infant, is the Virgin Mary. Indeed, the halo above her head suggests as much. Accordingly, the infant to her right (the viewer's left) is baby Jesus. He, too, sports a halo. His left arm rests upon Mary's, and his right draws up a cloth—reminiscent, perhaps, of the "swaddling cloth" mentioned in the Luke 2:7, 12.

Above Mary's right shoulder (to the viewer's left) is the only non-haloed member of this group. Its ethereal positioning and winged framing indicate that this figure is a cherub. In keeping with Luke's story, perhaps he is intended to signify the angel Gabriel, the messenger from God who first appeared to Mary and announced to her the "good news" of her impending pregnancy (1:26).

Immediately behind Mary (to the viewer's right) is a man who also has a halo. Given his stature and proximity to Mary, one might be tempted to assume that this is her husband, Joseph. (Indeed, that was my initial thought.) But a number of clues suggest otherwise. His long hair, long beard, and wrinkles denote a much older man. But more importantly, he is portrayed as turning his back to Mary and Jesus, away from them and toward yet another woman to the viewer's right. She, too, is haloed, but her facial features characterize her as a woman much older than Mary. This couple seems to belong together. But who are they?

Luke's narrative presents us with two possibilities. The first is Simeon & Anna. Shortly following Jesus's birth, his parents bring him to the Jewish Temple in Jerusalem to offer a sacrifice to God in fulfillment of the prescriptions of their religious Law (the Torah). While at the Temple, the family crosses paths with Simeon, "a righteous and devout man" who had been "awaiting the consolation of Israel" (2:25). That Simeon is older is implied by the fact that "it had been revealed to him by the holy Spirit that he should not see death before he had seen the Messiah of the Lord" (2:26). Upon encountering the infant, Simeon takes Jesus into his arms and declares:

> Now, Master, you may let your servant go in peace, according to your word, for my eyes have seen your salvation, which you prepared in sight of all the peoples, a light for revelation to the Gentiles, and glory for your people Israel (2:29-32).

Immediately thereafter, the family comes to meet Anna, a prophetess. According to Luke, "she was advanced in years, having lived seven years with her husband after her marriage, and then as a widow until she was eighty-four" (2:36-37). Like Simeon, she, too "gave thanks to God and spoke about the child to all who were awaiting the redemption of Jerusalem" (2:38).

So the elderly figures behind Mary in this relief could be Anna and Simeon. However, the remaining half-figure behind Jesus (on the viewer's far left) suggests another couple altogether. That half-figure is also a child, similar in age to Jesus, but slightly older. He too has a halo (so he's not a cherub). Who is he? Again, Luke's account provides us with the answer.

Luke doesn't begin his Gospel with Jesus's birth. Rather, his opening pages narrate the origins of John the Baptist. According to Luke, John's father was a Temple priest named Zechariah and his mother was Elizabeth. "Both were righteous in the eyes of God, observing all the commandments and ordinances of the Lord blamelessly. But they had no child because Elizabeth was barren and both were advanced in years" (1:6-7). One day, as Zechariah was ministering in the sanctuary, the angel Gabriel appeared to him and promised that Elizabeth would give birth to a son—one destined to "prepare a people fit for the Lord" (1:17). Despite Zechariah's understandable skepticism, this miraculous event does indeed come to pass. Following Gabriel's instructions, Zechariah names his newborn son "John."

Many biblical commentators are quick to draw parallels between John and Jesus. But the way that Luke has crafted his narrative suggests a more primary correspondence between Zechariah and Mary. Consider that the angel Gabriel appears to both, who are initially "troubled" by their encounter with him. Gabriel enjoins them to "be not afraid" and announces to them the advent of their sons. Given their circumstances (Elizabeth is barren; Mary is a virgin), both conceptions are considered miraculous works of God. Gabriel describes the unique mission for which each child is destined, and informs the parents of their names. In response to the news, both Zechariah and Mary question Gabriel. And both deliver a canticle of praise to God. All of these parallels are hardly coincidental. Rather, what Luke is establishing here is a pattern of gender symmetry (similarities balanced along gender lines) that he will continue to develop throughout the rest of his gospel.[50]

So if this second infant in the relief is indeed John the Baptist (and I don't know who else it could be), then the elderly couple that appears behind Mary is most likely John's parents, Zechariah and Elizabeth. In this respect, the back-to-back arrangement of Mary and Zechariah does considerable justice to Luke's gender symmetry motif. But one main character seems to be missing. Where is Jesus's father, Joseph? To be sure, he plays a decidedly supportive role in Luke's account, especially compared to his headliner role in the Gospel of Matthew. Nevertheless, he is conspicuously absent from this tableau.

My guess is that Joseph most likely appears in the missing section of this plaque. I find tremendous irony in all of this. For here we are presented with a popular and quintessentially Catholic scene where all the main characters are accounted for *except* for Saint Joseph. That void naturally begs the question: how should we fill in that

---

[50] For more, see Steven L. Bridge, *Getting the Gospels*, (Peabody, MA: Hendrickson, 2004), pp. 50-53.

space? But who better to serve as his proxy and stand in that gap than the very institution that bears his name?

Secondary Sources

- Bridge, Steven L. *Getting the Gospels* (Peabody, MA: Hendrickson, 2004).

- *The Gospel According to Luke* (esp. Luke 1:1-2).

Chapter 13
George Washington Inaugural Button, GWI 9-A (1789)

Among the thousands of artifacts that I have unearthed, the George Washington Inaugural Button is in a class by itself. To be sure, it is an outstanding example of the campus's material heritage. But beyond that, some might consider it a National Treasure.[51] George Washington Inaugural Buttons are considered to be THE Holy Grail of the hobby, and metal detector enthusiasts throughout the country have spent lifetimes in pursuit of them. Because of their scarcity and historical significance they have developed a cult-like status among collectors, and on the rare occasions when they come up for auction they fetch correspondingly high prices.

---

[51] There is a deliberate allusion here. In the 2004 Disney film of the same name, Benjamin Franklin Gates (played by Nicholas Cage) steals the Declaration of Independence in order to find a legendary Knights Templar treasure hidden by America's founding fathers. Although Washington Inaugural Buttons are not the object of Gates' quest, their rarity and value is nevertheless acknowledged by the screenplay. Dr. Abigail Chase, an archivist at the National Archives in Washington, D.C.—and Gate's love interest—is a collector. In an apparent act of kindness, Ben gives her a button that was missing from her collection. She is moved by the gesture, not knowing that it is really a ploy he is using to steal her password.

Surprisingly little has been written about these relics—which only compounds their mystique and allure. The standard reference works are J. Doyle DeWitt's *A Century of Campaign Buttons, 1789-1889* (Hartford, 1959), J. Harold Cobb's *George Washington Inaugural Buttons & Medalets 1789 & 1793* (Private printing, 1963), and Alphaeus S. Albert's *Record of American Uniform and Historical Buttons* (Boyertown, PA: Boyertown Pub. Co., 1969). (Currently, all of these books are out of print, and so have become collector's items unto themselves!) Of the three, Albert supplies the most information—but even then, it's only a dozen pages or so.

Technically speaking, these buttons weren't campaign buttons, per se. Washington never "campaigned" against any contenders. Rather, they were forged in honor of the Inauguration itself. Allow me to set the stage:

The year was 1789 and a new Government was being forged. Its organization was scheduled to have taken place on March 4, but back in those days, communications and travel were unreliable, slow, and difficult. Therefore, it wasn't until April 6 that a quorum of Congress finally reached New York (at that time, the nation's capital). The electoral votes were counted, and Washington was the unanimous choice. A messenger was dispatched to Mount Vernon to notify him of his election to the Presidency. Upon receiving word, he set out for New York immediately, and was greeted by the people in a triumphal procession all along the way. He took the Oath of Office as the first President of the United States on April 30. According to one eyewitness account of that event,

> It was one of those magnificent days of clearest sunshine that sometimes make one feel in April as if summer had come. At noon of that day Washington went from his lodgings, attended by a military escort, to Federal hall, at the corner of Wall and

Chapter 13 – George Washington Inaugural Button

Nassau streets, where his statue has lately been erected. The city was ablaze with excitement. A sea of upturned faces surrounded the spot, and as the hero appeared, thousands of cocked hats were waved, while ladies fluttered their white handkerchiefs. Washington came forth in a suit of dark brown cloth of American make, with silk hose and shoes decorated with silver buckles, while at his side hung a dress-sword. For a moment all were hushed in deepest silence, while the Secretary of the Senate held forth the Bible upon a velvet cushion, and the Chancellor Livingston administered the oath of office. Then, before Washington had as yet raised his head, Livingston shouted,—and from all the vast company came answering shouts,—"Long live George Washington, President of the United States!"[52]

Such is the context in which the Inaugural Buttons originally emerged. But exactly who created them, and where, remain the subjects of lively debate. It is not known how many were produced, or even how many different varieties exist. Indeed, classifying "varieties" depends on how one defines an Inaugural Button, and how closely one considers departures in details. It appears that around 30 different styles were created, but the slightest of discrepancies among these can push the number of "varieties" up much higher. Cobb, for instance, suggests "seventy or so," but readily acknowledges that "only four or five patterns of these buttons are commonly met with by collectors: the dated Eagle, GW in oval, Linked States, and Eagle and Star."[53] None of these are the type that I unearthed.

For more information about my button, I had to track down a present-day expert. And if the internet is any indication, then the country's leading authority on George Washington Inaugural Buttons would have to be Robert J.

---

[52] Albert, *Record*, pp. 383-84.
[53] Cobb, *Buttons*, p. 5.

Silverstein. He has devoted his life to studying them, and has amassed an enviable personal collection. His website, www.georgewashingtoninauguralbuttons.com, is a source of unparalleled information,[54] and he routinely provides professional evaluations of specimens for individuals, businesses, museums, and other organizations. I have never met anyone as intricately familiar with these artifacts as Robert. Take, for example, his description of the variety that I recovered:

> **GWI 9-A THE DOTTED SCRIPT "GW" MONOGRAM:** This button was manufactured in either stamped Brass or Copper. These early buttons were all cast as one-piece buttons, and had a soldered on loop shank....The button's pattern depicts a fancy *Dotted Script "GW" Monogram* in the button's center well. The "W" is adorned with a nice flamboyant *Colonial Swirl*, which circles around both letters. Surrounding the Monogram is a *Wide Flat Ring* which adds a sizable dimension to the button. The plain ring also helps emphasize the inner Monogram, and accentuates the outer Slogan. Outside of the Wide Flat Ring is a depressed channel. This contains the popular Slogan Livingston first said after administering the Oath to Washington, "*Long Live The President.*" This is written in raised Roman Font Capital Block Letters. In-between each of the three Slogan's words is a raised *Separation Dot*. This most likely was added for spacing, and to allow each word to stand out a little more boldly. In the bottom legend there is a raised *Six Pointed Star*, which is sometimes shown with Twelve encircling Dots. This obviously is the *representation of the original Thirteen States*.[55] Outside of the banner well is a slightly raised protective Border Ring. This small

---

[54] All of the information that appears in this chapter from Silverstein's website was publicly accessible when I first researched it, on July 18, 2014. Since then, some of it has (presumably) been moved to a members-only portal.

[55] There was still one state that had not yet ratified the Constitution when this button was produced. Rhode Island finally passed their vote on May 29, 1790, making it the last of the original 13 colonies to join the United States.

Chapter 13 – George Washington Inaugural Button 93

outside ring gives the slogan a little more emphasis, and helps protect the inner design.[56]

To this description, Silverstein appends two important remarks:

> First, this unique pattern is very similar to the Seal of Fredericksburg, VA Masonic Lodge.[57] The lettering, design, and the use of a Star surrounded by Dots is the same. Second, historical diaries indicate that this particular button was worn by George Washington's Elite Troops! This button was originally only found in the places of the soldiers who had served under Washington's direct command.[58]

The latter observation would explain why this button type is not as commonly encountered as some of the others. Of course, it also begs the question: To whom did it originally belong? I have a few ideas, but we'll return to that momentarily.

As I indicated above, I had the opportunity to meet Silverstein, and to have this button authenticated[59] and

---

[56] Taken from Silverstein's website. The only detail I would add (as Silverstein does elsewhere) is that the central well and depressed channel both feature stippled backgrounds.

[57] George Washington was known to have been a member of this Lodge. He was initiated an Entered Apprentice on November 4, 1752, passed to the degree of Fellowcraft on March 3, 1753, and raised to Master Mason—the highest basic rank—on August 4, 1753. He was then 21 years old.

[58] Silverstein, ibid.

[59] Given their popularity and value, these buttons have been the subject of later reproductions. (In fact, some of these are now collector's items!) The GWI 9-A has been reproduced at least twice. The easier one to spot is that in a series by Liberty Village (1974)—primarily because it is stamped on the back: "Repro 74 Liberty Village." A second reproduction is a bit more challenging to identify. Nevertheless, variations in lettering, metal, and design (notably, in the ending tail swirl beside the cursive "W" and 13 dots surrounding the star) offer certain

professionally evaluated by him. His characteristically meticulous report is as follows:

GWI 9-A Eval. Steven L Bridge Evaluation Sept 27 14   9/29/14 8:15 AM

GWI 9-A-1 THE DOTTED SCRIPT "GW" MONOGRAM

Color: An Olive Green with Orange Rusty Undertones.
Metal: Stamped Brass with Raised Lettering in the Legend.
Size: 35mm.
Rarity: R-3
Variety Type: Flat Wells, Dotted Tail Variety.
Present Condition: An Excavated Specimen, Strong Planchet Condition, Strong Impressions.
Obverse Button Analysis: This wonderful GWI 9-A specimen has retained all of it's original strike impressions from the steel die. The brass planchet is solid and flat, and shows no signs of metal fatigue or deterioration. The center well has a nice deep strike impression. The fancy Dotted Script "GW" Monogram is nicely elevated with crisp clear lines, and all of the individual dots are shown clearly, there is some flat pressed tops, but minor. The tail dots do show some die muteness, but again pleasing to the eye. The Colonial Swirl off the "W" is nicely raised without any smooth spots or broken lines in the swirl. The Wide Flat Border Ring does have some small minor corrosiveness, but it blends in nicely with the button's color. Unfortunately the narrow Banner Well lacks the clarity of it's stipples in the base. The Six Pointed Star is a bit worn and flat, but easy to see. The angled lines lack the clarity and border definition. Ten of the Twelve Dots show a strong image, and lack height elevation due to die fatigue during fabrication. Two of the lower dots in the star ring are worn smooth into the surface. The three raised Separation Dots are nicely elevated and still easy to see. All the Roman Font Capital Block letters have good height, and show strong straight letter lines that are easy to read. The narrow Edge is slightly wavy, but in strong condition without any nicks or cuts.
Reverse Button Analysis: This is flat a one-piece button with a soldered on loop shank. The shank is original straight and intact. The surface appears to be a bit granular.

Excavated by Steven L. Bridge at an old house foundation in Portland, Maine July 2014.

Robert J Silverstein
Isabela's George Washington Inaugural Buttons

clues. The dating of this second reproduction is unclear. Albert has it as 1943 (*Record*, p. 392), but Silverstein lists it as "America's Centennial Celebration 1889 Pewter Reproductions" (www.georgewashington inauguralbuttons.com).

Chapter 13 – George Washington Inaugural Button

A couple of explanations are in order. First, Silverstein uses the following Five-Point Scale for the planchet casting and strike impressions:

1) Exceptional
2) Strong
3) Good
4) Fair
5) Poor

The scale's highest rating (Exceptional) is normally reserved for non-excavated specimens. Therefore, the two "Strongs" earned by this button place it among the best of the excavated examples—and even higher than several of the non-excavated ones. In short, this artifact was found in exceptional shape! Its condition is due in large part to the especially fortunate environment in which it was buried. The site's terrain tends to consist mainly of richer, darker soil with healthy moisture content. For this reason, many of the metal objects I've unearthed there have been heavily corroded. However, this button was resting in a fairly small and isolated patch of very sandy soil (i.e., good drainage). And as fate would have it, it was lying on its side, perfectly perpendicular to the surface of the ground. Its face and shank were thus protected from the earth's natural pressures from above and below. Had it simply fallen elsewhere or otherwise, it certainly wouldn't have survived in the remarkable state that it did.

As for its rarity, Silverstein recently downgraded the GWI 9-A from an R-4 (11-25 specimens known) to an R-3 (26-50 specimens known). (Albert has it as an R-4.) Given this relatively recent downgrade, the actual number is probably closer to the lower end of the R-3 range—so perhaps only two to three dozen GWI 9-A's are known to exist.

Given its historical significance, condition, and rarity, the question of monetary value inevitably arises. (Not that this one is for sale!) Firm numbers are elusive, and estimates can only be made on the basis of past recorded sales—if and when they can be found. But one prime example comes from Harold Cobb's own collection. According to the website dedicated to it,

> Harold passed the collection to his son Lloyd, before his death in 1969. Lloyd died the following year, and the collection went to Lloyd's wife Joan. She kept the collection for her children until her recent death in August, 2002....The collection has now been sold in Stack's of New York January 21-23, 2003 Americana sale, lot numbers 1326-1365.[60]

At this Stack's auction, one such "Script GW" (GWI 9-A) specimen went up for sale. Granted, it was in remarkable condition (graded as "About Uncirculated"), but it garnered one of the highest bids of the entire collection. It achieved a "Hammer Price" of $17,000—to which a 15% buyer's fee was also added. Although this auction took place in 2003, this price can probably still be considered the upper end of the GWI 9-A's worth. Historically, the "average" GWI 9-A seems to go for anywhere between $4,000 and $7,000, with better specimens going for more, and poorer ones (bent planchets, broken shanks, worn features, etc.) for far less. As with most collectibles, condition is a big factor. But so, too, is provenance. Which brings us back to the question: To whom did this button belong?

Theoretically, anyone could have owned it, so long as their presence at the given site could be established within

---

[60] Taken from kirkmitchell.tripod.com/CobbGW/.

Chapter 13 – George Washington Inaugural Button

the correct time period (ca. 1789 to the mid-1800s). But if Silverstein is correct and this variety of Inaugural Button was primarily bestowed upon those who served under our first Commander-in-Chief, then the potential domain shrinks considerably. Assuming that premise, then the question becomes this: is there anyone associated with the campus who had any sort of connection to George Washington himself? It is precisely this question that has driven much of my historical research into our former property owners. And in the process, I discovered that this campus has some truly remarkable predecessors....

Secondary Sources

- Albert, Alphaeus S. *Record of American Uniform and Historical Buttons* (Boyertown, PA: Boyertown Pub. Co., 1969).

- Cobb, J. Harold. *George Washington Inaugural Buttons & Medalets 1789 & 1793* (Private printing, 1963).

- DeWitt, J. Doyle. *A Century of Campaign Buttons, 1789-1889* (Hartford, 1959).

- Mitchell, Kirk. *J. Harold Cobb's George Washington Inaugural Button Collection* website: http://kirkmitchell.tripod.com/CobbGW/.

- Silverstein, Robert J. *Isabela's George Washington Inaugural Buttons* website: www.georgewashingtoninauguralbuttons.com.

Introduction to (Some of) Our Remarkable Predecessors

In order to determine who preceded us here on campus, I had to track down hundreds of former deeds involving the purchase and sale of the campus's nearly 500 acres. This was no small feat. For now, however, I will spare the reader these details (which can be found in Part II of this book). By the time it was finished, this investigation uncovered around 160 previous property owners.

My next step was to conduct further research into some of the names on that list. Initially, I was looking for any sort of relationship between them and George Washington. (Spoiler alert: I found three!) But as this undertaking progressed, I came to discover a much richer heritage than I had ever expected. As it turns out, some truly amazing individuals occupied these grounds before us, and their stories were practically begging to be told.

So what appears next is a series of profiles designed to introduce the reader to some of our campus's more remarkable predecessors. The 11 featured here represent merely a sample of the whole. But my hope is that these biographical sketches will engender within readers a profound appreciation for some of the men and women in whose footsteps we now walk. (Oh, and just for the sake of closure, we'll be sure to return to the question of the Inaugural Button ownership at the conclusion of these profiles!)

Chapter 14
Moses Pearson (1697-1778)
Former Owner of Lots 63, 52, and 37

Moses Pearson was the seventh of ten children born to Jeremiah and Priscilla (Hazen) Pearson in Newbury, Massachusetts, on March 26, 1697. He became a joiner (a carpenter/builder) by trade, and married Sarah Titcomb in 1719/20. Together, they had six daughters: Mary, Elizabeth, Sarah, Eunice, Anne, and Lois. Each went on to marry men of considerable social prominence: Ephraim Jones, Dr. Joseph Wise, Daniel Dole, Rev. Samuel Deane, Benjamin Titcomb, and Joshua Freeman, Jr., respectively. We will revisit some of these individuals in subsequent profiles. What should be noted is that Moses Pearson had no sons...technically speaking. However, Ebenezer Shaw, who was orphaned at an early age, was raised in Pearson's household and apprenticed with him until he turned 21. Shaw was clearly influenced by Pearson, who afforded him some unique opportunities. Remarkable in his own right, we'll return to Ebenezer Shaw a bit later.

In 1728, Moses moved his family from Newbury to "Falmouth Neck" (Portland's Old Port area), where he resided for the remainder of his life. Pearson was accepted as a Proprietor there in 1730. His intelligence and business savvy did not go unnoticed, and Moses was soon tapped for various positions of civic responsibility. Over the next decade or so, he served on the Arbitration Committee, was elected Town Clerk, became a Selectman and a Notary Public, held an Innkeeper's License, was appointed Town Treasurer, and functioned as the First Naval Officer of the Port of Falmouth (Portland). He also represented the town in General Court in 1737, 1740, and 1749.

As previously mentioned, in 1745 Moses raised a company of 40 men from Portland to participate in the siege of the French fortress at Louisbourg.[61] Following their victory, Captain Pearson was appointed Agent of Sir William Pepperell's regiment and Treasurer of the nine regiments employed in the siege to receive and distribute the spoils of victory. Moses remained at Louisbourg, superintending the construction of barracks, a hospital, and repairs to the fortification until 1746, when he was sent home by Governor Shirley to procure additional materials to complete these projects.

On the heels of his leadership at Louisbourg, Moses Pearson became increasingly responsible for safeguarding the populace. For example, Willis describes how, in the fall of 1746, the residents of Portland, fearing the imminent invasion of a powerful French fleet, turned to Pearson to defend them.[62] Given his reputation for protecting and serving the public, it should come as no surprise that when Cumberland County was founded in 1760, Moses was chosen as its first Sheriff. He acted in this capacity for the next eight years (1760-68). Following that, Pearson was appointed Judge of the Common Court of Pleas (1770-75)—despite the fact that he wasn't even a lawyer!

An early Proprietor of Portland, Pearson was actually one of the original Proprietors of Gorham. At the first recorded meeting in 1741, Moses was chosen Moderator, and eventually elected Clerk. Over the next three decades, he served on the most important committees of the Proprietary and

---

[61] Those names can be found in a list provided by Henry Sweetser Burrage in *Maine at Louisbourg in 1745* (Augusta, Maine: Burleigh & Flynt, 1910), p. 85

[62] Willis, *Portland*, pp. 416-17. Miraculously, the prayers of the Portland residents were answered and disaster averted when an epidemic struck the fleet and gale force winds scattered it, scuttling some of the strongest ships in the process.

was involved in laying out the lots, maintaining the fort, building the first meeting house/church, and hiring the first minister.

Pearson's wealth of experience with the Proprietaries in Portland and Gorham prepared him well for his involvements in Standish. As noted, Moses was not merely one of the original Proprietors here; he was the driving force behind the very creation of this township. As Sears observes,

> Of the active Proprietors interested in the development and settlement of the town, Moses Pearson was by far the most energetic in its affairs....Pearson was an exceptionally active, enterprising and methodical man....[and] it was undoubtedly because of his personal efforts that Pearsontown was settled as soon as it was after its establishment by the general court.[63]

Pearson was elected Clerk and Treasurer of the Proprietary, and, as in Gorham, was chosen to serve on the most important of the Overseers' committees. Since Sears's book details the many roles that Moses Pearson played in the development of Standish, I shall not rehearse them all here. But suffice it to say, no one was more dedicated to this area than he was.

One measure of Moses's deep, personal investment in the town is reflected in his real estate holdings. Originally, Pearson was granted only one lot—#101—in the First Division of properties (1752). However, by 1773 Pearson had amassed no less than 26! This entitled him to draw another 26 Second Division properties as well. Pearson was generally inclined to pass such real estate along to his children. He

---

[63] Sears, *Founding*, p. 3.

granted three lots to each of his six daughters, sold one, and retained the rest:[64]

1st Division 30 Acre Lots	2nd Division 100 Acre Lots	Recipients
7	11	Mrs. Jones
8	48	MP
11	15	Mrs. Jones
19	97	Exchange with Eno. Isley for No. 100. Mrs. Jones
22	85	MP
24	69	Mrs. Freeman
30	40	Sold to Butterfield
38	107	Mrs. Titcomb
41	54	Mrs. Dean
52	62	MP
62	116	Mrs. Dean
63	22	Mrs. Dole
64	9	MP. 100 acres exchanged with Capt. Fuller? for 100 acres No. 61
65	38	Mrs. Dole
70	102	Mrs. Titcomb
88	81	Mrs. Freeman
89	44	MP
98	63	Mrs. Dean
101	49	MP

[64] I happened upon this previously unpublished listing, dated March 8, 1773, among Moses Pearson's personal papers in the Andrew Hawes Collection of the Maine Historical Society (Coll. 64, Supp. III, Box 10, Folder 47). This is especially valuable information, given that the original grantees of the Second Division properties were never officially recorded. The document, which includes lots 63, 52, and 37, also predates their aforementioned deeds in the Registry. This would make it (so far as I know) the earliest known reference to any of the campus's lots.

103	56	Mrs. Wise
108	52	Mrs. Dole Mrs. Wise
111	98	Mrs. Wise
114	8	Mrs. Dole
115	72	MP
118	108	Mrs. Titcomb
123	37	Mrs. Freeman

Given that Moses Pearson personally owned around 21% of the entire municipality, there can be little doubt that he was committed to the progress of this area. And clearly, the Proprietors appreciated all that he had done on behalf of their settlement. Not only did this town originally bear his name, the membership also granted to Pearson the whole of Frye's Island (as if he needed any more real estate!) in recognition of all of his efforts.

Moses Pearson lived to be 82 years old. He died on June 5, 1778, and now lies buried beside his wife Sarah in Portland's Eastern Cemetery. The epithet on his tombstone reads:

> Having lived an exemplary and
> useful life and served his Country
> to acceptance in a variety of
> offices civil and military.
> His works of Piety and Love
> Remain before the Lord.
> Honour on Earth and joys above
> Shall be his sure Reward.

While I cannot speak to any "joys above" that Pearson may have received, his "Honour on Earth" remains to be seen. As Sears remarks,

> It is a sad commentary on how soon one's endeavors and services are forgotten that his name is not commemorated in any way of the three towns in whose affairs he was so active.[65]

We know that this municipality, upon its incorporation in 1785, adopted the name Standish over Pearsontown. Given Moses's unparalleled contributions, this decision seems somewhat of an injustice. But it was undoubtedly the result of the political climate of that time. This was, after all, the period of the American Revolution, and Pearson was said to have been lukewarm towards that cause. As Sears explains it, Moses's neutrality was likely shaped by the offices to which he was appointed:

> It is also easy to understand during his service as sheriff and later as a judge in the period immediately preceding the outbreak of the Revolutionary War that, in performing his duties as a representative of the British Crown, he must have made not a few enemies, particularly among the ardent patriots, many of whose actions he could not overlook or condone.[66]

Ultimately, however, not even the Redcoats proved favorable towards him. Pearson's own home was one of the many destroyed by the British Royal Navy during the infamous "Burning of Falmouth (Portland)" on October 18, 1775.

Politics aside, Moses Pearson's extraordinary accomplishments—especially in the realm of public service—are certainly worth commemorating. And the fact that he personally owned three lots of the present-day campus now makes his story part of our own. For these reasons, I believe it only fitting that the College name something after him. Ironically, we already did! In light of this association, the

---

[65] Sears, *Founding*, p. 135.
[66] Ibid., p. 132.

"Pearson's Town Farm" and "Pearson's Café" labels become so much more than a mere nod to local history. Properly understood, those names rightly convey a facet of our own heritage. May they henceforth celebrate one of this campus's very own—and indeed, truly remarkable—predecessors.

Primary Sources

- Pearson, Moses. Miscellaneous papers, 1730-57, containing lists of proprietors of common lands in Falmouth, 1730: Falmouth tax lists, 1730-35; encompassing the county and province rates, the wolf rate, and the rates for support of the First Parish, ministers, and school masters; also papers relating to the siege of Louisbourg, during which Pearson was treasurer of the Army, including documents relating to the division of the spoils; a list of houses and buildings in Louisbourg, names of soldiers entitled to a share in spoils; lists of captured vessels; lists of prizes sold with names of purchasers and prices paid; accounts, muster rolls and other papers. Maine Historical Society, Coll. S-1276.

- *Andrews Hawes Collection* (1745-1860). Andrew Hawes is the collector and very few papers deal with Hawes himself. This massive collection (14 boxes, 3 half boxes, 9 vol., 2 cartons, 1 card file) includes papers collected by Hawes relating to 18th and 19th century Maine, particularly Falmouth, Me., together with a small amount of correspondence (chiefly genealogical); a travel diary (1860); and other papers, of Hawes. Also includes correspondence and legal, business, and family papers of Moses Pearson (1697-1778) first sheriff of Cumberland County; the Quinby family, especially John Quinby (1760-1806) relating to shipping; papers relating to the Revolution in Maine, the attack and surrender of Louisbourg (1745), and slavery in Maine; and other business, personal, and legal papers. Maine Historical Society, Coll. 64.

Secondary Sources

- Burrage, Henry Sweetser. *Maine at Louisbourg in 1745* (Augusta: Burleigh & Flynt, 1910), references throughout.

- McLellan, Hugh D. *History of Gorham, Me.* (Portland: Smith & Sale, 1903), references throughout, but esp. pp. 47-48.

- Quinby, Henry Cole. *New England Family History Vol. 2, No. 6* (New York: Hanover, 1908), pp. 137, 163-70.

- Ridlon, Gideon Tibbetts. *Saco Valley Settlements and Families, Volume 1* (Portland: Lakeside Press, 1895), pp. 120-23.

- Sears, Albert. *Early Families of Standish, Maine* (Westminster, MD: Heritage Books, 2010), pp. 196-98.

- ----------. *The Founding of Pearsontown (Standish), Maine* (Heritage Books, 2013), references all throughout, but esp. pp. 131-35.

- Willis, William. *The History of Portland, from 1632 to 1864: With a Notice of Previous Settlements, Colonial Grants, and Changes of Government in Maine* (Portland: Bailey & Noyes, 1865), references throughout, but esp. pp. 416-23.

Chapter 15
Samuel Deane (1733-1814)
Former Owner of Lots 63 and 52

Samuel Deane was born in Dedham, Massachusetts, on July 10, 1733, the oldest son of Samuel and his second wife, Rachel (Dwight) Deane. He attended Harvard and established himself as a highly respected scholar. Some of Deane's literary contributions were included in a prestigious volume of congratulatory addresses presented to King George III upon his accession to the English throne.[67] After

---

[67] The volume was entitled *"Pietas et Gratulatio Collegii Cantabrigiensis Apud Novanglos. Bostoni, Massachusettensium Typis J. Green and J. Russell, MDCCLXI."* According to Willis, the volume was better printed than any work that had previously been issued by an American press. "A prize of six guineas each was offered for the six best

graduating (A.B.) in 1760, Deane remained at Harvard for a few more years, where he continued on with his graduate work, obtaining his A.M. in 1763. During that time, he was employed as College Librarian (1760-62) and Tutor (1763-64).

In 1764, Samuel Deane accepted the invitation to serve alongside the Reverend Thomas Smith as Minister of the First Church in Portland. Smith had been the first established Minister of this Church; Deane thus became the second. Deane built his house near the Church on Back Street (today's Congress Street), and went on to pastor this congregation for the next 50 years, until his death in 1814. This included a stint from 1775 to 1782, when Deane, following the Burning of Falmouth (Portland),[68] temporarily relocated to Gorham, to his farm which he named "Pitchwood Hill."[69]

---

compositions, viz., an oration, poem, elegy, and ode in Latin, and a poem and ode in English; candidates were to be limited to members of the College, or graduates of not more seven years standing. The compositions much exceeded the number proposed, and the competition seemed to be, who could crowd the most flattery into the smallest space; they were all sufficiently loyal and laudatory to be perfectly disgusting at this day: and what is more they fell entirely short of their aim as the College never received the slightest patronage or aid, in even a smile from the royal pageant on whom they wasted so much ammunition, and towards whom, 14 years afterward, the halls of the College and the arches of the whole country re-echoed a totally different strain." Deane reportedly contributed an English poem, number ten in the series, and a Latin ode, number 21 (Willis, *Journals*, p. 290).

[68] Deane's home survived, but during that event, a shot went through the front of the house and landed in the chimney. A picture was hung to cover the hole in the panel over the fireplace, where it remained until Deane's death.

[69] In 1780, Deane devoted his longest poem (140 lines) to the subject of "Pitchwood Hill." It was published (without his consent) in the March 5, 1795 edition of the *Cumberland Gazette* and later republished (again, without his consent) in pamphlet form in 1806 (Willis, *Journals*, p. 295).

Chapter 15 – Samuel Deane

In 1766, Deane married Eunice Pearson, the daughter of Moses Pearson. Although they never had any children (she was five years older than he, and 39 at the time of their wedding), Samuel nevertheless made an indelible mark on history. He was known not for his theological treatises so much as for his agricultural advancements. As his biographer William Willis put it,

> In agriculture Dr. Deane pursued his labors zealously and scientifically and was consequently more successful than any other person in this region of the country.[70]

Deane's best known and most important literary contribution was a work comprehensively titled *The New-England Farmer; Or Georgical Dictionary: Containing a Compendious Account of the Ways and Methods in which the Important Art of Husbandry, in all its Various Branches, is, or May Be, Practiced to the Greatest Advantage, in this Country*. It was originally published in 1790.

In order for the reader to fully appreciate what Deane intended to accomplish, and just how enthusiastically he embraced his subject, permit me a somewhat lengthy quote from its Introduction. (I promise it's worth the read!)

> It is much to be regretted, that the most complicated of all the arts, in which the brightest genius may find sufficient room to exert and display itself, should be slighted and neglected, by a people not generally wanting in ambition. And it is equally strange and unaccountable, that the most useful and necessary of all employments should have been considered, even by the enlightened people of Newengland (sic), as below the attention of any persons, excepting those who are in the lowest walks of life; or, that persons of a liberal or polite education should think it

---

[70] Willis, *Journals*, p. 296.

intolerably degrading to them, to attend to practical agriculture for their support.

Perhaps, one occasion of the low esteem in which husbandry has been held, in this country, may have been the poor success which has most commonly attended the labours of those who have embraced the profession. Not only have most of them failed of rapidly increasing their estates by it, but too many have had the mortification of making but an indifferent figure in life, even when they have used the strictest economy, and worn out their constitutions by hard and incessant labour. The misfortune has been, that a great proportion of their toil has been lost by its misapplication. To prevent this evil in future is a leading design of the present publication. And since many among us begin to be convinced of the urgent necessity of having the attention of the publick (sic) turned to agriculture, it is hoped that the following attempt to promote the knowledge of its mysteries, and a spirited attention to the operations of it, will meet with the greater approbation and success. And as a very respectable Society in the Commonwealth of Massachusetts have undertaken to propagate the knowledge of husbandry, the day may be at hand, when the employment of the farmer shall no more be treated with contempt; when the rich, the polite, and the ambitious, shall glory in paying a close attention to their farms; when respectable persons shall confess it is one of the noblest employments to assist nature in her bountiful productions; when it shall be our ambition to follow the example of the first man in the nation, who does not think an attention to husbandry degrading; and when, instead of being ashamed of their employment, our laborious farmers shall, as a great writer says, "toss about their dung with an air of majesty."[71]

In what then follows, Deane presents an agricultural reference book of encyclopedic proportions. His *magnum opus* contains nearly 500 separate entries, from "Agriculture" to "Zest" ("an apartment in a barn, where corn to be thrashed is laid up," in case you were wondering), and everything in between. While at times Deane waxes eloquent

---

[71] Deane, *Farmer*, p. 1-2.

and philosophical, most of his content is decidedly pragmatic. His fundamental aim is to improve upon the traditional farming methods that, while effective back in the Old Country, proved inadequate for the unique challenges of New England's soil and climate. The vast majority of his instruction, be it on Apples, Beer, Compost, Grubs, Milk, Potatoes, Sheep, Rotation of Crops, Wheat, etc., is as applicable today as it was over 225 years ago. Other entries, while less pertinent to the present, serve as time-travel windows to peer into the past. Topics like Outhouse, Cart, and Waggon (sic) are good examples. But my personal favorite for demonstrating just how remarkably times have changed is this Wolf entry:

> A wild beast of the dog kind. This animal is very fierce, equal in size to a large mastiff, and has much the same appearance. Wolves are gregarious, go in droves, and surprise the nightly traveler with their hideous yelling. No beast of prey in this country is more formidable; they sometimes attack men. Newengland (sic), even from its first settlement, has been much infested with wolves. And, notwithstanding the bounties that have been given by government for destroying them, the settlements bordering on the wilderness are still subject to their mischievous incursions; so that there is little safety for sheep in these situations. Almost whole flocks in a night are sometimes destroyed by them. This exposure to wolves is equal to a heavy tax upon our frontier plantations. To secure the sheep from this enemy, it is necessary that they be pastured in the open fields by day, and housed in strong places every night: And even these precautions do not always prove effectual. Some say, that smearing the heads of sheep with a composition of tar and gun powder will prevent their being attacked by the wolves; but I cannot certify this from my own experience.[72]

---

[72] Ibid., p. 392.

Deane's publication was extremely well received and set the standard by which subsequent works were measured for decades to come. *The New-England Farmer* was "universally consulted" and "influenced to a large extent the character of our agriculture."[73]

Samuel Deane's stellar reputation as an erudite scholar led to a number of high-level appointments and prestigious accolades. Consequently, he wound up keeping company with some of the most prominent men in American colonial history. In 1780, Deane became one of 62 Charter Members of the American Academy of Arts and Sciences.[74] (Others included John Adams, Samuel Adams, James Bowdoin, and John Hancock.) Deane also belonged to the American Board of Agriculture, which was then presided over by future US President James Madison. Within that body, Deane served on the Committee of Correspondence in Massachusetts, along with his colleague and future US President John Quincy Adams.

Deane himself accepted two Presidential posts. He was elected the very first President of the Bible Society of

---

[73] Willis, *Journals*, p. 296; Samuel Lane Boardman, *Agricultural Bibliography of Maine: Biographical Sketches of Maine Writers on Agriculture, with a Catalogue of Their Works* (published by the author, 1893), p. 10.

[74] "The American Academy of Arts and Sciences, established by the Massachusetts legislature on May 4, 1780, is one of the oldest learned societies in the United States....From its beginnings, the Academy has engaged in the critical questions of the day. It has brought together the nation's and the world's most distinguished citizens to address social and intellectual issues of common concern and, above all, to develop ways to translate knowledge into action. Since 1780, Academy members have included both those who discover and advance knowledge and those who apply knowledge to the problems of society. Working together, they have established a legacy of leadership that continues to produce reflective, independent, and pragmatic studies that inform public policy and lead to constructive action" (from their website, https://www.amacad.org/).

Maine,[75] and the first President of the Portland Benevolent Society.[76] Deane nearly became President for a third time. He served as a Founding Trustee and Vice President of Bowdoin College for 20 years (1794-1813), but turned down the offer of its Presidency in 1801. Perhaps his best Presidential association, however, came in 1790, when Samuel Deane was awarded an Honorary Doctorate in Divinity (D.D.) from Brown University.[77] Included among the other Honorary Degree recipients that year was none other than the newly inaugurated US President, General George Washington.

---

[75] "This was the fourth Bible Society established in the United States. The first was at Philadelphia, the second at Hartford, Conn., and the third at Boston. It was formed in August, 1809, and incorporated in March, 1810. It has no funds that draw interest, but is supported by subscriptions, donations, and contributions. The Trustees meet every two months, and have sub-committees for the purchase and distribution of Bibles, under their direction; but the extent of their business has been reduced by the recent establishment of independent Societies in every County in the State, except that in the County of Oxford, which is auxiliary to this. By a vote of the Society, at a meeting held at Portland, on the 16th of October, 1816, it became auxiliary to the American Bible Society" (Willis, *Journals*, p. 455).

[76] "This society was incorporated in the year 1803. Its design was to relieve and assist those who might require relief in a manner different from that which is by law provided for the support and employment of the poor. It was not to go into operation until the sum subscribed should amount to $6000. This sum was obtained by subscriptions of from five to fifty dollars a year, and one prompt payment of twenty dollars. Managers are annually appointed to distribute the sums received. They meet once every month during winter for this purpose" (Willis, *Journals*, p. 455).

[77] Deane's Brown University connection raises some potential confusion between him and another Samuel Deane (1784-1834) who graduated from Brown in 1805. Though 50 years younger, this latter Samuel Deane had much in common with the former. He, too, was born in Massachusetts and went on to become an ordained Minister, serving 24 years at the Second Church in Scituate. He was also a published poet ("The Populous Village") and author (*The History of Scituate, Massachusetts*).

It seems only natural, given Deane's many powerful connections, that he would be tapped for some sort of political service. And indeed he was. In 1787, Deane was chosen by the Town of Falmouth (Portland) to attend the Convention in Massachusetts for the adoption of the National Constitution. For whatever reason, he declined. However, Deane did accept the position of Chairman of the Committee to consider and report on the advantages and disadvantages of a separation of Maine from Massachusetts. The State of Maine's very existence is owed, in part, to the work of this Committee. Their even-handed Final Report was published in 1791 and is explicitly dedicated to Samuel Deane.

Accolades aside, the historical sources also offer us a glimpse of Deane's physical stature, his manner of conduct, his personal beliefs, and his character. According to Willis,

> Dr. Deane was in person tall, erect and portly, of good personal appearance, and of grave and dignified manners; he was possessed of a keen wit,[78] and fond of social conversation, in which he could always make himself agreeable. His style of preaching was calm, and without much animation; his sermons were brief, plain, and practical, and without ornament or display; they were well written, but not calculated to kindle or excite an audience. He aimed more to convince the understanding than to alarm the fears or arouse the passions.[79]

---

[78] Deane's sense of humor is illustrated in an anecdote from his time as Tutor at Harvard. Deane was showing a stranger the curiosities in the Museum of the College and came upon a long and rusty sword. When the stranger asked the history of the sword, Deane replied that he believed it was the sword with which Balaam threatened to kill his ass. The stranger objected that Balaam had no sword, he only wished for one. "Oh true," said Deane, "*that* is the one he wished for!" (Willis, *Journals*, p. 292).

[79] Willis, *Journals*, p. 296. Deane's preaching style and content evidently failed to impress John Quincy Adams, who once complained

Chapter 15 – Samuel Deane

As for his theological tendencies, Samuel Deane

> had no sectarian zeal or bigotry about him; he was ready to commune with kindred spirits, and sincere lovers of God, whatever may have been their speculative belief in regard to his nature and mode of existence. His faith in God, in the mediation and atonement of Jesus, in the influences of the Holy Spirit, and the salvation of the just, was clear, firm, and unwavering; but he did not believe himself to be infallible nor that it was his office to judge his neighbor for modes of belief, provided his conduct was right, nor pronounce him condemned of God, for any mistake on a metaphysical dogma. His language was, "The Deity will not punish us in another world for not having understood in this what cannot be understood."[80]

Eunice Deane, Samuel's wife and companion of 46 years, passed away in 1812. He died two years later, on November 12, 1814. His last words were, "Death has lost all his terrors; I am going to my friend Jesus, for I have seen him this night." He was interred at the church he had so faithfully served for over half a century. The following obituary article ran on November 28, 1814, in the *Portland Gazette* (pp. 3/4):

> To his immediate friends and parishioners he was an object of peculiar respect and veneration. They loved him for his sincerity and ingenuousness, they respected him for his independence and firmness, and they venerated him for his wisdom and learning. His mind, naturally strong and intelligent, was much impaired [i.e. improved] by observation, reflection and literary research. His

---

that Deane "spoke with a whining sort of tone, which would have injured the sermons if they had been good" (http://firstparishportland.org/historydata.html). Readers, however, can judge this for themselves, as some of Deane's published sermons and can be found in the bibliography below.

[80] Willis, *Journals*, 298.

disposition was mild and conciliatory, and his judgment remarkably sound and discrimination....In his society the aged found themselves improved and enlivened by his social and engaging conversation, and the young were amused and instructed by his wit and learning.

Like the Reverend Thomas Smith before him, Samuel Deane had also kept a diary. They were published together in 1849, and are especially valuable for the historical and genealogical information that they provide. Deane's spans 53 years, from February 1, 1761, until October 18, 1814. It consistently records information about the weather, marriages, and deaths, but is otherwise fairly concise and remarkably devoid of emotional content.[81] In his records, Deane mentions several trips that he made to Pearsontown (Standish).[82] These entries are not very detailed, but they may well signal at least some of the occasions on which he visited his property—our campus.

Primary Sources

- Davis, Daniel. *An address to the inhabitants of the District of Maine: upon the subject of their separation from the present government of Massachusetts / by one of their fellow citizens. Dedicated to the Rev. Samuel Deane.* (1791) Maine Historical Society QJ M 081 C91d.

---

[81] For example, his daily entries surrounding the infamous Burning of Falmouth (Portland) read: "*October* 17. Mowatt's fleet worked up to the town; he sent a letter ashore that he would burn the town in two hours. 18. Wednesday. The town destroyed: fine day. 19. Rainy." Those around the death of his wife read: "*October* 14. Mrs. D. departed half past 4, P.M. 16. Funeral of Mrs. D.; full house." It seems Deane reserved his enthusiasm primarily for agricultural matters!

[82] Specific dates include January 29 & 31 and February 3, 1767; January 28 and July 15 & 16, 1783; and September 7, 1814.

Chapter 15 – Samuel Deane

- Deane, Samuel. *Four sermons to young men from Titus, 2, 6: preached at Falmouth* (1774). Maine Historical Society QJ 040 C685 v. 52.

- ----------. *Pitchwood Hill: a poem written in the year 1780.* Maine Historical Society QJ M 081 D06d.

- ----------. *The way to cure ye evils of ye tongue.* A sermon written by Rev. Samuel Deane in 1784, based on James 3:8. Andover-Harvard Theological Library, Divinity School bMS 732.

- ----------. *The New-England farmer: or, Georgical dictionary containing a compendious account of the ways and methods in which the most important art of husbandry, in all its various branches, is, or may be practiced to the greatest advantage in this country* (Worcester, Mass.; Isaiah Thomas & Company: Boston, 1790).

- ----------. *An oration delivered in Portland, July 4th, 1793: in commemoration of the independence of the United States of America.* Maine Historical Society QJ Mo P837.18.

- ----------. *A sermon preached before His Honour Samuel Adams, Esq., Lieutenant Governor: the honourable the Council, Senate, and House of Representatives of the Commonwealth of Massachusetts, May 28th, 1794: being the day of general election.* Maine Historical Society QJ MS 252.6 D346.

- ----------. *The death of an aged servant of God, considered and improved: in a funeral discourse delivered at Portland, May 31st, 1795, being the Lord's Day after the funeral of the Rev. Thomas Smith, senior pastor of the First Church in Portland, who departed this life, May 23, in the 94th year of his age.* Maine Historical Society QJ M 081 C95ds.

- ----------. *A sermon preached February 19th, 1795: being a day of national Thanksgiving appointed by the President of the United States.* Maine Historical Society QJ M 081 C95d.

- ----------. Sermons preached by Samuel Deane of Falmouth, Maine, between 1767 and 1802. Some sermons preached several times. Sermon # 524 delivered after proclamation of peace between Great Britain and the United States (27 April 1783). Maine Historical Society Coll. 940, Box 1/5.

- ----------. Sermons preached by Samuel Deane of Portland, Maine between 1790 and 1811. Maine Historical Society Coll. 940, Box 1/6-7.

- Willis, William. *Journals of the Rev. Thomas Smith and the Rev. Samuel Deane, pastors of the First church in Portland: with notes and biographical notices and a summary history of Portland* (Portland: Joseph S. Bailey, 1849).

Secondary Sources

- Broadman, Samuel Lane. *Agricultural Bibliography of Maine: Biographical Sketches of Maine Writers on Agriculture, with a Catalogue of Their Works: and an Index to the Volumes on the Agriculture of Maine, from 1850 to 1892* (Published by the author, 1893), pp. 10-11.

- First Parish Church. Online information about Samuel Deane can be found at the following website: http://firstparishportland.org/historydata.html.

- Potter, Alfred C., and Charles K. Bolton. "The Librarians of Harvard College. 1667-1877" in the *Catalogue of English and American Chapbooks and Broadside Ballads in Harvard College Library, Issues 52-54* (Cambridge: Library of Harvard University, 1902) 4:52, p. 27.

- Sibley, John Langdon. *Biographical Sketches of Graduates of Harvard University in Cambridge, Massachusetts* (Cambridge: University Press, 1873) Vol. 14, pp. 591-98.

Chapter 16
Sarah Jones Bradbury (1740-1824)
Former Owner of Lot 64

Sarah Jones was born to Ephraim Jones and Mary Pearson (the daughter of Moses Pearson) on January 7, 1740. Raised in Portland, she was the eldest of ten children. In 1762, Sarah married Theophilus Bradbury (the subject of our next profile). Two years later, they purchased from Pearson a lot of land on the corner of Middle and Willow streets (in the Old Port district), where they built their house. They resided there until the infamous Burning of Falmouth (Portland) in 1775. They relocated to Windham for a time (1775-79), but eventually settled in Newbury, Massachusetts (where Theophilus was originally from). In 1786, they bought property on the northwesterly side of Green Street and there they built their family estate.

Together, Theophilus and Sarah had the following seven children: 1) Theophilus, who married Harriet Harris and died childless;[83] 2) William, who died at St. Domingo, unmarried; 3) Francis;[84] 4) George;[85] 5) Harriet, who married

---

[83] The historical sources (e.g., *The Essex Antiquarian* and the *History of Newburyport*) frequently confuse this Theophilus Bradbury with his cousin, Theophilus Bradbury, son of Jonathan Bradbury and Abigail Smith. Both lived in Newburyport, Massachusetts, and shared a common grandfather: Theophilus Bradbury. However, the son of Jonathan and Abigail became a rather well-regarded silversmith, and two of his sons (John and Ebenezer) followed their father's footsteps into that trade as well.

[84] Francis Bradbury was born on December 14, 1766, in Falmouth (now Portland), Maine. He married Hannah Jones on October 6, 1803, and together they had six children. Much like his grandfather, Theophilus, Francis was, for a time, a sea merchant who maintained a small fleet of shipping vessels. The French commandeered one of them, *Confidence*, which Francis had co-owned with his father, Theophilus (for more on this, see Greg H. Williams, *The French Assault on American Shipping, 1793-1813* [Jefferson, NC: McFarland & Co., 2009] p. 109). In 1809, Francis relocated his family to Vergennes, Vermont. There, he secured a perpetual lease of waterpower and assigned the lease to the

Thomas W. Hooper of Newbury;[86] 6) Charles, who married Eleonora Cumming of Portland; and 7) Frances, who died at Newburyport, unmarried.

It is truly unfortunate that, when looking back into the past, "history" is often just that: "his story." For whatever reasons, information about females is usually sparse, and the female perspective is even rarer. Indeed, had I to rely solely on the typical sources for information, my entry on Sarah Jones Bradbury would effectively end here. Fortunately, however, that's not the case. As it turns out, Sarah kept a diary. What has survived—and has been released to the public[87]—is not terribly lengthy. (It spans

---

Monkton Iron Company. In 1810, Francis purchased the gristmill on the island in Otter Creek. He also operated a store on the west side of the creek most of his business life. Francis's brothers, George and Theophilus, also had an interest in Vergennes. Francis kept a journal (1818-22) in which he makes various references to his father, mother, and brothers (see Primary Sources, below). He died in Vergennes on April 10, 1837.

[85] George Bradbury will be the subject of an upcoming profile.

[86] Prior to her marriage to Hooper, Harriet caught the eye of another man, a young lawyer in Newbury (and eventual US President) by the name of John Quincy Adams. His March 5, 1788 entry describes her and her companions as "a sett [sic] that are almost always together and who have at least more personal beauty than any equal number of other unmarried ladies in this town." After describing one of them (Sarah Wigglesworth) in particular detail, Adams concludes: "Thus much for the present. I will take some other opportunity to mention the other stars that form this constellation." Indeed, Adams seems to have made good on this promise. He penned a poem entitled "A Vision" in which he mused on the graces and follies of some of these ladies. It was subsequently published (without his permission) and created quite a stir. Harriet is thought to be the subject of one 14-lined stanza, by which Adams refers to her as "Corinna" (see Currier, *Newburyport*, p. 544 for text and notes).

[87] Excerpts from the diary were originally published in the *Portland Sunday Courier-Telegram* on May 22, 1898, with the following introduction: "The most diligent inquiry has failed to locate the author of the following sketch, if it be such, or to disclose any knowledge as to this diary. The data used is all fact, but whether we have here extracts from Mrs. Bradbury's diary or a quaint and pretty story drawn from local

about six and a half single-spaced pages in a Word document.) However, it's enough to grant us privileged insights not only into the societal customs and practices of the times, but also into her intimate thoughts and feelings about some of her most important life events. Sarah's budding romance and youthful innocence are charmingly endearing, and they serve to make her one of the most accessible and relatable individuals among the profiles.

The subjects of Sarah's first entry are Lois Pearson and Joshua Freeman. They, too, were once owners of the College's property (Lot 37). But Sarah's preoccupation is with Joshua's fashion ensemble. It's an entertaining read. However, since Joshua Freeman is the subject of an upcoming profile, we'll return to this a bit later.

Sarah's next entry, dated January of 1757, goes into considerable detail over "a trick played upon the party folks last night, by, as it is suspected, that wild fellow S., although he doth deny that he had aught to do with it." The "trick" is a fairly harmless ruse that "S." undertook in retaliation for being excluded from a social gathering. Basically, he lured a pack of party-goers out onto the hard crust of some very deep snow. Having weakened it, the crust collapsed, and into the snow they went. Brigadier-General Preble, who was among the victims, "at first broke out into angry oaths." However, his reaction proved to be the exception:

> It is said, the laughter of those who escaped the pitfall was not more hearty than those who had fallen therein. Some of the young men were boisterous in their merriment, and there was some wrestling in the snow, so that when they were rescued from their predicament they were completely covered with snow like

---

history, the reader must decide, since we know no more than the public. So many requests have been made for this material that we herewith offer it to interested readers. –[Ed.]"

unto miller-men. Ladies seemed to enjoy the affair as well as the beaux, albeit their dresses were grievously wrinkled.

Following that, Sarah's entry of Monday, August 18, 1760, reflects on the Sunday prior. Sarah conveys some of the controversy surrounding "Mr. Clark," a newly installed minister, and shares her opinions about the clothing choices of some of her female companions. Sarah also introduces the subject of Mr. Theophilus Bradbury, in whom she has evidently taken an interest:

> There were quite a number of gentry present from the Neck, among which was Mr. Theophilus Bradbury, the school master who solicited the favor of accompanying me home, which I granted. We did not return as I went, but proceeded directly to the ferry through the woods and bushes which was shorter and pleasanter. Mr. Bradbury made himself exceedingly agreeable by his sprightly talk. I think on the whole the day was most happily and profitably spent.

As a bit of an afterthought, Sarah concludes her entry with this reminder to herself:

> <u>Mem.</u> I must not forget to flavor my next pies with cinnamon which condiment Mr. Bradbury thinks is a great improvement. Likewise to clear starch my lace ruffles.

Unfortunately, Sarah's next record is undated. Nevertheless, she describes a memorable outing spent among the islands off Portland's coast (long before the town was as developed as it is today):

> Yesterday our family with the Pearsons went to the Island – had a delightful – a fine day and agreeable company, and all seemingly bent on enjoying the occasion. There was just breeze enough to send us gaily on our way without creating an unpleasant sea, although in crossing from Poopooduck [sic] point Annie Pearson

Chapter 16 – Sarah Jones Bradbury

complained of dizziness caused by the boat's motion. We passed some large mast ships newly armed, and anchored in the stream, from which we received cheerful greetings. I don't believe there is to be found a more beautiful scene than the Neck presents from the ship Channel—a dense mass of foliage with here and there a picturesque opening; sometimes I fancy the whole peninsula covered with dwellings and ware-houses and its streets filled with a busy people. Will such a time ever arrive?

But Sarah's attention soon turns to Theophilus Bradbury and their morning together:

Mr. Theophilus Bradbury of Newbury, who is here on a visit and is a member of our party, kindly volunteered his services to assist me in gathering berries, in quest of which we soon started. They were so very abundant that in a short time we had gathered two brimming milk pails of the finest berries I ever saw. Covering them with leaves and placing them in a shady place, we strayed to a high bluff over-looking the ocean and whence we had a fine view of all the islands adjacent. While sitting there enjoying the scene, Mr. Bradbury recounted many interesting facts concerning the Indian. He described to me a great battle fought on Munjoy's Island off against us, in which a great many white were slain. He told me also of the inhabitants of the Neck once fleeing to refuge on the Island (which were then called James Andrew's Islands) were attacked by the savages who completely sacked the town, leaving it a heap of ruins. This was more than eighty years ago (1681). Afterwards we visited the remains of an old fort, thrown up there in the trouble by reason of which, the island was known as "Fort Island."

The party next reconvened for a hearty lunch of fresh chowder, which Sarah describes in some detail. Then,

after the repast, leaving the gentlemen to the enjoyment of the pipes and their punch, we ladies strolled among the trees which plentifully abound. We found their shade a grateful relief from the sun's scorching beams, which made sad havoc with our faces, and such parts as were exposed, in some instances raising painful blisters. I have kept my face and neck bathed in cream today, which is an excellent emulcient [sic], howbeit, the tips of my ears and nose still continue to burn and had begun to peel. A sad plight to [be] in should any call, especially Mr. B.

And this is where the narrative takes a surprising—and unforgettably romantic—turn:

We had not been very long in our stroll, when some of the young men joined us. Soon after which Mr. B. proposed to me we should go in search of the berries we had that morning gathered. I saw at once that it was a device that we might be by ourselves, which I was disposed to follow. It took us a long time to find the spot where we had left our pails, not having marked it particularly, as we should have done. I think we must have passed it many times in our rambles, by reason of our attention being otherwise engaged. In sooth our conversation became deeply interesting. I know not how it was, but presently our minds were so absorbed in other matters that we gave no heed to the berries. Mr. B. had mentioned that it was his purpose to leave his native town and take up his present residence at the Neck, while persuing [sic] his law studies. He said he had engaged to take charge of the school as it is the custom with law students. It was his intention however, to enter upon his profession the ensuing year. In such manner I think the conversation commenced. Upon my asking if, when his studies were over, he would still remain in Falmouth [Portland], he made answer much to my wonderment, "as for that Miss Jones it all rests with you." Thereupon seeing how astonished I was, he made avowal of his love, declaring that if I regarded his suit favorably he should hereafter make the Neck his home. Otherwise he should not abide there. In my confusion I know not what answer I made him, only that he seemed abundantly satisfied with it, in as much as he emboldened "to seal the compact," as he called it, which request I saw no reason to deny. Just then there came a loud call from the shore, that everything was in the boat in readiness to leave. Having recovered the berries, we hastened to obey, marveling that the afternoon had sped so quickly. All the party were awaiting us at the Beach. Right pleased was I to have for an excuse the boiling sun, for my heightened color, of which I was unpleasantly conscious. Albeit some jeered me, saying it was strange the shade should more effect my complexion than the sun's rays. I took their playful discourse in good part being in a pleasant mood, and when we set sail I said in my heart, "This day deserves to be marked with a white stone!" for it is the happiest day of my life.

(Isn't that the best?!?!) Sarah concludes this entry with the following, which presumably occurred within the next few days:

> While I was busied in the kitchen this forenoon making jam, my looks by no means improved over the fire, Mr. B. called. I was greatly fluttered for the moment, as he only desired to see mother. I readily divined the nature of his errand, and awaited with no little anxiety its result. He detained her a long time, as it seemed to me, though she says his call was short. When mother returned to the kitchen she embraced me warmly, saying, her interview with Mr. B. had occasioned her great joy. That she and my father heartily sanctioned his proposal and she hoped the connection might be even more fruitful of happiness than my own fond anticipations. Dear Mother! I know her heart was filled with a sad sort of joy, by the tears that gathered in her eyes and the tremor of her voice.

Sarah and Theophilus were married on August 26, 1762. Her next entry is from that day. It is short, but somewhat humorous. Given all that she could be thinking about and feeling, her mind is on the minister and the potential length of the ceremony:

> This evening I am to be married. Mr. Smith will perform the service. I do hope he will not have as much "assistance," as he styles it, in his prayers, as he had at the last wedding I attended, when he prayed for nearly an hour. I did so pity the poor bride. I would get Mr. B. to give him a hint on the subject if I did not think the good man would take it so amiss.

The remainder of Sarah's diary is dedicated to two separate events—both of which were parties held among the socially elite. The latter one, which took place in February of 1766, Sarah did not attend. Rather, her entries relate her concern for a rather large group of Portland revelers (including Colonel Waldo, Brigadier Preble, and Captain Ross) who were stranded for ten days by a snowstorm at King's Tavern.[88] Eventually, all returned safe, sound, and in remarkably good spirits.

But it was the former party—the one that Sarah did attend—that became the subject of an even greater controversy. She offers a firsthand account of it in her December 20, 1765 entry:

> Attended a dancing party at Joshua Freeman's last night,[89] there was a goodly company present. Brig. Preble, Col. Waldo and their wives and many others all of the "quality." We had a merry time and most excellent music. Two fiddles and a base viol. We enjoyed it all the more by reason that many straight laced ones have set their faces against amusements of this kind, and have threatened to enforce the laws prohibiting dancing in places of public resort. It was like participating of stolen fruit, which according to the proverb, is the sweetest.

Much to her chagrin, Sarah's observations about the "straight laced ones" proved to be correct. The very next day, she discovers that:

---

[88] In the Reverend Smith's journal, it is called "Rings" Tavern (at "Blackpoint," probably near Spurwink) and the event is dated to February, 1763 (Willis, *Journals*, p. 195).

[89] The "Joshua Freeman" Sarah refers to here is the father of the aforementioned Joshua Freeman. Freeman Sr. ran a popular Portland tavern on the corner of Middle and Fish (now Exchange) Streets. We'll return to him a bit later in his son's profile.

Chapter 16 – Sarah Jones Bradbury

> There is a great commotion about the dancing party, M, literally denouncing it as an infringement of the laws. He tells his determination to have it brought before the court. He is a man of very crabbed disposition, and furious upon all entertainments, however rational they may be. He says, which is very true, that the gentry have no more right to slight the laws than have the common people. I think in his present action he is more prompted by spite than principal, as he has on divers occasions sought to gain a footing with the quality, and because they give him no countenance, he embraceth [sic] this opportunity to retaliate upon them. Some of the ladies feel much chagrined and disheartened at the thought of what may happen. Mr. B laughs at their fears and says there will be no harmful results.

"Mr. B," of course, is Sarah's husband, Theophilus. But his casual dismissal appears to have underestimated the will of his adversaries. As we learn in Sarah's entry of January 13, 1766,

> M. has made good that he threatened. Mr. Deering, Mr. Wait and my husband with most of the leading men and their wives have been indicted for dancing at "Freeman's Tavern" on the evening of 17 December last year. Mr. B has been engaged to plead the indictment. It has caused a great stir. The community upholds the suit, and say [sic] jeeringly, "what is sauce for the goose is sauce for the gander," yet would they be wroth [sic] if this same justice were meted out to them for their frequent dancing and junketing in Fiddle Lane.[90]

Two weeks later, the matter did indeed go to court. On January 31, 1766, Sarah reports its outcome:

> Mr. B. was in court today to plead to the indictment. The Kings attorney, Mr. David Wyer, made a strong argument in support of it, and was unnecessarily severe on the dancing party. My

---

[90] As a later notation in the diary explains, "Fiddle Lane" probably refers to Franklin Street.

husband, I am told, managed the case with great shrewdness. He maintained that the room where the dance took place had been hired by the season by private individuals, and, therefore, could not be considered a place of public resort, but only a private apartment, and that those assembled there had a perfect right to meet in their own room, and, if so disposed, to dance. His plea was sustained by the court and so the matter comes to an end, greatly to the relief of the ladies as may be supposed. I asked Mr. B if he did not make use of subterfuge in asserting that the room was hired by private persons. "My dear, In law as in war, all things all shifts are pardonable" making use of some legal maxim, which, being in Latin, I did not, or failed, to understand.[91]

With their indictment successfully overturned, "the 'quality' danced to their heart's content ever after."[92] As for Sarah, nothing further appears in her diary beyond 1766. She outlived her husband (who died in 1803) and is listed on the May 15, 1811 deed of sale of their family home. She also outlived both her daughter Frances (d. 1801, who is buried beside her father), and her son Theophilus (d. 1818), about whose death her other son, Francis, wrote to her.[93] The last reference I could find to Sarah is this brief note in Francis's journal: "My mother now lives at Portland with my brother George, and will be 82 years old the 7th January, 1822—and from last accounts enjoyed her wanted good health."[94] Sarah actually lived for two more years. She died on May 22, 1824, and is buried in Portland's Eastern Cemetery.

---

[91] For another, more official version of these events, see James D. Hopkins's *An Address to the Members of the Cumberland Bar: Delivered During the Sitting of the Court of Common Pleas, at Portland, June Term, 1833*, (Portland: Charles Day & Co., 1833), p. 34.

[92] Herbert M. Sylvester, *Olde Cascoe: Ye Romance of Casco Bay* (W.B. Clarke., 1909), p. 180.

[93] Francis Bradbury papers (Vermont Historical Society, Leahy Library, Barre VT, MSA 284:1-2).

[94] Ibid.

Chapter 16 – Sarah Jones Bradbury

Primary Sources

- Bradbury, Francis. Papers, 1812-27. This collection consists of two folders, one containing Francis Bradbury's journal (1818-22) and miscellaneous papers, and the other containing Francis Bradbury's daybook for September to October 1812. Bradbury's journal includes information on the weather, occasional religious observations, accounts of his business affairs, particularly his mill, and of his agricultural endeavors. It also includes genealogical material relating to both the Bradbury and Jones families, as well as transcriptions of letters written on November 28, 1818, by Bradbury to his mother and his brother George, notifying them of the death of his brother Theophilus. The miscellaneous papers contain an account of a sea voyage to Malta and Smyrna written by Francis Bradbury, Jr. in 1827, addressed to his brother John, and two drawings, one a color pencil drawing of George Bradbury's house (the brother of Francis Bradbury) and the other, a water color of a street scene possibly somewhere in the Mediterranean. The daybook contains financial records relating to the iron foundry business, the store, and the grist mill. The accounts include boarding costs for the workers, as well as the sale of refined iron ore and the purchase of supplies, such as bar iron and pig iron. Vermont Historical Society, Leahy Library, Barre VT, MSA 284:1-2.

- Bradbury, Sarah Jones. Diary (1750-66). Extracts were published in the May 22, 1898 edition of the Portland *Sunday Courier-Telegram*. There is also a holograph copy of excerpts (with variations in text) which were read at the Fortnightly Club in Chicago in 1888. Both of these sources can be found at the Maine Women Writers Collection in the Abplanalp Library, at the University of New England's Portland campus. The Maine Historical Society also has a typeset copy of the diary in its collection (Coll. S-5081).

- Adams, John Quincy. *Life in a New England Town, 1787, 1788: Diary of John Quincy Adams While a Student in the Office of Theophilus Parsons at Newburyport* (Boston, Mass.: Little, Brown & Co., 1903) throughout, but esp. p. 107.

Secondary Sources

- Currier, John James. *History of Newburyport, Mass., 1764-1905, Volume 2.* (Newburyport, Mass.: Printed for the Author, 1909), throughout, but esp. pp. 265-66; 468-73; 540-44.

- Hopkins, James D. *An Address to the Members of the Cumberland Bar: Delivered During the Sitting of the Court of Common Pleas, at Portland, June Term, 1833* (Portland: Charles Day & Co., 1833), p. 34.

- Ilsley, Charles Parker. *Centennials of Portland, 1675, 1775, 1875 and 1975* (Somerville, Mass.: George B. King, 1876), p. 56.

- Lapham, William Berry. *Bradbury Memorial: Records of some of the Descendants of Thomas Bradbury* (Portland, Maine: Brown, Thurston & Co., 1890), pp. 88-89.

- Perley, Sidney. *The Essex Antiquarian, Volume 10* (Salem, Mass.: The Essex Antiquarian, 1906), pp. 149-50.

- Sylvester, Herbert M. *Olde Cascoe: Ye Romance of Casco Bay* (Boston, Mass.: W.B. Clarke., 1909), p. 180.

- Willis, William. *Journals of the Rev. Thomas Smith and the Rev. Samuel Deane, pastors of the First church in Portland: with notes and biographical notices and a summary history of Portland* (Portland: Joseph S. Bailey, 1849), pp. 243, 304.

Chapter 17
Theophilus Bradbury (1739-1803)
Former Owner of Lot 64

Theophilus Bradbury was born in Newbury, Massachusetts, on November 13, 1739, the son of Captain Theophilus Bradbury and Ann Woodman. Theophilus graduated from Harvard in 1757; following that, he studied law and taught grammar school in Falmouth (Portland). As mentioned, he married Sarah Jones (the granddaughter of Moses Pearson) in 1762, and together they had seven children.

Bradbury rose through the legal ranks quickly. He was admitted Attorney to the recently-established Cumberland Inferior Court in May 1762, Attorney to the Superior Court of Justice in June 1765, and Barrister in June 1767.[95] In 1768, Theophilus was appointed as Justice of the Peace. He was, it seems, a "big fish in a small pond," being the first educated lawyer to establish himself in the territory between York and Pownalborough (modern-day Dresden, Alna, Jefferson, and Wiscasset).[96] But he didn't have this region entirely to himself. He was followed one year later by another Harvard graduate, David Wyer:

> As these were the only lawyers in the county, until 1774, they engrossed the business,[97] and were always employed on opposite sides. Their characters were as much at variance as was the current of their practice: Bradbury was grave and dignified; Wyer, gay and full of satire, and the shafts of his wit did not always fall

---

[95] By the end of the 18th century there had been only 53 lawyers admitted to practice in Maine; of these, Theophilus Bradbury was one of only eight who had reached the rank of Barrister (according to Charles Warren, *History of the Harvard Law School and of Early Legal Conditions in America, Volume 1* [New York: Lewis Publishing Co., 1908], p. 292).

[96] William Willis, *A History of the Law, the Courts, and the Lawyers of Maine* (Portland, Maine: Bailey & Noyes, 1863), p. 93.

[97] This observation is corroborated by eventual US President John Adams in a letter to his wife Abigail, dated June 29, 1774: "Bradbury at Falmouth, they say, grows rich very fast."

harmless from the shield of his adversary. They were both good lawyers, and their forensic struggles afforded gratification, and often amusement, to the attendants upon the courts. Bradbury was a better special pleader, and his character and manners gave him much influence with the jury. Wyer, by his brilliant sallies, often carried the audience, if he did not win his cause.[98]

It was during this time that Theophilus Bradbury trained another young lawyer for his legal career: Theophilus Parsons. Parsons graduated from Harvard in 1768 and apprenticed with Bradbury until the end of 1773. As stellar

---

[98] Willis, *Law*, pp. 93-94. Willis goes on to describe Bradbury as "an earnest Congregationalist." Indeed, Theophilus is listed as the First Parish Clerk from 1773 to 1779, a position that his son, George, would eventually occupy from 1819 to 1821. Like most New England Protestants of his day, Theophilus Bradbury wasn't known to be especially fond of Catholics. In 1801, he and Justice Samuel Sewall "penned an opinion that expressed the icy magnanimity of the prevailing mood: 'Catholics are only tolerated here, and so long as their ministers behave well, we shall not disturb them. But let them expect no more than that.' The Massachusetts Attorney General, James Sullivan—himself the son of a Catholic and bitterly outspoken against his father's faith—had brought charges against Father de Cheverus for the crime of performing an illegal marriage, that is, a Catholic marriage, between two Catholic parishioners. Although the indictment was eventually thrown out, Father de Cheverus had been jailed for a time, and Justice Bradbury, who had presided at the unsuccessful trial, publically expressed his disappointment at losing the opportunity to consign a priest to the pillory" (Michael Ponsor, *The Hanging Judge: A Novel* [Open Road Media, 2013] 1:16; see also William Byrne, et. al., *History of the Catholic Church in the New England States, Volume 1* [Boston, Mass.: Hurd & Everts Co., 1899] pp. 27, 491). It is worth noting that Theophilus's son, Francis, gracefully overcame the biases of his father. Twenty years later, he wrote in his journal: "Bishop Cheverus the Roman Catholic Bishop delivered an address at the court house to a full audience, this man has done much good at Boston, he is a man much esteemed for his amiable character, as well as for his abilities.—Prejudice and superstition has counteracted the blessed effects of our Religion. It is to be hoped, that the prejudices will soon disappear and charity reign in their place" (August, 1822).

Chapter 17 – Theophilus Bradbury

of a career as Bradbury had, it is generally acknowledged that Parsons's eventually eclipsed that of his mentor.[99]

One of the most portentous events in Bradbury's life—and certainly one of the most significant in the history of Portland itself—was the so-called "Burning of Falmouth (Portland)." As it turns out, Theophilus played a key—if not reluctant—role in it.

In the spring of 1775, in the early stages of the Revolutionary War, the British army was besieged in Boston. They were being supplied by the Royal Navy, under the command of Vice-Admiral Samuel Graves. To further their own cause, local Patriots captured several supply ships headed for Boston and seized the British sloop *Margaretta* in Machias, killing its commanding officer. In response, Graves was ordered to "carry on such Operations upon the Sea Coasts ... as you shall judge most effective for suppressing ... the Rebellion." So he, in turn, ordered Lt. Henry Mowatt to "lay waste, burn, and destroy such Sea Port towns as are accessible to His Majesty's ships...and particularly Machias where *Margueritta* was taken."[100]

Following these orders, Mowatt set sail from Boston in early October aboard his 16-gun sloop *HMS Canceaux*, accompanied by the 20-gunship *Cat*, the 12-gun schooner *HMS Halifax*, the bomb sloop *HMS Spitfire*, and the supply ship *HMS Symmetry*.[101] Presumably en route to Machias,

---

[99] See, for example, Hopkins, *Address*, pp. 51-52; reprinted in B.B. Edwards & W. Cogswell, *The American Quarterly Register, Volume 12* (Boston, Mass.: Perkins & Marvin, 1840), pp. 278-79. Among his many other accomplishments, Parsons eventually went on to become Chief Justice of the Massachusetts Supreme Court.

[100] Roger F. Duncan *Coastal Maine: A Maritime History* (New York: Norton, 1992), p. 216.

[101] William Goold, *The* Burning *of Falmouth (now Portland), by Captain Mowatt in 1775* (Boston, Mass.: Maine Historical Society, 1873), p. 12.

this squadron anchored itself in the harbor of Portland—where several acts of violence had previously occurred, and where Mowatt himself had been briefly detained. On October 17, one of Mowatt's men ferried ashore a letter of his intent. This is where Theophilus Bradbury comes in:

> The Rev. Jacob Bailey, who was officiating in Falmouth, in place of Mr. Wiswell, in a letter published in vol. v., p. 441, of the Maine Historical Collections, says the officer "landed at the lower end of India Street amid a prodigious assembly of people, which curiosity and expectation had drawn together from every quarter." He says the officer was conveyed with uncommon parade to the town house, and silence being commanded, "a letter was delivered and read by Mr. Bradbury, a lawyer, but not without such a visible emotion as occasioned a tremor in his voice." This was Theophilus Bradbury, who moved to Newburyport after the destruction of the town, and became a judge in the Supreme Court. Mr. Bailey adds "It is impossible to describe the amazement which prevailed upon reading this alarming declaration; a frightful consternation ran through the assembly a profound silence ensued for several moments."[102]

The content of Mowatt's fateful letter, which Theophilus Bradbury read (with "a tremor in his voice") to his fellow Portland residents, is as follows:

> *Caxceau*, Falmouth, October 16, 1775
>
> After so many premeditated attacks on the legal prerogative of the best of sovereigns, after the repeated instances you have experienced in Britain's long forbearance of the rod of correction, and the manifest and paternal extention of her hands to embrace again and again, have been regarded as vain, and nugatory; and in place of a dutiful and grateful return to your King and parent State, you have been guilty of the most unpardonable rebellion, supported by the ambition of a set of designing men, whose

---

[102] Willis, *Portland*, p. 517.

insidious views have cruelly imposed on the credulity of their fellow creatures, and at last have brought the whole into the same dilemma; which leads me to feel, not a little, the woes of the innocent of them in particular on the present occasion, from my having it in orders to execute a just punishment on the town of Falmouth, in the name of which authority I previously warn you to remove without delay, the human specie out of the said town, for which purpose I give you the time of two hours, at the period of which, a red pendant will be hoisted at the main top gallant mast head, with a gun. But should your imprudence lead you to show the least resistance, you will in that case, free me of that humanity so strongly pointed out in my orders, as well as in my inclination.

I do also observe, that all those who did on a former occasion fly to the king's ship under my command, for protection, that the same door is now open to receive them.

The officer who will deliver this letter, I expect to return immediately unmolested.

I am, &c., H. MOWATT[103]

In response, the town sent a delegation to meet with Captain Mowatt, with the hopes that the threat could somehow be averted. Mowatt claimed that his orders were irreversible, and that they did not even authorize him to give the inhabitants any warning. He did insinuate, however, that the decision could be revisited if the town were to surrender all of its cannons, small arms, and ammunition. The delegation could not agree to that, but they did manage to afford the residents another 24 hours to remove as much of the populace and property as possible. Around 9:30am the next day, Mowatt gave order, and all the vessels in the harbor opened fire with discharges of incendiary

---

[103] Willis, *Portland*, p. 517.

cannonballs, bombs, carcasses, shells, grape shot, and musket balls. The barrage continued throughout the day, until 6pm. Mowatt then dispatched his men from the vessels to set fire to any houses or buildings that still stood. The residents were so preoccupied with moving their families and properties to safety, that the soldiers encountered little resistance.[104] According to Mowatt, "the body of the town was in one flame."[105]

Of course, news of the attack caused outrage in the colonies and only made the Revolutionary forces all the more determined to vanquish their British overlords. As for Bradbury, his house was one of the few that survived. It was set on fire several times, but repeatedly extinguished by great effort. Nevertheless, he temporarily relocated to Windham,[106] even while he continued his law practice in Portland. He was named Attorney General of Cumberland County in 1777, and served in this capacity until 1779, when he moved his family back to his hometown of Newburyport, Massachusetts. There he would reside until his death.

---

[104] Willis, *Portland*, pp. 519-20.

[105] Nathan Miller, *Sea of Glory: The Continental Navy fights for Independence 1775-1783* (New York: David McKay, 1974), p. 48.

[106] Windham is the location given by Sibley (p. 144), but I have been otherwise unable to confirm this. A survey of the Registry's deeds prior to 1775 indicates that Bradbury owned multiple properties in Falmouth (Portland), Harpswell, and Pearsontown (Standish), but not in Windham. On July 2, 1778, Bradbury did purchase land in Windham, but he only held it for 14 months (until October 14, 1779). In fact, following Mowatt's attack, Bradbury appears to have become much more involved in the affairs of the town of Standish. On March 25, 1776, the Pearsontown Proprietors appointed Bradbury, Enoch Ilsley, and Joseph Noyes to sell those lots whose owners were delinquent in their back taxes (see, e.g., 10:143; 10:171). This role may explain how Bradbury originally came to acquire Lot 64, and raises the possibility that he may have briefly resided in this area between his stints in Portland and Windham.

Chapter 17 – Theophilus Bradbury

While Bradbury had certainly done well for himself in Portland, his career ascended to an even higher plane in Newburyport. In 1780, he was chosen to serve on a committee to review the newly proposed Constitution of Massachusetts. Thereafter, he became increasingly involved in state and national politics. He was elected a member of the Massachusetts State Senate, a position he held from 1791 to 1794. His term ended when he was elected US Congressional Representative from Massachusetts. Bradbury served in that capacity during the Fourth and Fifth Congresses, under George Washington's administration, from March 4, 1795 until July 24, 1797.

It was during this period that Theophilus sent a letter to his daughter, Harriet (wife of Major Thomas Hooper). The full text of the letter, which was addressed from Philadelphia and dated December 26, 1795, was eventually released to the public.[107] In it, Bradbury describes a memorable Christmas Eve dinner, hosted by George and Martha Washington:

> Dear Harriet: In compliance with my promise I now sit down to write, and, though I have nothing material to communicate[!], I am influenced by the pleasure it gives me, at this distance, of conversing with my children in the only way which I can. Last Thursday I had the honor of dining with the President, in company with the Vice-President, the Senators the Delegates of Massachusetts, and some other members of Congress, about 20 in all. In the middle of the table was placed a piece of table furniture about six feet long and two feet wide, rounded at the ends. It was either of wood gilded, or polished metal, raised about an inch, with a silver rim round it like that round a tea board; in the centre was a pedestal of plaster of Paris with images upon it, and on each end figures, male and female, of the same. It was

---

[107] It first appeared in the *Pennsylvania Magazine of History and Biography* 8, no. 2 (June 1884), pp. 226-27.

very elegant and used for ornament only. The dishes were placed all around, and there was an elegant variety of roast beef, veal, turkeys, ducks, fowls, hams, &c.; puddings, jellies, oranges, apples, nuts, almonds, figs, raisins, and a variety of wines and punch. We took our leave at six, more than an hour after the candles were introduced. No lady but Mrs. Washington dined with us. We were waited on by four or five men servants dressed in livery.

Bradbury's letter next goes on to describe Philadelphia's Congress Hall (the seat of the US Congress prior to its move to Washington D.C. in 1800) and its environs. Given the level of detail that he provides, Bradbury obviously spent considerable time there and knew it well:

Perhaps you have a curiosity to have a description of Congress Hall; it is a large, elegant brick building, the north end on Chestnut street. The Representative's room is on the lower floor. The Speaker sits in a large arm chair with a table before him like a toilette, covered with green cloth, fringed. The Speaker's seat is elevated about 2 feet and is on the west side of the hall. The members' seats are 3 rows of desks, rising one above another in the form of a semi-circle, opposite the Speaker; these are writing desks with large armed chairs with leather bottoms. There is a lock and key to each desk and places on the desks for ink, pens, sand and a plentiful supply of paper. There are two fireplaces, on each side of the hall with stoves.

There is a good deal of room outside the semicircle, or, as we speak, "without the bar," to which we introduce strangers to hear the debates, and where considerable numbers are always in attendance, as well as in the gallery which is at the north end. At the south end, without the bar, there is an area or half circle with three large windows looking into a large square or walk, the only mall in the city, and two doors from the hall open into it. There are holes for the Southern and Eastern mails into which we deposit our letters to be carried to the Post Office by the doorkeeper. The Senate chamber is over the south end of the hall; the Vice President's chair is in an area (like the altar in a church) at the south end.

Chapter 17 – Theophilus Bradbury

> The Senators' seats, two rows of desks and chairs, in a semi-circle, but not raised from the floor. The floors of both halls are covered with woolen carpets. The lower room is elegant, but the chamber much more so. You ascend the stairs leading to the chamber at the north end and pass through an entry having committee rooms on each side; in that on the east side of the Senate chamber is a full length picture of the King of France, and in the opposite room is one of his Queen; the frames are elegantly carved and gilt. They are superbly dressed, with the insignia of royalty; hers, I think, is the finest picture I ever saw. She is tall and a fine form; her eyes are blue and her countenance expressive; she approaches near to a beauty. Alas! How little did they dream of the dreadful catastrophe awaiting them when they sat for these pictures. They were presented by the king. There is a building on the east side of the hall on Chestnut street for offices, connecting the hall with Pennsylvania state house, in which their general court is now sitting; this is as large a building as Congress Hall, and these buildings form the north side of the square or mall.

Finally, Bradbury concludes his letter with the hope that he might soon hear back from his daughter and her husband:

> But I suppose you are tired with my description. In my present want of a social domestic circle, the pleasure of it would in some measure be supplied by letters from my children and friends, and I doubt not you will consider this a motive for writing. You will give my sincere regards to Maj. Hooper and tell him that by employing a leisure hour in writing to me he would give me great pleasure. I am your affectionate parent, Theoph Bradbury

Bradbury's meteoric rise wasn't over just yet. He resigned from Congress in order to accept an appointment as Justice of the Supreme Court of Massachusetts in 1797. In 1798, he was elected a Fellow of the American Academy of Arts and Sciences. And in 1800, Theophilus Bradbury was chosen a member of the Electoral College, serving as President Elector for the State of Massachusetts.[108]

Unfortunately, Theophilus's extraordinary career was cut a bit short. In February of 1802, at the age of 63, Bradbury suffered a paralytic stroke. He was subsequently removed from the bench by legislative address in July of 1803.[109] He died in Newburyport on September 6, 1803, and was interred there beside his daughter, Frances (d. 1801), at the Old Hill Burying Ground. The following obituary article ran in the newspaper and was found pasted into the journal of his son, Francis:[110]

> JUDGE BRADBURY.
> In the *Centinel* of Wednesday we mentioned the death of the Honorable THEOPHILUS BRADBURY, of *Newbury-port.*—The following obituary notice thereof, is copied from the "*Repertory.*"— "In his private and public life—as a friend or as a magistrate; as a citizen or Legislator; a subject or statesman, Judge BRADBURY claimed and received the love of his acquaintance, and the gratitude and respect of his country. He devoted his early days with industry and success to the study and practice of a profession, which raised him to the honourable [sic] stations he afterwards filled. In later years he resigned the emoluments of that profession for the limited, and (as it proved) the precarious reward of a servant of the public. When a sudden and unforeseen event rendered him incapable to perform the duties of his high and responsible office, he was refused the pittance for which he

---

[108] In case you were wondering, Massachusetts' electoral votes that year went to the incumbent candidate (and close acquaintance of Bradbury's), Federalist John Adams. However, Adams was defeated in the general election by the up-and-coming Democratic-Republican candidate, Thomas Jefferson.

[109] The text of the corresponding address and its formal responses can be found in the *Massachusetts Law Quarterly, Volume 2* (Boston, Mass.: Massachusetts Bar Association, 1916), pp. 508-10.

[110] Francis Bradbury, Papers (Vermont Historical Society, Leahy Library, Barre VT, MSA 284:1-2).

had sacrificed former prospects of wealth and ease.[111] He was intelligent, serious and faithful in executing the laws of his country.—To his family, his connexions [sic] and friends, he was warmly attached, and affectionately endearing. His recent firmities [sic] deprived the public of a just and honest servant; his sudden death has bereaved his friends and acquaintances of a man they esteemed and loved."

Primary Sources

- Bradbury, Francis. Papers, 1812-27. (See Sarah Bradbury for fuller description.) Vermont Historical Society, Leahy Library, Barre VT, MSA 284:1-2.

- Bradbury, Theophilus. Letter to his daughter, Mrs. Thomas Hooper, Philadelphia, December 26, 1795. *Pennsylvania Magazine of History and Biography* 8, No. 2 (June 1884), pp. 226-27.

- Adams, John. *Familiar Letters of John Adams and His Wife Abigail Adams, During the Revolution: With a Memoir of Mrs. Adams* (New York: Hurd & Houghton, 1876), pp. 2-3, 17.

- Adams, John Quincy. *Life in a New England Town, 1787, 1788: Diary of John Quincy Adams While a Student in the Office of Theophilus Parsons at Newburyport* (Boston, Mass.: Little, Brown & Co., 1903), throughout, but esp. pp. 38, 40, 91. For those occasions that John Quincy Adams passed the evening at Theophilus Bradbury's house, see pp. 96, 106, 118, 131, 138, and 140.

---

[111] "He was refused pittance...etc." refers to the series of events following Bradbury's stroke. Despite being incapacitated, Bradbury fought his own removal from the bench and hired Theophilus Parsons to represent his case. They argued that the law allowed for the removal of judges only when misconduct was involved. Bradbury offered to resign voluntarily, but only if he was given a pension in lieu of his $1,166 salary. The Governor decided against him and issued a writ of *supercedeas*.

Secondary Sources

- Currier, John James. *History of Newburyport, Mass., 1764-1905, Volume 1.* (Newburyport, Mass.: Printed for the Author, 1906), throughout.

- ----------. *History of Newburyport, Mass., 1764-1905, Volume 2.* (Newburyport, Mass.: Printed for the Author, 1909), throughout, but esp. pp. 265-66; 468-73; 540-44.

- Hopkins, James D. *An Address to the Members of the Cumberland Bar: Delivered During the Sitting of the Court of Common Pleas, at Portland, June Term, 1833* (Portland: Charles Day & Co., 1833), pp. 34, 47.

- Lapham, William Berry. *Bradbury Memorial: Records of some of the Descendants of Thomas Bradbury* (Portland, Maine: Brown, Thurston & Co., 1890), pp. 88-89.

- *Memorials of the Essex Bar Association* (Salem, Mass.: Newcomb & Gauss, 1900), p. 243.

- Perley, Sidney. *The Essex Antiquarian, Volume 10* (Salem, Mass.: The Essex Antiquarian, 1906), pp. 149-50.

- Sibley, John Langdon. *Biographical Sketches of Graduates of Harvard University in Cambridge, Massachusetts.* (Cambridge: University Press, 1873), Vol. 14, pp. 143-46.

- Willis, William. *A History of the Law, the Courts, and the Lawyers of Maine* (Portland: Bailey & Noyes, 1863), pp. 92-95.

- ----------. *The History of Portland, from 1632 to 1864: With a Notice of Previous Settlements, Colonial Grants, and Changes of Government in Maine* (Portland: Bailey & Noyes, 1865), throughout, but esp. pp. 372-73, 516-20, 619-25.

- ----------. *Journals of the Rev. Thomas Smith and the Rev. Samuel Deane, pastors of the First church in Portland: with notes and biographical notices and a summary history of Portland* (Portland: Joseph S. Bailey, 1849), pp. 243, 304.

- Wroth, L. Kinvin and Hiller B. Zobel, eds. *Legal Papers of John Adams, Volume 1* (Cambridge, Mass.: Belknap Press, 1965), pp. xcvii-xcviii.

Chapter 18
George Bradbury (1770-1823)
Former Owner of Lot 52

George Bradbury was born to Theophilus and Sarah (Jones) Bradbury in Portland on October 10, 1770. Of all of Theophilus's children, George was the one who most closely followed in his father's footsteps. Like Theophilus, George attended Harvard, where he studied Law. While there, he delivered an oration entitled "On the Learned Professions" to the Phi Beta Kappa Honor Society in 1787, and was selected for membership into the college's chapter in 1789.[112] George graduated with his AB in 1789 and went on to earn his AM in 1792.[113]

Following Harvard, George worked out of his father's law office in Newburyport, where he honed his legal skills. He was admitted to the Bar in the County of Essex, where he practiced for several years. On June 15, 1800, he married Mary Kent of Portland, and together they had five children. Like his father, George also became involved in politics, and was elected a member of the Massachusetts Legislature, representing Newburyport in 1802.

Geographically speaking, George's career was mirror-opposite that of Theophilus's. Whereas Theophilus had been born in Newburyport, launched his practice in Portland, and ended up in Newburyport, George had been born in Portland, launched his practice in Newburyport, and ended up in Portland. George returned "home" to Portland in 1803 (the same year in which his father died) and settled there

---

[112] *Catalogue of the Harvard Chapter of Phi Beta Kappa, Alpha of Massachusetts* (Cambridge, Mass.: Riverside Press, 1912), pp. 9, 63.

[113] According to Willis, "But three town [of Portland-] born young men previous to 1800 had graduated at any college. These were the sons of the Rev. Mr. Smith [John and Peter] and George Bradbury. To obtain an education was a much more expensive and difficult undertaking than it now is, and but few persons of that day, in comparison with the present, were liberally educated" (*Portland*, pp. 742-43).

until his own death in 1823. This watercolor painting of his house was found among the papers of his brother, Francis:[114]

While George's career was not quite as illustrious as his father's, it was nevertheless distinguished in its own right. Shortly after relocating to Portland, George was appointed Attorney for the Government in the County of Cumberland, a position he held for a few years. Locally, he served as a Portland Town Officer (1805, 1806, and 1808); Justice of the Peace; and, as previously mentioned, First Parish Clerk (1819-21).

Bradbury also continued to remain active in politics. He returned to the Massachusetts Legislature (this time as a representative for Portland) from 1806 to 1810 and 1811 to 1812. George resigned that position upon being elected to

---

[114] Courtesy of the Vermont Historical Society, Leahy Library, Barre VT, MSA 284:1-2.

Congress. He served as a Federalist for Massachusetts' 15th Congressional District (Maine) for two consecutive terms. This was from March 4, 1813, until March 3, 1817, being the 13th and 14th Congresses—both under James Madison's presidency. However, Bradbury's bid for re-nomination in 1816 was unsuccessful.

Following his departure from Congress, George went back to his legal practice. He served in Portland, along with Judge Freeman, as Associate Clerk of the Judicial Courts from 1817 until 1820, when Maine officially separated from Massachusetts. He was also an Overseer of Bowdoin College from 1815 until 1821. But his political career wasn't quite finished. He was elected to represent Cumberland County in the Maine State Senate in 1822, and even served as its President during a part of that year.

Unfortunately, much like his father, George Bradbury's career was also cut short. On November 7, 1823, he died rather unexpectedly at the age of 53. He is interred in Portland's Eastern Cemetery. And while his professional aspirations may not have reached quite the lofty heights as his father's, George's manner and character certainly left a lasting impression upon his colleagues:

> [George Bradbury] was respected and very highly esteemed by all who knew him. Amiable in private life, and ever affable and faithful in the discharge of his duties in public situations; -- perhaps he never had an enemy. Happy reminiscences will be associated with his name, and long continue to remind us of the universal regret at his sudden and unexpected decease.[115]

---

[115] James D. Hopkins, *An Address to the Members of the Cumberland Bar: Delivered During the Sitting of the Court of Common Pleas, at Portland, June Term, 1833* (Portland, Maine: Charles Day & Co., 1833), p. 64. These sentiments seemed to be shared by John Quincy Adams, a friend of the Bradburys whose diary entries speak positively of both Theophilus and George.

Primary Sources

- Adams, John Quincy. *Life in a New England Town, 1787, 1788: Diary of John Quincy Adams While a Student in the Office of Theophilus Parsons at Newburyport* (Boston, Mass.: Little, Brown & Co., 1903), pp. 38, 77, 90-91, 124.

- Bradbury, Francis. Papers, 1812-27. (See Sarah Bradbury for fuller description.) Vermont Historical Society, Leahy Library, Barre VT, MSA 284:1-2.

Secondary Sources

- *Catalogue of the Harvard Chapter of Phi Beta Kappa, Alpha of Massachusetts* (Cambridge, Mass.: Riverside Press, 1912), pp. 9, 63.

- Freeman, Samuel. *Extracts from the journals kept by the Rev. Thomas Smith* (Portland: T. Todd & Co., 1821), pp. 105, 106, 112.

- *General Catalogue of Bowdoin College and the Medical School of Maine, 1794-1912* (Brunswick: Bowdoin College, 1912), p. 6.

- "George Bradbury" on the *Wikipedia* website: https://en.wikipedia.org/wiki/George_Bradbury

- Hopkins, James D. *An Address to the Members of the Cumberland Bar: Delivered During the Sitting of the Court of Common Pleas, at Portland, June Term, 1833* (Portland, Maine: Charles Day & Co., 1833), p. 64.

- Lapham, William Berry. *Bradbury Memorial: Records of some of the Descendants of Thomas Bradbury* (Portland, Maine: Brown, Thurston & Co., 1890), pp. 118-19.

- *Proceedings of the Massachusetts Historical Society, Series 2, Volume 16* (Cambridge: John Wilson & Son, 1902), p. 362.

- Willis, William. *The History of Portland, from 1632 to 1864: With a Notice of Previous Settlements, Colonial Grants, and Changes of Government in Maine* (Portland: Bailey & Noyes, 1865), pp. 742-43.

Chapter 19
Joshua Freeman, Jr. (1731-96)
Former Owner of Lot 37

Joshua Freeman, Jr. was born in May of 1731, to Joshua and Patience (Rogers) Freeman in Harwich, Massachusetts. His father, Joshua Freeman, Sr. (known as "Fat Freeman" for his size), kept a popular tavern in Portland on the corner of Middle and Fish (now Exchange) Streets before the Revolutionary War.[116] As previously mentioned in Sarah Jones Bradbury's profile, this tavern was the site of the infamous dancing incident. Albert Sears confuses father and son by claiming that Joshua Sr. acquired nine lots in Pearsontown's Second Division (including Lot 37) and four in the Third Division.[117] However, given the year of his death (1770), this would have been impossible. Rather, these deeds belonged to his son, Joshua Freeman, Jr.

While it falls well beyond the scope of this work to examine the genealogies of our property owners, Joshua is a bit of an exception—primarily because this work has already been done. Joshua comes from fairly remarkable stock, and a few of his ancestors are worth mentioning. His father is a direct descendant of Elder William Brewster, who originally arrived here, along with his daughter, Patience Brewster, aboard the *Mayflower*. Patience married Thomas Prence, the Governor of Plymouth Colony. Their daughter, Mercy Prence, was Joshua Freeman, Jr.'s great-great grandmother. Joshua's mother's side (the Rogers line) is even more impressive. She was a direct descendant of Thomas Dudley,

---

[116] The Maine Historical Society has a powder horn inscribed "Joshua Freeman March 27/1767" and decorated with images of a bird, flower, squirrel, bear, buck and rattlesnake. This artifact was carved for Joshua Sr. by Joseph Weir, a scout and Indian fighter who often stopped at the Freeman Tavern. It can be seen online at https://www.mainememory.net/artifact/6044.

[117] Sears, *Families*, p. 84.

Governor of the Massachusetts Bay Colony; Reverend John Rogers, Fifth President of Harvard College; Major General Daniel Denison, Commander-in-Chief of the Colonial Forces; the Reverend Jose Glover, the first to introduce the printing press to New England; and many others. In fact, so distinguished are Joshua Freeman, Jr.'s bloodlines, that several can be traced with certainty all the way back to 12th century England.[118]

Joshua grew up in Plymouth, but around 1740, at the age of eight or nine, he moved with his family to Falmouth (Portland). There he would reside for the rest of his life. In the spring of 1750, Joshua began courting Lois Pearson, the daughter of Moses Pearson. Sarah Jones Bradbury's first (purported)[119] diary entry affords us a rare glimpse into this period:

> Spent the afternoon and part of the evening with Lois Pearson, and had a very agreeable visit, for it is a truly pleasant family. Miss Pearson is engaged and will shortly be married to Joshua Freeman. After tea while we were walking in front of the house, and looking at Capt. Ross' mast ship newly arrived in the harbor, Mr. Freeman joined us. He was very loudly "drest," so much so, that I could but observe him with more particularity than usual. He wore the usual cocked hat and full buttoning, which

---

[118] Henry Cole Quinby, *Genealogical History of the Quinby (Quimby) Family in England and America* (Rutland, Vermont: The Tuttle Company, 1915). See pp. 213 & 215 for family trees, and p. 218 for his explanation.

[119] There are several good reasons to question the authenticity of this particular entry, which is dated Friday, July 21, 1750. If this date is to be believed, Sarah would have been only ten years old at the time. However, the style and eloquence of her writing seems well beyond that age. Indeed, it is more consistent with the next entry, which is a good seven years later, when Sarah would have been 17. The date itself is also problematic, since Joshua and Lois were married on June 19, 1750. However, a month later, Sarah is here describing them as still "engaged." Finally, as we shall see, the content of Sarah's entry is suspiciously similar to Willis's source.

Chapter 19 – Joshua Freeman

marvelously became him. Also a scarlet cloak, thrown over in Spanish style gracefully across one shoulder. His coat was scarlet, the cuffs of which reached to the elbow, and his hands were half hidden in ruffles. I observed he wore drab small clothes, the color most effected by the gentry. Albeit some prefer buckskin, most fancifully embroidered with exceedingly deep pocket flaps. White silk hose, silver knee buckles, ingeniously wrought, shoes similarly adorned, completed his toilet. Surely a marvelously foppish display. Moreover he wore two watches, one on each side. Such fondness for outward adornment in a young man, and he hath not yet reached his twentieth, would seem to indicate a light and frivolous mind. Yet he is spoken of as a youth of exceedingly good and clean parts. Certes his conversation savors of exceeding excellent sense. Nevertheless, were he beau of mine, I should greatly prefer that he made himself less conspicuous in dress. It does seem in this respect our young men go to extremes, and try to emulate the ladies in their vain frippery.

This depiction of Joshua Freeman is strikingly reminiscent of William Willis', which he draws from Isaac Ilsley:

> It may show something of the style of an early day to describe the dress of Joshua Freeman, when he went a courting in 1750, as given by himself to Mr. Isaac Ilsley. He said he wore a full bottomed wig and cocked hat, scarlet coat and small clothes, white vest and stockings, shoes and buckles, and two watches, one each side. That surpasses any foppery of the present day: the wearer of this dress was then twenty years old.[120]

Freeman's ostentatious outfit may have been more than just a display of "peacocking" for Lois. As it just so happens, his flamboyant wardrobe was quite comparable to that of his prospective in-laws:

---

[120] Willis, *Journals*, p. 135.

> In our town [Portland] the persons who were distinguished by the cocked hat, the bush wig, and the red cloak, the envied marks of distinction, were the Waldos, the Rev. Mr. Smith's family, Enoch Freeman, Brigadier Preble, Alexander Ross, Stephen Longfellow, Dr. Coffin, Moses Pearson, Richard Codman, Benjamin Titcomb, William Tyng, Theophilus Bradbury, David Wyer, and perhaps some others. The fashionable color of clothes among this class was drab; the coats were made with large cuffs reaching to the elbows, and low collars. All classes wore breeches which had not the advantage of being kept up as in modern times by suspenders; the dandies of that day wore embroidered silk vests with long pocket flaps and ruffles on their breasts and over their hands. Most of those above mentioned were engaged in trade, and the means of none were sufficiently ample to enable them to live without engaging in some employment. Still, the pride of their caste was maintained....[121]

Whether Joshua Freeman was seeking to make a good impression upon Lois, her family, or both, he evidently succeeded. The two were married on June 19, 1750, and built an impressive house at 25 Granite Street (formerly 210 Deering Avenue).

Together, Joshua and Lois Freeman had 13 children.[122] One of these, Eunice Freeman, would go on to marry Captain John Quinby, another owner of College property, and the subject of our next profile.

As for Joshua, he appears to have lived a relatively quiet life in Falmouth (Portland). He is listed as a member of the Falmouth (Portland) Militia on August 16, 1757, serving as the Clerk of Captain Isaac Ilsley's Back Cove Company.[123]

---

[121] Willis, *Portland*, pp. 776-77.

[122] For a list of names and dates, see Henry Cole Quinby, *New England Family History* Vol. 2, No. 6 (New York: Hanover, 1908), p. 287.

[123] Marquis Fayette King, *Baptisms and Admission from the Records of First Church in Falmouth, now Portland, Maine* (Portland, Maine: Maine Genealogical Society, 1898), p. 171.

Chapter 19 – Joshua Freeman

But perhaps his most significant role came in 1760, when Massachusetts' York County, which originally encompassed the entire "District of Maine," was subdivided into three. The first Officers of the newly formed Cumberland County were sworn in on December 3, 1760. They included Enoch Freeman as one of the Judges of Common Pleas, Moses Pearson as Sheriff, Stephen Longfellow as Clerk of the Courts, and Joshua Freeman, Jr. as Crier of the Courts.[124] Beyond this, Freeman's only other record of public office is that of Selectman.

Joshua Freeman, Jr. died on November 11, 1796. He is buried in Eastern Cemetery in Portland beside his wife, Lois, who passed away on March 21, 1813. His tombstone describes him simply as

> A Gentleman of Excellent Character
> and an exemplary Christian.[125]

---

[124] Quinby, *New England*, p. 286. In case you were wondering what a "Crier of the Court" is: "The Supreme Court of the United States appointed a 'Cryer' on the second day of its opening term in February 1790. Nine years later, Congress enacted a law (1 Stat. 626) directing the district and circuit courts to appoint such officers. The statute contained no description of the criers' duties, but these officers followed their predecessors in English and colonial courts by performing various ceremonial functions, such as introducing judges, calling witnesses to the stand, and announcing the opening and adjournment of court sessions" (www.fjc.gov/history/home.nsf/page/admin_03_13.html). This role is still operational in the US Supreme Court today. At the beginning of each session, the marshal of the Court (or Court Crier) announces: "The Honorable, the Chief Justice and the Associate Justices of the Supreme Court of the United States. Oyez! Oyez! Oyez! All persons having business before the Honorable, the Supreme Court of the United States, are admonished to draw near and give their attention, for the Court is now sitting. God save the United States and this Honorable Court" (https://en.wikipedia.org/wiki/Oyez).

[125] Quinby, *New England*, p. 286.

Primary Source

- Bradbury, Sarah Jones. Diary (1750-66). For bibliographic details, see the listing under Sarah Jones Bradbury's entry.

Secondary Sources

- King, Marquis Fayette. *Baptisms and Admission from the Records of First Church in Falmouth, now Portland, Maine* (Portland, Maine: Maine Genealogical Society, 1898), p. 171.

- Quinby, Henry Cole. *Genealogical History of the Quinby (Quimby) Family in England and America* (Rutland, Vermont: The Tuttle Company, 1915), pp. 213, 215, and 218.

- ----------. *New England Family History Vol. 2, No. 6* (New York: Hanover, 1908), pp. 284-87.

- Sears, Albert. *Early Families of Standish, Maine* (Westminster, MD: Heritage Books, 2010), p. 84.

- Willis, William. *Journals of the Rev. Thomas Smith and the Rev. Samuel Deane, pastors of the First church in Portland: with notes and biographical notices and a summary history of Portland* (Portland: Joseph S. Bailey, 1849), pp. 135, 187, 467.

Chapter 20
John Quinby (1758-1806)
Former Owner of Lot 64

John Quinby was born on May 12, 1758, in Portland to Joseph II and Mary (Haskell) Quinby. The Quinby family was a prosperous one. Both John's father and his grandfather, Joseph Quinby I, had been involved in the shipping business. John would likewise follow in their footsteps.

John was educated at the Portland public schools and was, at the age of 13, enrolled in Master Parson's class (1771). (Recall that Theophilus Parsons was, at that time, Theophilus Bradbury's legal understudy.) Parson's schoolhouse was on the west side of King Street (now India Street) just above Middle Street. By 1774, Quinby was a pupil of Mylo Freeman at South School.

In 1775, the Quinbys lost their home in the Burning of Falmouth (Portland). So John's father moved his family to Saccarappa (now Westbrook), where he became part-owner of a mill there. When he died the following year, John inherited it, along with his father's considerable real estate holdings in and around Portland.[126] John thus returned to Portland where he launched his own career as a merchant mariner.

As previously mentioned, John Quinby married Eunice Freeman, the daughter of Joshua and Lois (Pearson) Freeman. They tied the knot at the First Parish Church on October 31, 1782. The ceremony was officiated by Eunice's uncle, the Reverend Samuel Deane. Together, John and Eunice had six children. These included one daughter, Eunice (b.1783–d.1862) and five sons: Thomas (b.1784-d.1802), Moses (b.1786-d.1857), Levi (b.1787-d.1829), George (b.1789-d.1790) and an infant son born around

---

[126] For a copy of the will and a full list of John's inheritance, see Quinby, *Quinby*, pp. 144-45.

December 12, 1790. Tragically, John and Eunice lost their 16-month old, George, in a drowning accident on September 21, 1790. As if this wasn't enough grief to bear, John then lost both his 29-year-old wife and their newborn infant to a complicated childbirth less than two months later. (Seriously, can you imagine?) These three are interred in Portland, at the Stroudwater Burial Ground.[127] Rounding out his family, John Quinby also had a nephew, Thomas Seal, who was brought up in his household. Seal was the illegitimate son of Quinby's sister, Rebecca. His father was purportedly an English captain. Seal eventually went on to work for Quinby in his shipping business.[128]

Five months after his marriage (1783), John Quinby bought some property in Stroudwater, where many of his relatives were living, and began the construction of his home. This served as the Quinby family's permanent residence. Long after John's death, the house was moved to the northwesterly corner of State and Pine Streets in Portland.

The same year that John broke ground on his new house, he and his business partner, Archelaus Lewis, purchased land and mill rights on the waterfront in Stroudwater and began to establish their shipping enterprise. By 1796, they had built a two-story shop on the wharf at Town Landing, where they manufactured and

---

[127] Of the surviving children, Eunice went on to marry Major Ezekiel Day, and Thomas died at Port Republic (now Port au Prince), Haiti on October 22, 1802. His obituary notice in *Jenk's Gazette* (Falmouth, December 20) called him "a promising and enterprising young man." I have no further information about Moses or Levi.

[128] Preceding information taken from Quinby, *Quinby*, pp. 218-19 and from the Maine Maritime Museum website http://archon.mainemaritimemuseum.org/?p=creators/creator&id=61.
Note that as it currently stands, the museum website has confused the information about the dates of the deaths of George, Eunice, and the infant son.

Chapter 20 – John Quinby

outfitted all manner of sailing vessels.[129] Quinby himself was either full or part owner of at least 13 crafts, including the *Friendly* (brig), *Falmouth* (brig), *Maine* (brigantine), *John* (bark/ship), *Almira* (brig), *Diamond* (brig), *Mentor* (brig), *Mary* (schooner), *Eunice* (ship), *Dispatch* (sloop), *Superb* (brig), *Good Intent* (brig) and *Industry* (sloop).[130] From Europe, South America and the West Indies, Quinby imported cigars, indigo, flour, corn, rice, coffee, molasses, rum, brandy, gin, chocolate, sugar, and shoes. Such merchandise was delivered to his store by gundalows (flat bottom cargo vessels) up the Fore River via Portland. In turn, Quinby exported lumber, shingles, staves and fish. To further facilitate his commerce, Quinby also played an active role in the development of the Stroudwater-Portland highway. In 1793, he proved instrumental in building the bridge over the Fore River, which previously separated the two localities. And in 1802, Quinby became one of the original incorporators of the Maine Turnpike Association.[131]

In addition to his business ventures, John Quinby also served time in the military. In 1787, he was commissioned by Massachusetts Governor James Bowdoin as Lieutenant of the Sixth Company, First Regiment, in the County of Cumberland in the Sixth Division of the Militia. In 1794, he was commissioned by Massachusetts Governor Samuel Adams as Captain in the First Regiment of the Second Brigade, Sixth Division, Militia of Massachusetts, counties of

---

[129] Ibid., p. 216. The building itself remained intact for 50 years or so, when it was removed in 1845 to the junction of Frost and Congress streets and used as a shop and dwelling by Captain Dexter Brewer. It was eventually relocated to Tate Street in Portland where it continues to function as a private residence.

[130] According to the Maine Maritime Museum website: archon.mainemaritimemuseum.org/?p=creators/creator&id=61.

[131] Quinby, *Quinby*, p. 217.

York and Cumberland, in the District of Maine. He eventually resigned from this latter position and was Honorably Discharged on June 1, 1796.[132]

Shortly after Captain Quinby's discharge, two of his vessels were captured by the French during an undeclared naval war with the United States. (Also known as the "Quasi-War," and the "XYZ Affair," it lasted from approximately 1798 to 1800.) One of these, the schooner *Mary*, was captured "in sight of Margaretta," a West Indies island just off the coast of Venezuela. It was captained by James Blake and valued at $5,500. The second ship, *Eunice*—named for Quinby's wife and daughter—was captained by his nephew, Thomas Seal. On June 14, 1797, *Eunice* left Liverpool, England bound for Philadelphia with her cargo of salt (145 tons), copper, coal (21 tons), dry goods, and ceramic Liverpool-ware. She never arrived at her destination. Rather, *Eunice* was seized by the French privateer *L' Intrepide* on July 7, 1797, and taken to Nantes. The French commandeered the ship and its freight on the specious grounds that it lacked an official passenger list. Quinby filed a claim against France with the US State Department in 1799. A treaty negotiated between these two countries in 1800 granted compensation to the claimants of French spoliations. However, Congress proved glacially slow in moving on their behalf. Before he died, Quinby willed his French claim to his sons, Moses and Levi. They, too, died before seeing the payout, as did their sons and daughters—all except one: Almira Quinby. It was to her that the US Court of Claims finally, in the year 1900, granted John Quinby's claim for the sum of $11,938.[133]

---

[132] Ibid., pp. 214, 216.
[133] Ibid., pp. 217-18.

Chapter 20 – John Quinby

In 1804, John Quinby contracted what was then called "consumption" (or today, tuberculosis). He died two years later, on September 27, 1806, at the age of 48. He was laid to rest near his wife and sons at the Stroudwater Burial Ground in Portland. On his gravestone are etched the words:

> That life is long which answers life's great end.[134]

Primary Sources

- Quinby, John. Papers (1724-1802). Maine Maritime Museum Manuscript Collection, Bath, Maine (MS-186). The John Quinby papers consist of a single box of manuscript records mostly pertaining to his 18th century shipping business. The papers are organized into three series. Series I (Folders 1-3) relate generally to John Quinby's shipping business. Series II (Folders 4-29) are all vessel related papers. And Series III (Folders 30-31) are personal papers. Quinby's trade with local residents in merchandise and his involvement in the shipping industry are well documented. Papers capture shipbuilding activities, labor exchanges, purchases, repairs and shipping. A number of receipts show Quinby was also a surveyor of lumber. Some of the other receipts are handwritten by Portland Customs officials for clearance of vessels. In general business correspondence are proposals for the selling of a ship and the sale of the ship by Quinby. Moreover, there are letters from captains aboard vessels to Quinby concerning cargo, weather, damage, expenses, market trends and bills. The papers exhibit domestic and foreign trade, especially in the West Indies. The personal papers include a heartbreaking receipt for digging the grave and tending to the funeral of John Quinby's wife on December 10, 1790 (folder 30).

- Quinby, John. Account book "B" and daybook (1795-98). Many entries pertain to Falmouth and Casco Bay. Includes several entries for the ship *Eunice* and the schooner *Mary*. Also discusses

---

[134] Ibid., p. 218.

shipbuilding in Portland, Maine. Maine Historical Society, Coll. 1081.

- *Andrews Hawes Collection* (1745-1860). Andrew Hawes is the collector and very few papers deal with Hawes himself. This massive collection (14 boxes, 3 half boxes, 9 vol., 2 cartons, 1 card file) includes papers collected by Hawes relating to 18th and 19th century Maine, particularly Falmouth, Me., together with a small amount of correspondence (chiefly genealogical); a travel diary (1860); and other papers, of Hawes. Also includes correspondence and legal, business, and family papers of Moses Pearson (1697-1778) first sheriff of Cumberland County; the Quinby family, especially John Quinby (1760-1806) relating to shipping; papers relating to the Revolution in Maine, the attack and surrender of Louisbourg (1745), and slavery in Maine; and other business, personal, and legal papers. Maine Historical Society, Coll. 64.

Secondary Sources

- Maine Maritime Museum website. Includes biographical profile and details of the John Quinby manuscript collection: http://archon.mainemaritimemuseum.org/?p=creators/creator&id=61.

- Quinby, Henry Cole. *Genealogical History of the Quinby (Quimby) Family in England and America* (Rutland, Vermont: The Tuttle Company, 1915), very thorough biography with pictures, esp. pp. 211-21.

Chapter 21
Jedediah Lombard, Jr. (1760-1842)
Former Owner of Lot 64

Jedediah, Jr. was born in Truro, Massachusetts, in 1760, the second of five children to Jedediah and Susan (Dorsett) Lombard. His father, Jedediah, Sr. (1728-1820), lived quite the adventurous life. The son of Solomon Lombard, he was

> a man possessed of great strength. He was a sailor following the sea for forty years, twenty of which was as mate. He was cast away on Cape Cod during a violent snow storm on March 29, 1769, but escaped without injury.[135]

Jedediah Sr. also saw considerable action in the Revolutionary War. Although he himself never owned any of the campus's property, his daring exploits may nevertheless be pertinent to it. Accordingly, it is worth reviewing here. The following account comes from Gorham historian Hugh D. McLellan:[136]

> During the war a privateer sloop was fitted out at Boston to cruise against the enemy, and on account of the scarcity of men she came into Portland to complete her complement. Meeting with poor success the Lieutenant came to Gorham. His business soon became known, and there was quite an assembly of men; after a consultation, some ten of them proposed going if Lieut. Cary McLellan would go with them. Accordingly, McLellan was offered the birth of lieutenant of marines, which he accepted, and on the next morning the sloop left Portland harbor. The cruise was not successful; they took one or two small prizes, but soon fell in with Capt. Mowatt, in a large vessel of very superior force. They were captured, and carried into New York, and confined on the, ever-to-be-remembered by Americans, prison ship *Jersey*.

---

[135] McLellan, *Gorham*, p. 633.
[136] Ibid., pp. 133-40. Given the heroic portrayal of Lieutenant Cary McLellan, I think we can safely presume that the author is a descendant. In any case, Cary appears to be the ultimate source of the information.

Here they, in common with the other American prisoners, were insulted, and assailed by hunger, disease, and sickness....

When this capture was made it was in the winter. The weather was cold, and the prisoners were deficient in comfortable clothing, and fires had to be kept to keep the men from freezing. The British captors made the wooding of the prison ship the work of the prisoners. They were compelled to go in boats a long distance on the Jersey shore, and under a guard of soldiers with loaded muskets and fixed bayonets, cut the wood, not only for their own use, but also for the use of the officers and crew of the ship. The treatment of slaves at this labor would have been good compared with what they received, and it is not to be supposed that the prisoners worked with a will; the wooding was a hard business, and they made it a slow one. A boat would be gone two days, with a strong gang of men, and when she returned the result would probably be as much wood as one of the same men would have procured in two hours, if allowed to work on his own account.

One afternoon, on the return of the boat with its load of wood, McLellan was looking over the side of the ship, and carelessly made the remark in the hearing of a stripling of an officer, that he did not think much of men that could not procure more wood in that time; they must be lazy. The officer immediately turned to him and said, "Well, you rebel, do you think you could do any better? " The reply was "I think I could if I could have a good crew, and sharp axes." The officer at once told him sarcastically that he should have a chance to try his hand on the morrow, and that he might take the axes and grind as much as he pleased. This was precisely what McLellan desired. The axes were ground with a will; and when the morning came, the prisoners were mustered, and he was ordered to select his men, he chose Jedediah Lombard, Jonathan Simpson and William McLellan, Jr....With two privates and an orderly for their guard, the boat started on its voyage, which voyage Lieut. McLellan had determined should be a voyage for liberty or death for some of them. They landed at the usual wooding place, at some miles from New York, in a region of country occupied by many tory families. Before the landing no one of the crew had been made aware of Lieut. McLellan's plan. During the day, however, the

Chapter 21 – Jedediah Lombard Jr.

wooding went on well, and he had an opportunity of making known his plan to his companions.

It was usual for the wooding party to remain on the ground overnight, and occupy an old log house; one of the guard standing sentry, while the others slept; and they took sufficient provisions with them to last the two days. Toward the night on the first day, Lieut. McLellan told the orderly that he felt tired and should like a glass of something good to drink. The orderly replied that there was a store about a mile out, and if money could be raised, they could have some....Accordingly one of the guard was ordered to accompany Lieut. McLellan to the store, which was kept by a tory. Here he bought a new pail, and a gallon of the best West India rum the store offered. As the pail was so full of rum, he thought it was not prudent to add any water, but put molasses in to make it sweet and palatable. The guard tasted it and as well as himself pronounced it good. For this treat McLellan paid ten silver dollars, but counted the money of no value as it was to him the price of liberty....When they arrived at the camp...supper was prepared, and the rum went round. McLellan had cautioned his men to drink sparingly, if at all, but appearances at least must be kept up....The evening passed merrily enough with drinking and talking. A looker-on would hardly have believed that in that company there were prisoners and their guard.

As the reader can probably surmise, McLellan's scheme was effective. One by one, each of McLellan's men feigned passing out in a drunken stupor as two of the three British guards actually did. Once everyone appeared to be fast asleep, the third remaining guard also succumbed to temptation, and soon thereafter began to doze at his post. McLellan and his men quickly sprang into action. They procured the axes, took the guard's gun, and, one by one, bound the hands of their hapless, intoxicated captors. However, their plan to sail through the British lines under the cover of darkness was thwarted by the tide, which had left their boat high and dry. Thus, they returned to the house, fed their prisoners, and formulated a new plan.

When the tide had risen sufficiently to float the boat, the prisoners were made to lie flat in the bottom, and some green bushes were piled over them. As the boat was a man-of-war's boat, and on that account would be recognized immediately if seen in the light, it was necessary to disguise it in some way. Soft mud was taken, and the boat completely smeared over with it. The bushes were allowed to hang over the side, and everything was done to make it appear like a country boat....

In order to reach the American lines it was necessary to pass directly by one of the enemy's ships. They knew that no boat would be allowed to pass without being hailed, but to attempt to pass farther off would ensure their having a boat sent for them, and make capture certain. Consequently it was thought best to put a bold face on the thing and steer directly for New York, which path lay directly past the ship which lay at anchor about three miles from the city. The wind was fresh and the course was laid to leeward of the vessel. They expected to be ordered alongside, and Simpson was ordered to take care of the sail, and to loose the sheet and let it fly, thus making the boat unmanageable; consequently, as the wind blew from the ship, it would render it more impossible to obey the order from the ship. As anticipated they were hailed, to which the answer was made, "A country boat going to market with vegetables." As it was somewhat duskish the green boughs favored and proved the answer. When the orderly found his proximity to the ship he made an attempt to call for help, but Lieutenant McLellan put the heel of a stout boot into his mouth, which, with the loss of a tooth by the operation, caused him to groan and at once remain quiet. They were then ordered to come alongside as vegetables were wanted on board. This was the chance for the display of their seamanship; the sail blew out of Simpson's hands; all sprang to try and catch the sheet, while the boat drifted off, and Lieutenant McLellan called at the top of his voice that he could not get to the ship but wished they would send after the vegetables. At this the Lieutenant of the ship, with an oath, told them to go to the devil with their cabbages, and look out they did not get drowned. This was the order desired. At a proper time the boat was again under way, and made off in another direction, which if seen from the ship would doubtless be attributed to their *good seamanship*.

It was now light....Without hesitation they kept directly up the North River till they arrived within the American lines, and were hailed from the shore by one of the Continental guards, when they landed with their prisoners, and were marched to White Plains, the headquarters of George Washington, where they gave up their prisoners to the army, and sold their boat. Simpson and Lombard remained with the army, and the two McLellans came home on foot through the country.

Jedediah eventually returned back to Gorham. His home was on the western half of the hundred acre lot 105 on what has since been called Mighty Street. As mentioned above, he married Susan Dorsett and they had five children: three daughters (Sara, Phebe, and Salome) and two sons (Jedediah, Jr. and Hezekiah)—the latter of whom was eventually lost at sea. Susan Lombard died on July 18 1784, and on October 20, 1784, Jedediah married Mrs. Susanna Libby, the widow of Joab Libby. Jedediah died on January 24, 1820, at the age of 92. He lies buried in Fort Hill Cemetery in Gorham, Maine.

As for Jedediah, Jr.—the former owner of campus property—he moved from Truro, Massachusetts, to Gorham, Maine, with his family, and like his father, he also enlisted in the Revolutionary War. He served as a Private for nearly seven years, beginning with a three year stint from January, 1777 until December, 1779 in Captain Richard Mayberry's company, Colonel Tupper's regiment. He then re-enlisted in the spring of 1780 and was assigned to Captain Whitmore's company, Colonel Sproat's regiment until the war's end in September, 1783.

After the war, Jedediah, Jr. married Lydia Rand, the daughter of Jeremiah and Lydia Rand, on July 12, 1785. He took up faming and fathered ten children: Marcy, Nathaniel, Betsey, Hezekiah, John, Polly, Sargent, William, Esther, and Sally. By 1790 the family had relocated from Gorham to Standish Neck.

When the War of 1812 began, Jedediah enlisted yet again. On Dec. 28, 1812, he was assigned into Captain Smith Elkins' company, Colonel Denny McCobb's regiment and was stationed in Burlington, Vermont. However, in the summer of 1813, he was struck by an epidemic fever that left him completely blind in his right eye and partially blind in his left. Accordingly, Jedediah was honorably discharged that August, and he returned back to his home in Standish.

Jedediah's wife Lydia died on January 13, 1830, at the age of 61. He outlived her by twelve years before passing away on March 16, 1842. He was 82. They lie buried together in the small Lombard Cemetery next to the "Sebago to the Sea Trail" near its terminus at Sebago Lake in Standish.[137]

Secondary Sources

- McLellan, Hugh D. *History of Gorham, Me.* (Portland: Smith & Sale, 1903), pp. 133-40; 633, 635.

- Sears, Albert. *Early Families of Standish, Maine* (Westminster, MD: Heritage Books, 2010), p. 133.

---

[137] Ibid., p. 635; Sears, *Families*, p. 133.

Chapter 22
The Ebenezer Shaw Family
Former Owners of Lots 63, 51, and 52

Ebenezer Shaw (1713-82)

Ebenezer Shaw was born on October 7, 1713, as the eighth of nine children to Caleb and Elizabeth (Hillard) Shaw of Hampton, New Hampshire. Caleb was a sailor, and master of the sloop, *Mayflower*—not the Pilgrim one. In 1715 he perished at sea at the age of 44, when Ebenezer was only two. Elizabeth remarried Captain Joseph Tilton, but she died nine years later (1724), also at the age of 44. Thus, Ebenezer was left orphaned at the age of 11. It was then that he came to live and apprentice with Moses Pearson, first at Newbury, and then in Falmouth (Portland). Upon turning 21, Ebenezer returned home to Hampton, where he married Anna Philbrick in 1738. Reportedly, Ebenezer preferred a somewhat exclusive and puritanical lifestyle:

> After his marriage, and as children were born to them, he, being of a religious turn of mind and a zealous churchman, was so desirous of bringing them up in a God-fearing manner, that...he removed from Hampton to Sargent's Island, in order that they might grow up uncontaminated by the impure associations of the town.[138]

Together, Ebenezer and Anna had nine children, all born in New Hampshire. Indeed, that is likely where they would have remained had Moses Pearson not contacted Ebenezer some twenty years later.

Following the Fall of Quebec and the ending of Indian hostilities in the area, the Proprietors of Pearsontown agreed on January 21, 1762, to set aside a 100-acre lot for the construction of a sawmill. To sweeten the pot, they also

---

[138] Harriette Favoretta Farwell, *Shaw Records: A Memorial of Roger Shaw, 1594-1661* (Bethel, Me.: E. C. Bowler, 1903), p. 106.

reserved another 100 acres of land for anyone who could successfully build and operate it by October of that year. Four days later, Moses sent a letter to his former apprentice in Hampton and invited him to take advantage of this opportunity. Shaw accepted Pearson's offer. Ebenezer and his oldest son, Josiah, arrived later that year, and in just nine days they built Pearsontown's first sawmill on the upper reaches of the north branch of the Little River. Shaw then constructed his own house and moved his entire family here. For this reason, many historical sources consider him to be the first true resident of Pearsontown.[139]

As previously mentioned, the steady supply of board lumber contributed greatly to the fledgling development. But so, too, did Shaw's influence, as wave after wave of settlers connected to him by blood, marriage, or friendship began emigrating from New Hampshire over the next few years.

Ebenezer Shaw died on March 13, 1782, and lies buried in the Standish Village Cemetery. His widow, Anna, outlived him by 22 years (d. 1804). Incredibly, at the time of her death, Ebenezer and Anna's descendants numbered 201! They included nine children, 82 grandchildren, 109 great-grandchildren and one great-great-grandchild. As far as the history of the College's campus goes, these are the real subjects of our inquiry, because although Ebenezer Shaw never owned any of the College's property, at least 16 of his descendants did. Of the 160 former landowners, the Shaw family is by far the most represented. Members of this clan account for nearly 14% of that population. But the

---

[139] See e.g., W.W. Clayton, *History of Cumberland Co., Maine* (Philadelphia: Everts & Peck, 1880), pp. 372-73 and Diane and Jack Barnes, *The Sebago Lake Area: Windham, Standish, Raymond, Casco, Sebago, and Naples* (Portsmouth, New Hampshire: Arcadia, 1996), p. 26. Obviously these sources overlook those individuals who resided in the Pearsontown Fort from 1754 to 1759.

Chapter 22 – The Ebenezer Shaw Family 171

connection between the Shaw Family and the College is not as broadly scattered as one might assume. Rather, a relatively concentrated line runs through only one of Ebenezer's sons, and only two of his grandsons (see chart at the end of this chapter). So it is to those individuals that we now turn.

Ebenezer Shaw, Jr. (1749-1836)
Former Owner of Lot 51[140]

Ebenezer Shaw, Jr. was born on January 3, 1749, in Hampton, New Hampshire, as the fifth of nine children to Ebenezer and Anna (Philbrick) Shaw. Ebenezer, Jr. and his siblings were somewhat renowned for their longevity. His obituary, which ran in the August 25, 1836 issue of Portland's *Christian Mirror*, notes that none of the 11 Shaw family members who came to settle in Standish lived less than 65 years. The article, which ran just two weeks after Ebenezer, Jr.'s death at 87, puts their average age at 79.

In addition to his longevity, Ebenezer, Jr. is also one of the most prolific Shaws on record. Between his two wives, he sired an astounding 26 children! Ebenezer first married Sarah Wood of Gorham in 1771. Over the next two decades,

---

[140] There is some degree of ambiguity as to the precise identity of the owner of the campus's Lot 51. The two pertinent deeds (48:552 and 145:306) simply list an "Ebenezer Shaw, Jr." Theoretically, this could refer to either this Ebenezer or his son (who is technically Ebenezer III, but elsewhere also referred to as Ebenezer, Jr.). At the time of the original sale (1806), the former would have been 57 and the latter only 19, so there is good reason to believe that it was the father and not the son. Indeed, the Registry contains at least one other property sale around this same time period that is clearly the father's, since it is co-signed by his wife, Salome (61:286). However, the deeds involving Lot 51 are not co-signed at all. This is probably an omission, but it can be noted that the son was not married until 1816, six years after the sale of this property (1810), and thus would have had no spouse with whom to co-sign.

she bore at least ten children before passing away on July 8, 1792. The following year, the 44-year-old widower married 21-year-old Salome Green of Gorham. They went on to have at least 14 more children. (I was unable to account for two of the 26.) Ebenezer, Jr. himself died on August 11, 1836, and is buried in the Standish Village Cemetery.

There aren't a lot of details about Ebenezer, Jr.'s life in the historical sources. Occupationally, he is listed as a brick maker, mason, cooper, and farmer.[141] And for two months and 20 days, he was also a Continental Soldier in the Revolutionary War. His brief service was as a Private in the 1779 Penobscot Expedition in Captain Joshua Jordan's Company within Colonel Jonathan Mitchell's Regiment.[142] But perhaps Ebenezer, Jr.'s greatest legacy, so far as the College is concerned, is the number of his direct descendants (15) who would go on to become landowners of the campus. Of his 26 children, one of them, Samuel Shaw, became particularly invested in this area, and a second, Ebenezer III, had grandchildren who did.

Samuel Shaw (1775-1848)
Former Owner of Lot 63

Samuel Shaw was born on December 10, 1775, to Ebenezer, Jr. and Sarah (Wood) Shaw, the third of their ten children. He married Mary Phinney of Gorham and together they also had ten children, whom they raised on their homestead on Lot 63.[143] Three of Samuel's sons would go on to own College property. Joseph P. owned Lot 52, Ebenezer (a farmer, teacher, and stonecutter) owned Lot 63, and Leonard (a

---

[141] Sears, *Families*, p. 239; Farwell, *Memorial*, p. 120.

[142] *Collections and Proceedings of the Maine Historical Society* (Maine Historical Society: The Society, 1899), pp. 158-59.

[143] Sears, *Family*, p. 239; Farwell, *Memorial*, p. 166.

farmer) owned Lots 64, 63, and 52.[144] Furthermore, some of their children (Samuel's grandchildren) carried on the Shaw tradition by also owning these lots. Two of Joseph P.'s children (Henry and Zilpha) owned Lot 52. All three of Ebenezer's children (Mahlon, Rebecca, and Nancy H.) owned a 25-acre section of Lot 63. And two of Leonard's children (Charles H. and Albert S.) owned a 55-acre section of Lot 63. Samuel also had a fourth son, Caleb, who did not possess any College property. However, Caleb's son (Samuel's grandchild), Winthrop M. Shaw, did (Lot 52).[145] Altogether, Samuel Shaw and 11 of his direct descendants were previous owners of campus parcels.

Ebenezer Shaw III (1787-1860)

Ebenezer Shaw III was born on July 21, 1787, the eighth of Ebenezer, Jr. and Sarah (Wood) Shaw's ten children. Between his two wives, Ebenezer III fathered nine children. His first wife, Rebecca Yates of Standish, bore seven. Shortly after her death on July 31, 1832, Ebenezer III married her sister, Mary Yates. Mary had two children, but neither of them survived to maturity.[146]

Neither Ebenezer III nor any of his children went on to own College property. However, three of his grandchildren did. Sumner P. Shaw, son of Leander Shaw (farmer), owned various parcels of Lot 52. Sumner was a farmer, butcher, cattle dealer and an "itinerant peddler of meats," as a charming circa 1895 photo of him and his meat wagon on Whites Bridge illustrates.[147]

---

[144] For Ebenezer, see Farwell, *Memorial*, p. 183; for Leonard, see ibid., pp. 183-84.
[145] For Caleb, see ibid., p. 182.
[146] Sears, *Families*, pp. 239-240; Farwell, *Memorial*, pp. 166-67.
[147] See Barnes, *Sebago Lake*, p. 9.

Sumner's brother, Alvin C. Shaw (farmer), also owned a parcel of Lot 52. Ebenezer's third grandchild who owned campus land was Harriet D., the daughter of Curtis Shaw (farmer & fur trader). She owned Lot 51.[148]

****

It is easy to underestimate the effect that Moses Pearson and Ebenezer Shaw had upon the ownership of campus property. However, the following chart illustrates at least some of the extent of their influence. Note that not all genetic descendants are included, but only those who either owned College land (their Lot numbers are in parentheses) or were otherwise necessary to connect those who did.

---

[148] For Leander and Curtis, see Farwell, *Memorial*, p. 185. For Sumner P. see ibid., p. 190; for Alvin C. see ibid., pp. 190-91; and for Harriet, see ibid., p. 185.

Chapter 22 – The Ebenezer Shaw Family 175

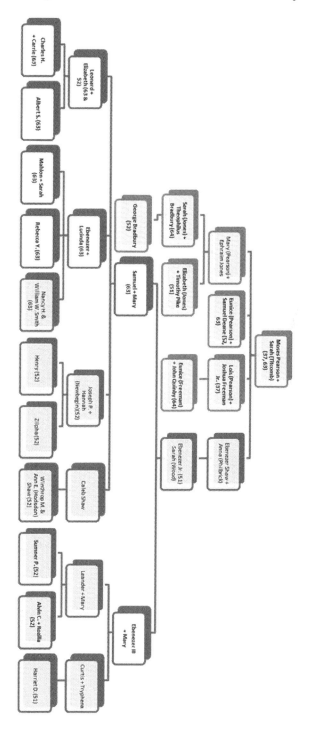

In conclusion, it is worth acknowledging that most of the aforementioned Shaws tended to be farmers (and their families) who lived relatively humble and unassuming lives. For this reason, they don't merit much attention in the literary records of the past. Nevertheless, their roots run quite deep here. As we will see, the Shaw family continuously owned one particular parcel (Lot 63) for nearly a century (1813-1911). During that time, they undoubtedly came to know this campus well. But perhaps no one knew it better than the subject of our next profile: Leonard Shaw.

Secondary Sources

- Clayton, W.W. *History of Cumberland Co., Maine* (Philadelphia: Everts & Peck, 1880), pp. 372-73.

- Barnes, Diane and Jack. *The Sebago Lake Area: Windham, Standish, Raymond, Casco, Sebago, and Naples* (Portsmouth, NH: Arcadia, 1996)

- Farwell, Harriette Favoretta. *Shaw Records: A Memorial of Roger Shaw, 1594-1661* (Bethel, Me.: E. C. Bowler, 1903), an exquisitely detailed treatment of the Standish Branch on pp. 106-91.

- Metcalf, Henry Harrison and John Norris McClintock. *The Granite Monthly: A New Hampshire Magazine Devoted to History, Biography, Literature, and State Progress, Volume 12* (1889), pp. 77-83.

- Ridlon, Gideon Tibbetts. *Saco Valley Settlements and Families, Volume 1* (Portland: Lakeside Press, 1895), pp. 124-25.

- Sears, Albert. *Early Families of Standish, Maine* (Westminster, MD: Heritage Books, 2010), thorough coverage on pp. 234-43.

- ----------. *The Founding of Pearsontown (Standish), Maine* (Heritage Books, 2013), references all throughout, but esp. pp. 21-24.

Chapter 23
Leonard Shaw (1815-92)
Former Owner of Lots 64, 63 & 52

To be honest, compared to the other individuals whom I have profiled, Leonard Shaw lived a fairly inconspicuous life. He wasn't born into a privileged class; he never attended an Ivy League school; he wasn't elected to political office; nor did he achieve much professional success. In all these respects, Leonard Shaw was decidedly unexceptional.

But what makes Leonard Shaw so remarkable is his relationship to this campus. As it turns out, Leonard Shaw was born here, grew up here, got married here, and raised both his children and his grandchildren here. For over half a century, he cultivated this very soil for his family's subsistence. He spent his entire life—all 77 years of it—right here on campus. And when he passed away, he did so here, and was subsequently—and quite appropriately—buried here as well. In this regard, Leonard's connection to the College's campus is unparalleled. As I said, nobody would have known this place more intimately than Leonard Shaw.

As for his particulars, Leonard Shaw was born on May 14, 1815, to Samuel and Mary (Phinney) Shaw, the eighth of their ten children. Samuel Shaw had purchased campus property in 1813 and subsequently built his house here. (Thanks to the residential maps of Standish and a little bit of fieldwork, we know precisely where it stood.) So Leonard Shaw was not merely raised here; in all probability, he first arrived into this world on the premises of our College.

In 1835, Samuel Shaw (then 60 years old), legally turned his homestead over to his 27-year-old son, Ebenezer. Samuel, Mary, Leonard, and the rest of the Shaw family continued to reside there. In 1839, Leonard (then 24) assumed ownership of the property. This was the same year that he married Elizabeth "Betsy" Hamblen of Standish.

Together, they had eight children. According to Farwell's work, these included: Ellen S., Charles H., Mary S., Frankie (d. infancy), Albert S., Lydia M. (d. infancy), Lucy H., and Eudora.[149]

It is interesting to compare this list with the information given in the Standish censuses. Leonard himself is not named in the 1840 Census; rather he is likely the 20 to 30-year-old male residing in Samuel Shaw's household. However, Samuel died in 1848; thereafter, Leonard is registered as the Head of Household in the 1850, 1860, 1870, and 1880 Censuses.[150] (He would also have been listed as such in 1890, but no census was conducted that year.) We can briefly review each of these Censuses in turn:

1850
Leonard Shaw, 35, farmer, $1200 worth of real estate owned
Elizabeth Shaw, 29
Ellen Shaw, 7, in school
Charles Shaw, 4, in school
Susan Shaw, 2
Mary Shaw, 69
Martha Crocket, 85
Joanna Crocket, 52
Andrew Crocket, 50, farmer, idiotic
Samuel Shaw, 22, millman [sic]

As evidenced by the 1850 Census, Leonard Shaw was hardly overseeing a traditional nuclear family. Many others were dependent upon him. Nor could he be considered particularly wealthy. His $1,200 worth of real estate is estimated to be roughly equivalent to a $36,700 standard of living in today's economy.[151] His wife, Elizabeth, and two

---

[149] Farwell, *Memorial*, pp. 183-84.
[150] Census information obtained online from www.mocavo.com.
[151] Online calculator found at www.measuringworth.com.

school-aged children, Ellen and Charles, match the previous list. As for the two-year-old, this must be the "Mary S."[usan] referred to by Farwell. She probably went by Susan to avoid being confused with her grandmother, Mary, who also lived with them. In the 1860 Census, she is referred to as "Susan M."[ary].

Leonard Shaw bought the neighboring 40-acre lot in 1846. Shortly thereafter, he mortgaged it to Ephraim Crockett.[152] According to the terms of their agreement, Shaw was responsible for the maintenance and support of Ephraim and his wife Martha, as well as their children, so long as Ephraim and Martha survived. This Census confirms that Shaw kept his promise. By 1850, Ephraim had passed away, but Leonard continued to provide for the man's family. This included his son, Andrew, which the Census labels as "idiotic." This was a sub-category which also included those who were "deaf and dumb, blind, insane,...pauper, or convict." Presumably, "idiotic" was a reference to mentally challenged individuals—but obviously prior to the age of political correctness!

The final name in Leonard's 1850 household is Samuel Shaw. This was Leonard's younger brother, the last of his siblings still residing in their ancestral home.

---

[152] Leonard's grandmother (his mother's mother) was Susanna Crockett, but I have been unable to determine how (or if) she is related to Ephraim Crockett.

> 1860
> Leonard Shaw, 45, farmer, $1500 real estate, $800 personal property
> Elizabeth Shaw, 40
> Ellen Shaw, 17, teacher com. schools, in school
> Charles H. Shaw, 13, in school
> Susan M. Shaw, 11, in school
> Albert S. Shaw, 5, in school
> Lydia C. Shaw, 3, in school
> Nancy M. Shaw, 11 months
> Francis B. Shaw, 13
> Joan Crockett, 63, servant, pauper

By 1860, Leonard's reported holdings had grown a bit more. So had his immediate family. Ellen, Charles, and Susan were joined by three new siblings: Albert S., Lydia C. and Nancy M. The latter two names differ from the family records, which list a Lydia *M.* and a *Lucy H.* The two Lydia's must be the same, although Farwell's note that she died "in infancy" must be interpreted a bit more loosely. (According to Lydia's gravestone, she was actually four when she died.) That Nancy M. is the same person as Lucy H. is suggested by their ages—according to Farwell, Lucy H. was born on September 7, 1858, and died February 25, 1864.[153] However, I am at a loss to explain the reason for such a discrepancy between these names. As for Francis B. Shaw, this was Leonard's nephew. Leonard evidently took him in following the death of his brother, Joseph P. Shaw (circa 1857).

By 1860, only one Crockett remained. Joan(na) evidently had no income, and apparently helped the family out around the house as best she could.

---

[153] Farwell, *Memorial*, p. 184.

Chapter 23 – Leonard Shaw

> **1870**
> Leonard Shaw, 56, farmer, $1200 real estate, $300 personal property
> Charles H. Shaw, 24, hack driver[154]
> Susan Shaw, 21
> Albert Shaw, 17, in school
> Dorah Shaw, 9, in school

The 1870 Census suggests a number of losses for Leonard Shaw; some were real, others were simply oversights. His wife Betsy, for instance, is not listed. (This is an oversight.) His property holdings were also downgraded. And while Charles, Susan, and Albert are all found here, Ellen, Lydia, and Lucy/Nancy are not. Sadly, the three of them all passed away in the 1860s, as, presumably, did Joan(na) Crockett. There was, however, one new addition to Leonard's family: his daughter (Eu)Dorah Shaw.

> **1880**
> Leonard Shaw, 65, husband, farmer
> Betsey Shaw, 60, wife, housekeeper
> Charles H. Shaw, 33, son, hostler[155]
> Albert S. Shaw, 25, son, farmer
> Lizzie B. Shaw, 26, daughter-in-law, housekeeper
> Carrie E. Shaw, 3, grandchild

The last Census record for Leonard Shaw is 1880. This time, his wife Betsy is included. Susan Shaw is not. She moved out, having married John Knight of Gorham. Charles also got married. But rather than move out, he moved his wife, listed here as "Lizzie B." (Farwell has her as "Carrie

---

[154] This occupation refers to one who offers transportation for hire; the precursor to the cab-driver.
[155] This occupation refers to one employed to look after the horses of people who stay at an inn.

Horton") into the household.[156] Their daughter, Carrie E., also joins the family. As for Albert, he remained unmarried and continued to follow in the farming footsteps of his father. Leonard Shaw would eventually (1892) entrust both the homestead and his wife Betsy into Albert's care.

Clearly, Leonard and Betsy Shaw ran a busy household! From 1850 to 1880, at least 15 other individuals resided with them. And as indicated, Leonard Shaw supported them all primarily by farming.

As you can probably imagine, 19th century Maine farmers didn't tend to leave many paper trails. But thanks to a competition sponsored by the Maine Board of Agriculture, we have a detailed account of at least one of the crops that Shaw raised during the 1859 season.[157] A report by the Committee on Grains and Vegetables, under the category of *Indian Corn*, declares:

> Although the present season has not been favorable to the growth of corn, June having been wet and cold, retarding its early growth and making it late upon wet land; a pretty sharp drought having occurred in the latter days of July and up to the 25th of August, very nearly ruining that growing upon sandy, dry soil; and a severe frost having put a termination to the corn season in most localities on the 15th of September; yet some favored places, aided by skillful cultivation, have produced crops of which the cultivators themselves, our county and State, need not feel ashamed. The quality of the samples on exhibition were all good, and some of them were excellent, full and well ripened. They were mostly of the eight rowed varieties; and we would here remark, that, in a climate like our own, where the seasons are so short, it is very desirable to select for cultivation early ripening varieties, having small cobs which will have lost their succulency [sic] by

---

[156] Farwell, *Memorial*, p. 183.
[157] *Agriculture of Maine: Annual Report of the Secretary of the Maine Board of Agriculture, Volume 4, Part 1859* (Augusta: Stevens & Sayward, 1959), pp. 41-42.

Chapter 23 – Leonard Shaw

the time the kernel has acquired that hardness which fits it for the crib; as there is danger of loss by mold if the cob is not well dried before cribbing. There were seven entries made, only four of which were accompanied with the necessary statements of cost, method of cultivation, &c., as *required by Statute*; and one of these, viz: that of Mr. Shaw of Standish, though very full and satisfactory, lacked the *certificate of oath*, which is *required by the rules* of the Society.

The competition, therefore, was between Amos Boulter of Standish, to whom we award the first premium; Coleman Harding of Gorham to whom we award the second premium; and Ithiel Blake of Gorham[158], to whom we award the third premium.

We recommend the publication, as a part of this report, of the statements, and the account current with the several crops, of the successful competitors and also those of Leonard Shaw of Standish; all of these documents being worthy a careful examination by the farmers.

This report is then followed by a series of "Statements" in which each "competitor" describes the process by which he raised his crop and submits an itemized record of his expenses and profits. Leonard Shaw's Statement reads accordingly:[159]

> My crop of corn, consisting of 37 ½ bushels of 60 pounds to the bushel, was grown on one half of an acre, being at the rate of 75 bushels to the acre. The soil on which it grew, was a moist gravelly loam, considerably stony, of a redish [sic] color, fine and mellow, plowed to about nine inches deep. The subsoil is rather a coarse gravel and from fifteen to eighteen inches from the surface.
>
> Two thirds of the land was broken up in the fall of 1857,— planted to potatoes without manure in 1858; the other third was broken up in the fall of 1858.

---

[158] The Ithiel Blake named here (of Gorham, son of Timothy and Susan [Higgins] Blake) is not the same Ithiel Blake (of Standish, son of Nathaniel and Mary [Fogg] Blake), who owned College property. They were, however, relatives (first cousins once removed).

[159] *Agriculture*, p. 44.

In May last I put on three cords of green barnyard manure and plowed it in; furrowed the rows three and one half feet apart, putting the hills the same distance. I put 1½ cords of compost manure in the hills—composted of muck and old yard manure; also, one bushel of plaster and the same amount of ashes put in the hills at the time of planting. Planted the 16th of May with a kind of corn that has been usually planted on this farm for fifty years; has no particular name; the ears are from eight to sixteen rows each. The seed had not been soaked. I cut the top stalks about the middle of September. Hauled in the corn and husked it the first of October.

Crop of Corn

DR.			CR.
Plowing once—2 days	$2 00	37 ½ bushels at $1.15	$43 12
3 cords barnyard manure	9 00	2 bushels unsound	1 00
1 ½ cords other manure	3 00	Fodder	2 00
Carting and applying the same	2 00	Manure left in soil for future crop, estimated at	5 00
Harrowing	50		
Furrowing and planting	75		
Cultivating twice	75		51 12
Hoeing twice—2 days	2 00	Deduct cost	26 17
Dressing and applying the same; plaster and ashes	50		
Cutting and harvesting	1 50		
Husking	3 00		
4 quarts of seed	17		
Interest on land	1 00		
Total	$26 17	Profit	$24 95

Leonard Shaw's profit of $24.95 would be roughly equivalent to the labor earnings of around $4,550 today.[160] If the estimated figures for Shaw's standard of living and labor earnings are correct, then this crop of Indian corn would

---

[160] Online calculator found at www.measuringworth.com.

have represented about 12% (or one-eighth) of Shaw's total income for that year. Exactly what other crops he may have cultivated (potatoes were mentioned), or livestock he may have raised (he included cattle and sheep in a real estate transaction with his brother Ebenezer), we can only guess.

In addition to farming, Leonard Shaw was also actively involved in the affairs of the neighborhood school. Standish District 1 was serviced by a schoolhouse originally located on Lot 62 (near the corner of the present-day Hearthside and Whites Bridge Roads). The schoolhouse lay half way between Leonard's residence and that of his cousin, Leander Shaw. Appropriately enough, this region was known as the "Shaw District." So many of the Shaw children attended it, they accounted for up to 80% of the student population in some years.

The earliest reference I could find to this particular school is in a deed between James Moody and Curtis Shaw (279:210) dated 1857, the same year that the school appears on a residential map of Standish. I have also tracked down nine of its Agent Returns (1864-92) and six of the School Committee's Reports (1870-81). According to this (admittedly fragmented) evidence, Leonard Shaw served as the School Agent in 1864, 1868-70, 1872, and 1890. During the period of Leonard's administration, the enrollment varied from as many as 28 students (in the 1860s) to as few as ten (in the 1890s), with the ages of its pupils ranging from four to 20.

Regrettably, District 1 had a decidedly negative reputation. It consistently received low marks from its assessors, and was repeatedly called out for the poor quality of its teachers, the dilapidated state of its schoolhouse, and the lack of progress among its students. To what extent Leonard Shaw was to blame for this is difficult to ascertain. (On the one hand, these are certainly the types of things for which the School Agent would be directly responsible. But on the other hand, Leonard was just one of at least five School Agents assigned to District 1 throughout this time.) By the early 1890s, District 1's enrollment had declined significantly. Shortly thereafter, it was assimilated into District 2, the so-called "Harding District." Their schoolhouse was located just down the street, on the corner of Whites Bridge Road and Route 35. (It still stands there today, where it functions as a private residence.)

Leonard Shaw died on January 10, 1892, at the age of 77. His cause of death is listed as "chronic cystitis," but this condition is rarely fatal. Therefore, it was probably also accompanied by some sort of prostate or kidney issues. Most likely, Leonard departed this world in the very same house where he first arrived. Fittingly, he was interred in a small cemetery just a stone's throw away from his lifelong home. There, he joined his sister, Hannah P. Shaw (d. 1843) and his children, Frank P. (d. 1855) and Lydia C. (d. 1860). Eventually, Leonard would be joined by a few other relatives, including his wife, Betsy (d. 1907).

It strikes me as particularly odd that someone's entire existence can be so inextricably tied to one place, and yet all memory of them completely vanishes after the passing of a mere generation or two. That seems something of an injustice. However, I can sleep a bit better now knowing that, at least in Leonard's case, this wrong has been righted.

Primary Source

- The Committee on Grain and Vegetables Report in *Agriculture of Maine: Annual Report of the Secretary of the Maine Board of Agriculture, Volume 4, Part 1859* (Augusta: Stevens & Sayward, 1959), pp. 41-42, 44.

Secondary Source

- Farwell, Harriette Favoretta. *Shaw Records: A Memorial of Roger Shaw, 1594-1661* (Bethel, Me.: E. C. Bowler, 1903), pp. 183-84.

Chapter 24
Owen P. Smith (1869-1943)
Former Owner of Lot 52

Owen Percy Smith was born in Hiram, Maine, on April 9, 1869, to William H. Smith, M.D., and Marcia (Hodgton) Smith. He was educated at the local schools and graduated among a class of 34 from Fryeburg Academy in 1888. At his Commencement Exercises, Owen delivered an address on "The Power of Habit" and subsequently put his self-discipline, ambition, and intellectual curiosity to good use. Following in the professional footsteps of his father, he graduated from Bowdoin Medical School in 1892.

Owen spent one year (1893) as an intern at Maine General Hospital in Portland before undertaking post-graduate studies at the University of Edinburgh and the University of Vienna. He became a Specialist in Otology, Rhinology, and Laryngology (i.e., of medical issues pertaining to the ear, nose, throat, and mouth). Smith's medical career was briefly interrupted by the Spanish-American War (April-August, 1898), during which he was appointed Assistant Surgeon of the US Navy aboard the *USS Montauk*. It was during this stint that Owen crossed paths with one of the most significant events in US history.

The *Montauk* (named after the small town in New York) was a 1335-ton, iron-clad, single-turreted, *Passaic*-class monitor. Built and launched in New York in 1862, it was a Civil War battleship which the Union Navy operated along the coastal waterways of Georgia, North Carolina, and South Carolina from 1863 to 1865. It saw action (and took dozens of hits) in the attacks on Fort McAllister (Georgia), Fort Sumter (South Carolina), and Fort Wagner (South Carolina). Following the surrender of the Confederacy on April 9, 1865, the *Montauk* proceeded to Washington, D.C., where it docked at the Naval Shipyard. On April 15, it played host to

President Abraham Lincoln, who toured the ship and was warmly received by its exuberant crew. Later that evening, Lincoln was fatally shot by John Wilkes Booth at nearby Ford's Theatre. In a tragically ironic twist of fate, within two weeks (April 27) the *Montauk* was being utilized as the site of Booth's autopsy and as a floating prison for six of his co-conspirators.[161]

The *Montauk* was decommissioned in December of 1865 at Philadelphia. However, it was reintroduced back into service after Congress declared war on Spain in 1898. It arrived in Portland Harbor on May 13 to help protect the coastal area from Spanish attacks. Sixty-five men (primarily local naval reservists) served on board while the *Montauk* was stationed near Fort Gorges. Owen was responsible for their medical care.[162]

Fortunately, the Spanish-American War was a relatively short-lived conflict (officially lasting less than four months), and Smith was discharged in September of 1898.

The following spring (April 4, 1899), Owen married Elizabeth Milliken. Together, they had two children (who were also campus property owners). Their daughter, Margaret Smith, went on to become a New York attorney. Their son, Owen Milliken Smith, graduated from Dartmouth College in 1923 and from Harvard Business School in 1925. He married Helen Probyn and became a Portland-based

---

[161] Information variously complied from www.ibiblio.org/hyperwar/OnlineLibrary/photos/sh-usn/usnsh-m/montauk.htm, www.navsource.org/archives/01/montauk.htm, and Timothy Sean Good, ed., *We Saw Lincoln Shot: One Hundred Eyewitness Accounts* (Jackson: University Press of Mississippi, 1996), p. 71.

[162] A record of his report can be found at the Maine Historical Society (see primary sources, below).

insurance agent and photographer.[163] Owen Sr. and Elizabeth owned some property in Raymond and Standish, but their primary home was located on 692 Congress Street in Portland.

Most of Owen's medical career was spent in the vicinity of Portland. He was a Surgeon at the Maine Eye and Ear Infirmary, the Maine General Hospital, and the Children's Hospital (all in Portland), the "Sisters' Hospital" (now St. Mary's Regional Medical Center) in Lewiston, and the Webber Hospital (now Southern Maine Health Care) in Biddeford. Smith was also appointed to the Board of Trustees for the Maine School for the Deaf, and served as its Treasurer in 1919.

In conjunction with his practice, Owen was an active member of several professional organizations, and held various offices within them. These include the Cumberland County Medical Association (for which he served as President from 1908 to 1909), the Maine Medical Association, the American Medical Association, the American Laryngological Rhinological, and Otological Society, the New England Otological, Rhinological and Laryngological Association (for which he served as Vice-President), and the American College of Surgeons. Smith frequently presented at the scholarly conferences associated with these organizations, and he was a regular contributor to their journals and publications (a sample of which appear in the primary sources below). In June of 1942, Owen was presented with the Maine Medical Association's Gold Medal in recognition of his 50 years of dedicated service as a physician.

---

[163] Some of his photographs are now housed in the Maine Historical Society, Coll 2437.

Smith was as actively engaged in his recreational pursuits as his professional ones. His real passion was agriculture, and more specifically, Jersey cows.[164] Owen pursued his hobby at "Lakeland Farm," a scenic and functional complex that he developed on the shores of Sebago Lake. The precise location of this farm was a bit of a mystery, but the extant sources offered some helpful clues. It has been described as "a rock-strewn New England homestead about 20 miles from Portland. It borders on Sebago Lake, and the view is beautiful across the large body of water to the White Mountains, with Mt. Washington in the middle of the picture."[165] According to one article (dated June 4, 1938), Smith had been breeding cows at this location "for more than 30 years."[166] This means he would have bought the land no later than 1908. Another article specifically locates Lakeland Farm in Windham.[167] However, this information contradicts the Registry of Deeds, which has no record of Owen ever owning any property in Windham. He did have holdings in Raymond and Standish, but divested himself of the Raymond real estate by March 16, 1908. That same day, Smith purchased 80 acres of Lot 62 (821:74), which is bordered by Sebago Lake and lies adjacent to the campus—constituting the Hearthside neighborhood today. That this property served as Owen's "Lakeland Farm" is all but confirmed by another article

---

[164] Smith also raised Berkshire swine at Lakeland. Four pedigreed animals are listed in the *American Berkshire Record*, Vol. 50 (1917), pp. 50, 312.

[165] "Dr. Owen Smith Honored by Jersey Club" in the *Lewiston Daily Sun* (May 16, 1942), p. 7.

[166] "Dr. Owen Smith, Lakeland Farms, Has Second Best Bull in Country," in the *Lewiston Journal Illustrated Magazine Section* (June 4, 1938), p. A-11.

[167] "Lively Jersey Interest in Western Maine," in *The Jersey Bulletin*, Vol. 41, Issue 2, p. 2140.

which directs "visitors from the eastern and southern parts of the State [to] go to North Windham village and to the farm by way of White's Bridge."[168] Smith owned Lakeland Farm until he died.[169] In 1927 he was able to expand it by acquiring the property across the street (i.e., the campus's Lot 52).

Smith's success as a Jersey breeder is exceptionally well documented. (The secondary sources cited below provide a good indication of this, but even these are not comprehensive.) He maintained a herd of at least 20 cattle, including "Premier Brown Bell Boy," the second-best ranked Jersey bull in the country. An animal achieves such a status by yielding very productive offspring. By 1922, the average heifer was, at its peak, producing around 523.81 lbs. of milkfat per year.[170] But "Premier Brown Bell Boy" had sired 15 daughters who were collectively averaging 721.45 pounds of milkfat in a 365-day period.[171] That's equivalent to approximately 901.8 lbs. of butter per cow, per year!

As he did in the medical field, Owen became highly involved with various organizations relating to agriculture

---

[168] "Maine Jersey Breeders to Meet at Sebago Lake - Dr. Owen Smith Will Entertain at Lakeland Farms" in the *Lewiston Evening Journal* (August 13, 1926), p. 14.

[169] In 1920, Smith must have intended to sell his farm, since the following classified real estate listing appeared several times in *The Outlook*, Vol. 125 (June 9, July 14, July 21, July 28): "Real Estate MAINE FOR SALE A BEAUTIFUL COUNTRY HOME On Lake Sebago, Maine. Fine view of lake and mountains. House has bathrooms, fireplaces, porches, garage, barn, orchards, woods, and sup't's house. Inquire Dr. Owen Smith, 690 Congress St., Portland, Me." For whatever reason, the sale never materialized, and Smith retained the property for another 23 years.

[170] C.W. Turner, "Method of Comparing Fat Records of Jerseys" in the *Jersey Bulletin*, vol. 41 (1922), p. 1151.

[171] "Dr. Owen Smith, Lakeland Farms, Has Second Best Bull in Country," in the *Lewiston Journal Illustrated Magazine Section* (June 4, 1938), p. A-11.

and husbandry. He was a member of the Western Maine Jersey Breeders Club, whose meetings he frequently hosted—to much acclaim—at Lakeland Farm. He also belonged to the Portland Farmers Club (for which he served as Secretary), the Maine Chamber of Commerce and Agricultural Society (for which he served as long-standing President before retiring in 1938), the Maine Dairymen and Livestock Breeders Association (for which he served as Secretary-Treasurer), and the Maine Committee for the 1939 World's Fair in New York (to which he was appointed Chairman). In conjunction with these organizations, Smith was a frequent speaker and guest lecturer.

Owen evidently had quite an effect on his audience. On one particular occasion, at a banquet at the State Dairy Conference in 1912, Smith spoke out against the heavy fees and taxes placed upon the small farmer.[172] In response to his speech, one of Smith's fellow panelists, the Hon. Charles Strout (son of the Maine Supreme Court Judge, Sewall Strout), paid this highly illustrious—if not altogether over-the-top—tribute to him:

> I have not even the claim to recognition as a farmer that Dr. Smith has given. He is one of our most expert men in his line of business here and we all look to him with a great deal of confidence in the most difficult cases; and yet he has told you tonight, not in so many words but inferentially, that he is one of the best, the noblest martyrs to farming we ever met. We have Socrates, who was a martyr to the ideal, Napoleon, who was a martyr to the warrior spirit, and Lincoln, who was a martyr to duty and to mankind. But the Doctor stands among them all as a martyr to farming. He may not go down to history as those

---

[172] Owen Smith, "Remarks by, at banquet, State Dairy Conference" in *Agriculture of Maine. Tenth Annual Report of the Commissioner of Agriculture of the State of Maine* (Waterville: Sentinel Publishing Co., 1912), pp. 123-25.

illustrious personages have, but he tells us frankly here that he works all day and collects those expert fees which are well earned and then he takes them out to his farm in Sebago and puts them into his farm and leaves them all there; and when he comes to study up the net profit he has to come back here and go to work again.[173]

In addition to Smith's numerous production records, gold and silver medals, and other accolades, in 1942 he was presented with the coveted Constructive Breeder Certificate on behalf of the American Jersey Cattle Club—the first breeder in the State of Maine to be so recognized.[174]

In 1942 Owen retired from his active medical practice after suffering from a heart attack. He died about a year later (on July 30, 1943) at Lakeland Farm. He was 74 years old. A short biography of Smith's is included in *Who's Who in New England* and his obituaries appeared in the *Bowdoin Alumnus* magazine, the *Journal of the Maine Medical Association*, and *The Jersey Bulletin*, the latter of which deemed him "a man of sterling qualities and sound convictions."

Primary Sources

- Smith, Owen P. "Harelip and Cleft Palate" in the *Transactions of the Section on Laryngology, Otology and Rhinology of the American Medical Association at the Seventy-First Annual Session, held at New Orleans, La., April 26 to 30, 1920* (Chicago: American Medical Association Press, 1920), pp. 140-49.

---

[173] Hon. Charles Strout, "Remarks by, at banquet, State Dairy Conference" in *Agriculture of Maine. Tenth Annual Report of the Commissioner of Agriculture of the State of Maine* (Waterville: Sentinel Publishing Co., 1912), p. 128.

[174] "Dr. Owen Smith Honored by Jersey Club" in the *Lewiston Daily Sun* (May 16, 1942), p. 7.

- ----------. "Complete Cleft Palate with Hare-Lip" in the *Transactions of the Twenty-First Annual Meeting of the American Laryngological, Rhinological and Otological Society held in Chicago, ILL. June 15th and 16th, 1915.* (New York: Published by the Society, 1915), pp. 202-12.

- ----------. Case Presentation in the *Journal of the Maine Medical Association Vol. V, No. 1* (August, 1914), pp. 8-9.

- ----------. "Abstract of Discussion" in the *Transactions of the Section on Laryngology, Otology and Rhinology of the American Medical Association at the Sixty-Fifth Annual Session, held at Atlantic City, N.J., June 23 to 26, 1914* (Chicago: American Medical Association Press, 1914), pp. 90-91.

- ----------. "Remarks by, at banquet, State Dairy Conference" in *Agriculture of Maine. Tenth Annual Report of the Commissioner of Agriculture of the State of Maine.* (Waterville: Sentinel Publishing Co., 1912), pp. 123-25.

- ----------. "Goitre" in the *Transactions of the Maine Medical Association, 1907-1908 Vol. XVI* (Portland: Stephen Berry Co., 1908), pp. 374-82.

- ----------. "Urano-Staphylorrhaphy" in the *Transactions of the Maine Medical Association, 1904-1906, Vol. XV* (Portland: Stephen Berry Co., 1906), pp. 293-300.

- ----------. *Statistical report of the U.S.S. Montauk, quarter ending Sept. 1898, issued at Philadelphia Naval Shipyard.* Maine Historical Society (Portland) Coll. 949, Series 3 (Box 1/ folder 18).

Secondary Sources (listed by date, with most recent first)

- "Necrologies. Owen Smith, M.D., 1869-1943" in *The Journal of the Maine Medical Association*, Vol. 34 (1943), p. 182.

- "Necrology. Dr. Owen Smith" in the *Bowdoin Alumnus* Vol. 17, No. 4 (August, 1943), p. 17.

- "Dr. Owen Smith Dies" in *The Jersey Bulletin*, Vol. 62, Part 2, (August 20, 1943), No. 16, p. 961.

- "Dr. Owen Smith Honored by Jersey Club" in the *Lewiston Daily Sun* (May 16, 1942), p. 7.

- "Maine Jersey Cattle Club Entertained by Dr. Smith," in the *Lewiston Daily Sun* (June 24, 1940), p. 2.

- "Good Records at Lakeland Farms," in the *Lewiston Daily Sun*, (June 20, 1940), p. 9.

- "Dr. Owen Smith, Lakeland Farms, Has Second Best Bull in Country," in the *Lewiston Journal Illustrated Magazine Section*, (June 4, 1938), p. A-11.

- "News from the Classes" in the *Bowdoin Alumnus* Vol. 12, No. 2 (January, 1938), pg. 64.

- "Improved Breeding Has Produced Dr. Smith's Excellent Jerseys," in the *Lewiston Journal Illustrated Magazine Section* (July 25, 1936), p. A-11.

- "Good Heifers Proving Worth in Dr. Smith's Jersey Herd," in the *Lewiston Journal Illustrated Magazine Section* (July 4, 1936), p. A-11.

- "Western Maine Club Meets with Dr. Smith," in the *Lewiston Daily Sun* (June 27, 1936), p. 6.

- "Chamber of Commerce Heads Interested in Raising Jerseys," in the *Lewiston Journal Illustrated Magazine Section* (Aug. 18, 1934), p. A-11.

- "Jersey Scenes at Lakeland Farm," in the *Lewiston Daily Sun* (Aug. 18, 1934), p. 6.

Chapter 24 – Owen P. Smith

- "Dr. Owen Smith Addresses Western Maine Jersey Ass'n" in the *Lewiston Daily Sun* (Nov. 3, 1932), p. 6. (His subject was "The Raising of Swine.")

- "Sebago Lake Jersey Production Winner," in the *Lewiston Daily Sun* (May 14, 1932), p. 6.

- "Jersey Club had Fine Meeting at Lakeland Farm with Dr. Owen Smith," *Lewiston Daily Sun* (June 24, 1931), p. 6.

- "Dr. Owen Smith Has New Gold Medal Jersey," in the *Lewiston Daily Sun* (July 12, 1930), p. 6.

- "Dr. Smith Has Another Register of Merit Jersey," in the *Lewiston Daily Sun* (Sept. 28, 1929), p. 6.

- "Dr. Smith's Purebred Jerseys Make Records" in the *New England Dairyman*, Vols. 12-13 (Andover, MA: NEMPA, 1928), p. unidentified.

- "Jersey Breeders Met at Lakeland Farm Sebago," in the *Lewiston Daily Sun* (Aug. 30, 1926), p. 12.

- "Maine Jersey Breeders to Meet at Sebago Lake - Dr. Owen Smith Will Entertain at Lakeland Farms" in the *Lewiston Evening Journal* (Friday, August 13, 1926), p. 14.

- "Lively Jersey Interest in Western Maine," in *The Jersey Bulletin*, Vol. 41, Issue 2, (1922), p. 2140.

- "Maine Breeders Meet," in *Home and Field*, Vol. 26 (January 1916), p. 84.

- "SMITH Owen (Percy)" in *Who's Who in New England*, Vol. 2 (2nd edition; Chicago: A.N. Marquis, 1915), p. 992.

Conclusion to Part I

Now that readers have had the opportunity to meet some our campus's remarkable predecessors, we can, as promised, revisit the question that first started this section: To whom did the George Washington Inaugural Button belong?

As previously mentioned, whoever lost this item must have been physically present at its particular excavation site sometime between 1789 and the mid-1800s. While that requirement certainly narrows the field a bit, keep in mind that potential candidates wouldn't necessarily have had to have been property owners. Theoretically, this button could have belonged to a friend, guest, or even a stranger passing through. However, these scenarios are statistically less likely and would be nearly impossible to account for.

If Silverstein's assertion is correct, then the original owner of this button had to have been someone connected to Washington himself. Among the campus's property owners, three individuals fit that bill: Jedediah Lombard, Jr., Samuel Deane, and Theophilus Bradbury. Moreover, all three meet the prerequisites of time and place. (Both Bradbury and Lombard actually owned the property on which this button was found, and Deane—who owned the next lot over—was certainly in close enough proximity.) We can consider each of their cases in turn.

Jedediah Lombard, Jr. was the only one of these three men to serve as a soldier in the Revolutionary War. In fact, he did so for nearly seven years. However, he never rose above the rank of Private, and was never directly under Washington's command. His father, on the other hand, not only met General Washington, but personally delivered three captured British soldiers to his headquarters at White Plains, New York. After doing so, Jedediah Sr. reportedly stayed on with Washington's troops (although it is not specified for how long). If Jedediah Sr. was given this button, then it seems likely that he would have eventually bestowed it upon his (only surviving) son. The main caveat to this theory is that Jedediah Sr. actually lived to be 92, passing away in 1820. But Jedediah, Jr. owned his campus property much earlier, and for only a brief period of time (1800-1802). This means that Jedediah Sr. would have had to have parted with his button decades before his own death, and Jedediah, Jr. would have had to have dropped it within a relatively short time span. All of this, of course, could have happened.

For his part, Samuel Deane had a more immediate connection to George Washington and, of the three, was with him closest to the time of the Inauguration. Both Deane and Washington were among a small class of Honorary Degree recipients at Brown University in 1790—just one year after the Inauguration. Is it possible that Deane obtained this button in anticipation of that meeting? Deane never "served" under Washington, but the two did have a number of high-ranking mutual acquaintances (e.g., Samuel Adams, John Hancock, James Madison, etc.)—not the least of whom was John Adams, Washington's first Vice-President. Given his distinguished network, and his many contributions to this country as a whole, it is certainly conceivable that this object somehow found its way into Deane's possession—and then perhaps back out of it while visiting his neighbor!

Of these three men, Theophilus Bradbury is the only one to have served directly under George Washington, doing so as a member of the fourth and fifth Congresses. Bradbury was also the most intimately acquainted with our First President, having celebrated Christmas dinner with him and his wife. However, Bradbury's documented relationship with Washington appears to have begun a half-dozen years after the Inauguration. Had Theophilus met Washington prior to that? I simply don't know. Nevertheless, like Samuel Deane, Bradbury and Washington ran in the same social circles (which included John Adams). And of these three candidates, Bradbury likely had the most contact with the property in question. He not only owned it, but may have held this lot for 20 years or more before selling it in 1795.

So whose button was this? It appears that we're left with three intriguing contenders. Personally, I lean towards Theophilus Bradbury. I'd estimate that particular likelihood at around 60%. However, I hesitate to press the matter any further, pending additional evidence. That's not to say this issue is over. Far from it. After all, one never knows what else might be out there, buried beneath the surface, just waiting to be unearthed....

****

Having reached the conclusion to Part I, readers should now have a much better sense of the rich history of the Saint Joseph's College campus. But in reality, this project has only scratched that surface. There are literally hundreds more items and names that have yet to be examined. Who knows what we might learn about them? Like pieces to a puzzle, each one has the potential to contribute something unique to the overall picture of our past.

Part II of this book is designed to help complete that puzzle. It contains the compiled results of my fieldwork and documentary research. These Site Reports and Chains of Ownership will introduce readers to the rest of the artifacts and predecessors that have occupied this campus. My hope is that they will prove valuable for future studies into our campus's material and ancestral heritage.

Part II

Site Reports

and

Chains of Ownership

Introduction to the Site Reports

As I previously mentioned, throughout the course of my fieldwork I've discovered 12 artifact-bearing sites within the campus's boundaries. All of these sites predate the College Era (1955 on). Some are more recent (1940s-50s); others go as far back as the late 1700s. They include a mix of accidental spills, intentional dumps, dug cellar holes, and house foundations. Each site is unique, and thereby contributes something distinctive to our understanding of the campus's past. But rather than offering comprehensive analyses of all 12 (which would take up entirely too much time and space), I've provided detailed Reports on four of the most prominent and representative ones. But before turning to these, permit me a few words regarding my methodological approach.

Generally speaking, prospective sites are often approached in one of two ways. At one end of the spectrum are what I'll call the "treasure hunters." Such individuals (usually hobbyists) scan an area primarily for items of significant monetary value. They tend to target nonferrous (non-iron) metals such as gold, silver, copper, and bronze—usually in the form of coins or jewelry. The goal of their hunt is either to acquire such objects for resale and profit, or to amass valuable collections for their own pleasure. In either case, such a goal is best achieved by covering large areas quickly and avoiding or disposing of all other "junk" items. For such individuals, their attachment to a particular site is dependent upon its yield; if one location isn't producing, they simply move on to the next.

At the other end of the spectrum are the professional archaeologists, whose goals are much different. In approaching a site, they seek to gather as much information about it as possible so as to advance a collective understanding of the identities, behaviors, practices, and economies of its previous occupants. To that end, they would undertake a thorough historical and topographical analysis first. Then, they typically dig a few test pits, grid out the area in question, and proceed to investigate it one square meter at a time. Larger items are photographed and recorded *in situ*. Excavated soil is removed and sifted through a series of successively finer mesh screens so that virtually nothing of potential interest is lost. Everything recovered is cleaned, tested (if necessary), identified, stabilized, reconstructed, documented, and catalogued. If expertly accomplished, it is often a painstakingly methodical process that involves a considerable investment of time, effort, and expense. Nevertheless, it also yields enormous amounts of valuable data for a wide variety of research purposes.

As a historical researcher, my own approach to these campus sites falls somewhere in between these two ends of the spectrum. Unlike the treasure hunter, I have proceeded much more systematically: recovering, cleaning, cataloguing, researching, documenting, and storing much of what I recovered. This includes thousands of "trash" items that would normally be left behind—shards of glass and porcelain, iron nails, wood fragments, bits of clay, etc. Although they lack monetary value, each is a unique puzzle-piece that contributes to the overall picture of the site's history. But unlike the archaeologist, I have not collected absolutely everything I have come across. I haven't gridded out the sites and progressed meter by meter, nor have I bothered to screen the soil. As careful and as conscientious as I have been, I am certain that I have overlooked much, and that much more remains to be accomplished...and discovered.

The four Site Reports that follow reflect my particular approach. They are far more comprehensive than one would expect from a mere hobbyist. (My strong affection for the College and ever-growing fascination with its past has virtually assured that outcome!) But despite their thoroughness, they nevertheless lack some of the more sophisticated and technical analysis that one might otherwise receive from a team of dedicated experts. If anything, I offer these Reports as "ground-breaking," yet preliminary, records. By documenting some of the material remnants that our predecessors left behind, I hope to bear witness to our campus's intriguing history, and provide some sort of foundation—and justification—for its continued study.

Procedurally I've arranged these Site Reports in reverse chronological order, moving backwards in time from latest to earliest. Each Report begins with a general description of the site. These descriptions include details about the site's layout, both in terms of its horizontal appearance as well as its vertical layers. I've deliberately chosen not to pinpoint any of these sites on a map or divulge their specific GPS coordinates. As useful as that information is, my overriding concern is to protect the integrity of these areas for ongoing and future research.

A comprehensive inventory of items follows the general description. To make things easier, I've broken each survey down into four main categories: Glass, Ceramics, Metal, and Miscellaneous items. Some important considerations about each of these categories are as follows:

Glass

The vast majority of glass artifacts that I found are bottles, jars, or lids. Dating such objects is not an exact science, but the best of experts can usually narrow the range of a given bottle down to a period of 10-15 years. I claim no such proficiency. However, there are a few helpful guidelines that I've gleaned along the way:

- If a bottle has a "pontil scar," this indicates that it was "hand blown" (or HB). A "pontil" (aka a "ponty" or "punty") is an iron rod on which molten glass is handled while being shaped or worked. Once this process was completed, the removal of the pontil left a ring-shaped scar on the base. (I like to think of these cute little scars as the bottles' "belly buttons.") Open pontil scars are found on the earliest of American bottles, and typically no later than 1855.

- If a bottle has a visible seam along its side which ends *below* its top lip (or mouth), this indicates that it was "blown in mold" (or BIM). In other words, molten glass was inflated with lung power into a preformed casting. The joining of the casts is what produced the visible seams. BIM bottles date from 1820 to 1915.

- BIM bottles can be further subdivided by the shape of their lips (or mouths). In the earliest stages of the BIM process, an extra bit of glass had to be used to form the lip after the blow pipe was removed. This is known as an "Applied Lip," and indicates a date between 1820 and 1890. After around 1890, bottle manufacturers tooled the glass of the neck after removing the blow pipe, so extra glass wasn't needed. These "Tooled Lip" bottles date from 1890 to 1915.

- If a bottle has a visible seam that continues *into* its top lip (or mouth), then it was produced by an Automatic Bottle Machine (ABM). This manufacturing process became widespread in the early 1900s, so such bottles date from that point forward. The earliest of the ABM bottles (1900-20s) tend to have more bubbles in their glass; bubble incidence declines significantly after 1930.

- Embossing (raised lettering) on bottles was popular from the 1850s to the 1930s. Some embossed bottles even mention their patent date, which is extremely helpful. In the 1940s, embossing gave way to enameled Applied Color Labeling (ACL), a practice that continues to this day.

- From 1935 to 1960, liquor bottles were required to indicate that "Federal Law Forbids Sale or Reuse of This Bottle." So bottles with such an inscription date to that period.

I must confess that the treasure-hunter in me is always more than a little crestfallen when I uncover a beautiful old bottle that had been shattered. As one might expect, there tends to be a direct correspondence between the age of the site and the percentage of the glass objects that are broken. This isn't surprising, considering that these fragile containers are continually subjected to the elements, especially the extreme frost-and-thaw-cycles of Maine's harsh winters. (As the Good Book says, "Time and chance happen to all.") But while broken shards of glass are monetarily worthless, even some of the smallest pieces can convey vital archaeological information pertinent to the site. They can not only tell us what sort of product was used and when, but also offer clues as to who may have been using it and why. Theoretically, any glass fragment has the potential to unlock this wealth of information. However, for non-specialists (like myself), glass fragments that are embossed or enameled are particularly helpful, since their identification tends to be far easier.

As we make our way through the survey, I will differentiate glass finds according to their identifying features. These include their overall condition (whole vs. fragments), labeling (embossed or enameled vs. unmarked), color, height, and manufacturing process (HB, BIM, or ABM). Where applicable, other recovered glass artifacts (non-bottles, jars, or lids) will also be mentioned.

Pottery/Ceramics

Many of the same observations that I made about the importance of glass likewise apply to pottery/ceramics, if not more so:

> The archaeologist attaches great importance to pottery, since ceramics is among the most informative kinds of material culture, in history and prehistory as well. Pottery is fragile yet indestructible: while it breaks easily, the fragments are highly resistant to corrosion and discoloration....The perishability of pottery when a part of the living world, and its longevity in the earth, means that the chances are good that any given piece was broken not a very long time after its manufacture, and that the archaeologist recovers large collections of ceramic materials that have a high degree of chronological precision....Small wonder that the analysis of ceramics sometimes occupies what might at first seem a disproportionate amount of the archaeologist's attention and time.[175]

Broadly speaking, "ceramics" covers three general classes of pottery: earthenware, stoneware, and porcelain.

---

[175] James Deetz, *In Small Things Forgotten: An Archaeology of Early American Life* (New York: Doubleday, 1996), pp. 68-69.

Introduction to the Site Reports 209

The former two types were in dominant use prior to 1800. Following that, porcelain became much more widespread. Nearly all of the ceramic items that I have unearthed are in pieces. However, the patterns are usually still vivid, and some of the fragments bear the maker's marks. (Those I am especially grateful to find!)

In the surveys that follow, ceramic pieces will be subdivided according to their class and then itemized according to their distinguishing features. If known, these include their maker (or company), place of origin, pattern, date, object type, extent recovered, and any other information that might be helpful for their identification.

Metal
Because I've relied on a metal detector to locate sites and pinpoint items, metallic objects are naturally going to enjoy greater representation than the other, "accidental" artifacts. Consequently, this category tends to be the largest. It could be subdivided any number of ways. I considered arranging items according to their use, with domestic (homestead) items in one category and nondomestic (farm and field) items in another. However, quite a few objects blur that distinction. Metal articles could also be subdivided according to their primary composition: iron, tin, pewter, aluminum, nickel, steel, brass, bronze, copper, silver, and gold. But such differentiation requires far more expertise in metallurgy than I currently possess.

For the sake of simplicity, therefore, I have assigned all such artifacts into one of two categories, iron-based (IB) or non-ferrous metals (NFM), with the vast majority belonging to the former group. Unfortunately, when iron and iron-alloys (like steel) are exposed to oxygen and moisture over time (as they inevitably are when buried in the ground), the result is iron oxide (rust). The rate of rust can vary due to a number of complicated factors. For this reason, the present condition of each metal artifact has been graded according to the following scale: Very Good (VG), Good (G), Fair (F), and Poor (P). Again, it's a bit heartbreaking to unearth a really unique object, only to discover that it's in such an advanced state of decomposition as to be beyond restoration. The good news is that, in some cases, rust can be somewhat undone by reverse-electrolysis.[176]

In the following surveys, I have listed all metal objects alphabetically. In addition to their metal composition and condition, I have also listed their dimensions and noted any engraving or other unique features that might further enable their identification.

Miscellaneous

This fourth, catch-all category encompasses any item that doesn't fit into the first three. These tend to be rare, but they include articles composed of bone, wood, stone, clay, plastic, leather, and (as we have seen) even paper.

---

[176] Reverse-electrolysis is the least destructive and most thorough method available to remove oxidation. The process removes no base metal and avoids more invasive products like grinders, wire wheels, scrappers, acids or sandpaper. When properly executed, reverse-electrolysis can remove rust and oxidation while leaving the appearance of "patina" so valued by collectors. The instructions for building reverse-electrolysis contraptions can be found online. I won't repeat them here, since they include some important precautions that need to be carefully followed. It should be noted that this method is designed *only* for iron-based metals and can have negative and harmful effects on NFM's. In my experiments with reverse-electrolysis, I've had varying results. Some objects have been dramatically improved and now reveal striking details that were otherwise obscured. But other objects—particularly those being held together by rust—suffered the loss of structural integrity. While this aspect of the project continues to be a work in progress, I've learned to adopt a *very* conservative approach to this—and any other—restoration endeavor.

Chapter 25
The "Curious Deer" Site

General Description

I happened upon this site in the spring of 2015, and I proceeded to excavate it for a couple of months. During that time, I was regularly visited by a very curious deer. I suppose that because I was usually working so low to the ground at such a slow, methodical pace, the doe correctly perceived me as no real threat. She simply foraged around me, and, as curiosity seemed to get the better of her, gradually approached close enough to sniff me out from about an arm's length distance. In honor of this encounter, I've nicknamed this the Curious Deer (CD) Site.

This is a U-shaped foundation that may have originally been dug as a simple root cellar. The banks are unreinforced earthen berms with no signs of any roofing, flooring, brickwork, or even nails that are so ubiquitous at other sites. The U opens to the West and measures only about 11 feet wide. Despite its small size, this site was rich in artifacts and appears to be the detritus of a fairly affluent family.

Vertically speaking, the site consists of three distinct layers: the dark brown top (six to eight inches thick) is overburden, the medium brown middle (ten to 12 inches thick) is the productive zone, and a light brown sandy/limey soil constitutes its "floor." I found nothing in the floor itself, except for dozens of beautiful (but unmarked) crown-topped "champagne style" or "bright green select" bottles (1925-29). Presumably, these were the first items to have been disposed of here.

Most of the objects unearthed here were glass bottles and porcelain tableware. The metal consisted primarily of heavily rusted cans, but some NFM pieces were recovered as well. From all indications, this appears to be a single-period site; the finds date from the late 1800s to the early 1930s.

Chapter 25 – The "Curious Deer" Site

Generally speaking, the condition of these objects is significantly better than those from the other sites.

Inventory of Artifacts

A. Glass

Happily, the majority of glass objects which I unearthed here were still whole. This is fairly remarkable, given that they are, on average, around 100 years old. None of the glass bottles were hand-blown. All were produced by ABMs, and therefore post-date 1900. On the other hand, none of the glass was enameled either, suggesting that they pre-date 1940.

Altogether, I recovered a total of 108 whole bottles and jars—far more than any other site on campus. Of these, the following 33 are readily identifiable according to their embossing:

Color	H (in)	Embossing, etc.
Aqua	9	INGALLS BROS. BOTTLING CO. / PORTLAND, ME. REGISTERED 7 ½ OZ
Clear	2¼	YARDLEY LONDON imprinted on base, round bottle (smelling salts?)
Clear	3	LISTERINE / LAMBERT PHARMACAL COMPANY w/cork
Clear	3¾	3i (on shoulder) OWENS 12 (on base)
Clear	4¼	HELLMAN'S BLUE RIBBON REGISTERED 3[0]8 (on base), screw top
Clear	4¼	LISTERINE / LAMBERT PHARMACAL COMPANY
Clear	5	EAU DE COLOGNE / No 4711 / MADE IN U.S. OF AMERICA hexagonal
Clear	5	LAVORIS / LAVORIS CHEMICAL COMPANY MINNEAPOLIS (mouthwash) (1920s) – a total of 2 of these
Clear	5½	CLEVELAND O-PEE-CHEE (on base) w/ screw cap
Clear	5½	FOSS' 2 OZ. FL. LIQUID FRUIT FLAVORS PORTLAND, ME. / FULL STRENGTH / STANDARD QUALITY (1930s) – A total of 6 of these were found (1 is slightly broken)
Clear	5½	No. 4711 wide mouthed (cologne)
Clear	6	ATLAS E-Z SEAL complete with lid, seal, and metal frame
Clear	6	CARBONA / 3 (on base) 12-sided bottle (cleaning oil)
Clear	6	LAVORIS / LAVORIS CHEMICAL COMPANY MINNEAPOLIS (mouthwash) (1920s)
Clear	6½	O-Cedar / Made in U.S.A. w/cork (wood furniture polish) (1919)

Clear	7	CARBONA / 7 (on base) 12-sided bottle (cleaning oil)
Clear	7	No. 4711 wide mouthed (cologne) – a total of 2 of these
Clear	7¼	FLY-TOX w/cork (insecticide 1920s)
Clear	9	J.H. HEINZ CO. PATD 57 (on base) – 8 sided
Clear	10	J.H. HEINZ CO. PATD 213 O inside square, 38 (on base) – 20 sided
Cobalt	5	MILK OF MAGNESIA / TRADE MARK / REG'D. IN U.S. PATENT OFFICE / THE CHAS.H.PHILLIPS CHEMICAL COMPANY GLENBROOK, CONN. (missing back)
Cobalt	5	MILK OF MAGNESIA/TRADE MARK / REG'D. IN U.S. PATENT OFFICE AUG. 21, 1906 THE CHAS.H.PHILLIPS CHEMICAL COMPANY GLENBROOK, CONN. (w/cap)
Green	7½	MOXIE / TRADEMARK REG US PAT OFFICE / REGISTERED CONTENTS 7 FL. OZ.
Green	7½	Straight-sided REGISTERED COCA COLA BOTTLING CO./7 ½ OZ./INGALLS BROS/PORTLAND, ME 26 N on base (broken top) (flavor bottle, 1926)
Green	9	Straight-sided REGISTERED COCA COLA BOTTLING CO./7 ½ OZ./INGALLS BROS/PORTLAND, ME, 26 N on base (flavor bottle, 1926)
Green	10	CLICQUOT CLUB TRADE MARK / REGISTERED / A B 27 N (w/an Eskimo figure, on base)
Lavender	2¼	YARDLEY LONDON imprinted on base, round bottle (smelling salts?) chipped lip

The following 55 bottles are largely unmarked. They have proven a bit more challenging—but not impossible—to identify:

Color	H (in)	Marks and notes
Amber	5	Unmarked W and triangle with W over T 21 on base
Amber	5	Unmarked W and triangle with W over T 30 on base, w/cap
Aqua	7¼	Unmarked wide-mouthed – 4 (on base)
Aqua	7¼	Unmarked wide-mouthed – 6 underlined (on base)
Aqua	7¼	Unmarked wide-mouthed – a total of 2 of these
Aqua	7½	Unmarked wide-mouthed – 1 (on base)
Aqua	9½	Unmarked A.B. Co. X 30S (on base) (American Bottle Co. 1930)
Aqua	9½	Unmarked R inside triangle, X C 48 9 (on base)
Aqua	9½	Unmarked R inside triangle, X C 85 9 (on base)
Clear	2	Unmarked cylindrical vial
Clear	2½	Unmarked wide-mouthed bottle H 4 on bottom
Clear	2¾	Unmarked G [circled diamond] 6 (on base)
Clear	3¾	Unmarked pear-shaped bottle w/ cap (onion-shaped tm on bottom)
Clear	4½	Unmarked bottle with 2 on shoulder and W T in triangle w/ U.S.A. 7 on base
Clear	4½	Unmarked bottle with W.T. Co./H/U.S.A. (on base) (Whitall, Tatum & Co., pharmacy bottle, 1901-24) slightly cracked
Clear	4½	Unmarked rect. bottle, screw top, 13 near bottom, circled diamond 6/9 (on base) cracks
Clear	5	Unmarked 4 sided bottle, 757 / T in diamond / 2 (on base) screw top
Clear	5	Unmarked 6 (on base) screw top
Clear	5	Unmarked I within a diamond, 1 (on base) w/cork

Chapter 25 – The "Curious Deer" Site 215

Clear	5¼	Unmarked wide-mouthed, 5380 near bottom, 1 HA (on base)
Clear	5¼	Unmarked wide-mouthed, hour-glass bottle HA 6 (on base)
Clear	5¼	Unmarked wide-mouthed, hour-glass bottle 6 (or 9?) (on base); faint remnants of label under lip, "...ER..."
Clear	6¼	Unmarked 8-sided wide-mouthed screw top, 8 near bottom
Clear	7¼	Unmarked O within a square 34 (on base) – a total of 2 of these
Clear	7¼	Unmarked wide-mouthed, label around neck
Clear	7¼	Unmarked wide-mouthed, 4 on base
Green	12	Unmarked wine bottle w/cork, 2 near bottom
Green	9½	Unmarked 25N (on base) (1925 – Newark, A.B. Co.)
Green	9½	Unmarked 26N (on base) (1926 – Newark, A.B. Co.)
Green	9½	Unmarked 27N (on base) (1927 – Newark, A.B. Co.)
Green	9½	Unmarked 28N (on base) - a total of 20 of these (1928 – Newark, A.B. Co.)
Green	9½	Unmarked 29N (on base) (1929 – Newark, A.B. Co.) – a total of 2
Green	9½	Unmarked R inside triangle, X C 64 9 (on base)
Milk	2½	Unmarked milk glass (cracked) HA on base

The remaining whole bottles from the CD Site consist of 20 unmarked (and as yet, uncleaned) clear glass storage jars.

In addition to whole bottles and jars, I also recovered a few embossed glass fragments. Since they, too, can provide helpful information for product identification and dating, I am including them here:

Color	Embossing/Notes
Aqua	PUTNAM 59 (canning jar base)
Clear	BAKER'S FLAVORING EXTRACT/BAKER EXTRACT COMPANY
Clear	BAKER'S FLAVORING EXTRACT/BAKER EXTRACT COMPANY/STRENGTH & PURI[TY]/FULL MEASU[RE]
Clear	DIRIGO BOTTLING CO. /D.B.CO/PORTLAND, MAINE/CONTENTS 7 ½ FL. OZS. (soda from the 1930s)
Clear	HELLMANN['S] BLUE RIBBON REGISTERED (on base)
Clear	HINDS HONEY AND ALMOND CREAM/A.S. HINDS CO. BLOOMFIELD N.J. U.S.A.
Clear	SMALLE[Y/]KIVLAN/ONTHANK/BOSTON/UNION MADE (canning jar base)

Rounding out the CD Site's glass inventory are a variety of other objects, most of which are connected to food preparation. The exceptions would be the marbles, lightbulb, and fuses:

Item	Color	Size (in)
Bottle top (broken) with wire frame and ceramic stopper	Clear	5 H
Bottle topper, screw top	Lavender	1½ dia.
Bottle topper, screw top, a total of 3	Clear	1½ dia.
Cup – drinking (HA 60 on base)	Clear	3 H 2 dia.
Cup - drinking, Depression glass (broken, 75% extant)	Light green	3¾ H 2¼ dia.
Decanter - for oil?	Clear	4½ H
Decorative bowl (2 pcs. – 85% extant)	Clear	5½ dia.
Fuses - 5 glass/6 other	Clear	1¼ dia.
Lid, canning	Aqua	3½ dia.
Lid, flat	Clear	2 dia.
Lightbulb, intact, WESTINGHOUSE [...]5W120V	Frosted	5 H
Marble	Amber swirl	½ dia.
Marble	Red swirl	½ dia.
Measuring cup (broken, 25% extant)	Clear	2¾ H
Salt & pepper shakers, a total of 2	Clear	3 H

B. Ceramics

Of the three classes of ceramics, porcelain is, by far, the most prevalent at this site. Although this is the smallest of the four sites that I will profile, it has yielded the greatest number of porcelain pieces. At least 18 different patterns are represented here, with some patterns appearing on up to a dozen different wares:

Company/ Origin	Pattern	Date (ca.)	Wares/Extent found	Notes
Carl Ahrenfeldt, France Richard Briggs Co., Boston	Unknown. Border of green maple-style leaves and tan il de fleur-style posts	1894-1930	Teacup 1 – 2 pcs. 100% Teacup 2 – 2 pcs. 100% Egg cup – 2 pcs. 100% Plate 1 – 3 pcs. 99% Plate 2 – 2 pcs. 95% Plate 3 – 3 pcs. 90% Plate 4 – 3 pcs. 80% Plate 5 – 4 pcs. 80% Plate 6 – 4 pcs. 45% Plate 7 – 2 pcs. 45% Plates – 25 pcs. Cups – 10 pcs.	French Limoges porcelain. It is double marked by both the French maker, and also carries the mark for the Richard Briggs Co, a Boston importer that catered to the wealthy patrons of the gilded age. The second mark on the plate is CA France. This mark can be traced to Carl

Chapter 25 – The "Curious Deer" Site

Maker	Pattern	Date	Pieces	Marks/Notes
Charles Field Haviland / Gerard, Dufraisseix & Abbott France	Unknown. Black square flag with green triangle border	1900-1941	Plate 1 – 6 pcs. 80% Plate 2 – 4 pcs. 75% Teacup – 2 pcs. 20%	Ahrenfeldt, a maker in France from 1859-93. Marks: "CH FIELD HAVILAND LIMOGES" (encircled) & "GDA" (cursive) over FRANCE
China.	Green & white floral	1892	Tea bowl – 3pcs. 30%	Red square mark *Tongzhi Nian Zhi* on the base, dated to 1892.
China.	Sky blue w/yellow and white floral, red trim	1898?	Stemmed bowl – 3 pcs. 95%	Red square mark *Guangxu Nian Zhi* on base, dated to 1898? Qianjiang Decoration?
China? Japan?	Outer: Blue & pink flowers Inner: mountains, boat, tree, village, people, landscape + 3 characters		Tea bowl – 3 pcs. 100%	Back mark, unknown encircled characters
F. Winkle & Co. England	Pheasant	1908-11	Plate – 8 pcs. 90%	"WHIELDON WARE"
Haviland & Co., Limoges, France	Unknown. Green stalks & small flowers	1876-89	Plate – 3 pcs. 80%	Simple design, but faded.
Haviland & Co., Limoges, France	Unknown. Red floral with gilt edge	1894-1931	Teacups – 9 pcs.	
Paul Muller China Company, Bavaria, Germany.	The Baronial	1920s	2 handled teacup – 3 pcs. 95%	22K gold trim on white porcelain. Crown and shield with cross design back stamp.
Ridgway England	Willow (Blue)	1891-1923	Creamer – 7 pcs. 95%	Backstamp: Ridgways England, Semi China (and impressed 3)
Theodore Haviland Limoges, France	Unknown. Red floral	1903-mid 1920s	Plate – 7 pcs. 100% Cup – 3 pcs. 10%	

Theodore Haviland, Limoges, France	Unknown. Blue floral	Ca. 1903	Teacup – 3 pcs. 95%	
Unknown Misc.	At least 3 different patterns		7 pcs.	
Unknown. Simple blue floral design on white	Blue Danube style (but earlier)		Bowl w/ scalloped edging – 7 pcs. 95%	Back marked "T. 8."
Unknown. China	Rose Medallion	Pre-1890	Platter- 6 pcs. 40%? Teacup - 6 pcs. 20%	No back mark. Beautifully painted birds, peonies, and Asians.
Unknown.	Textured white w/faded red flowers		Bowl – 6 pcs. 35%	Back mark cursive "T"
Unknown.	White w/broad cream edges		Serving dish – 4pcs. 30%	Back stamped "16 ½"

In addition to the porcelain finds, a few fragments of an earthenware bowl were also recovered:

Maker	Pattern – Glaze	Wares/Extent found
Unknown	White inside, brick red outer	Bowl – 4 pcs. 40%

C. Metal

Most of the metal that I encountered at the CD Site consisted of the greatly deteriorated—and otherwise unidentifiable—remnants of food cans and tins. However, there were a number of notable exceptions, as the following inventory demonstrates. Not surprisingly, the NFM artifacts tend to be in better condition than their IB counterparts:

Item	Size (in)	Comp.	Cond.	Engraving & other notes
Bottle top	1 dia.	NFM	G	Screw top, fancy H
Bottle top (talc?)	2¾ L	NFM	F	w/lid
Bottle top (talc?)	2¾ L	NFM	F	w/out lid
Buckle	½ L	NFM	G	Decorative patterning

Chapter 25 – The "Curious Deer" Site

Buckle	2 L	IB	F	
Compact case	2 dia.	NFM	VG	6-sided "Charles of the Ritz" (1920s-30s)
Disc/bowl	2 dia.	NFM	G	
Garter clip	2 L	NFM	G	"Gripmor"
Garter clip	2 L	IB	P	
Grommet	¾ dia.	NFM	G	
Label	1 ½ L	NFM	F	"E.T.BURROWES CO/ PORTLAND ME" "9-8-38/6-9-02"(?)
Label	2 dia.	NFM	F	Red trademark with "S.S.P. Co. Puritas et curia" and eagle w/lion shield (from S. S. Pierce Company, 1890s – 1920s)
Lamp burner	2 ½ dia.	NFM	F/P	
Ring	¾ dia.	NFM	G	non-ornamental
Ring	¾ dia.	NFM	F	non-ornamental
Shotgun shell	½ dia.	NFM	F	"REMINGTON EXPRESS 16 GA"
Silver spoon	6 L	NFM	G	"Bigelow, Kennard & Co. Sterling 925/1000" monographed "LD"
Silver spoon	6 L	NFM	G	"WM. Rodgers & Son"
Snap	¾ L	NFM	G	
Spoon	8 L	IB	P	Broken (2 pcs)
Tin – rectangle	1 ¾ L	IB	F	
Tin – round	1 ½ dia.	IB	P	
Tin plate	9 dia.	IB	F/P	
Wire	10 L	NFM	G	

D. Miscellaneous

Finally, rounding out our inventory are the following miscellaneous items. Aside from the comb, all appear to be related to food preparation:

Item	Size (in)	Comp.	Cond.	Engraving/Notes
Bones	Various	Animal	F-G	11 total; unidentified mammal remains
Bottle stopper	¾ H	Cork	F	
Comb	3 L	Plastic	P	Broken half
Disc	1 ½ dia.	Stone?	G	Smooth, white; unknown
Spoon	2 ½ L	Wood	P	Broken; missing handle

Chapter 26
The "1926 Site" Report

General Description

It is not always easy to date the artifacts that one recovers from a given excavation. Typically, one must settle for a range of years, decades, or, with really ancient sites, centuries or epochs. But this particular spot proves the exception to that rule. The items that I recovered tend to converge around one specific year: 1926—hence, its nickname. From all indications, this was a single-use site. There is no evidence of occupation prior to a mid-1920s time period, nor is there any after that. The objects recovered suggest that it may have been occupied by one male and one female, middle-aged or older. I found no evidence of any children having occupied this site.

The 1926 Site consists of the dug foundation of a small house and its immediate vicinity. The foundation is surrounded by a squarish, U-shaped berm of rock and earth that opens to the North. I measured the distance from the western entrance corner (the apex of the U) to the middle of the back "wall" (the trough of the U) at 31 feet. Some remnant plumbing is still in place. On the eastern half of the foundation, beneath several inches of overburden, I found rows of tin sheets (probably roofing) that ultimately served to protect some of the items beneath them.

The foundation itself was littered with the (mostly broken) remnants of hundreds of glass bottles and porcelain china. Assorted metal objects (primarily farming implements) were located in the "back" of the house, along the southern wall. Various objects were also found scattered outside of the foundation, especially in the higher ground behind it. Overall, the artifacts that came out of this site tended to be in relatively good condition.

Chapter 26 – The "1926 Site"

Inventory of Artifacts

A. Glass

To date, the 1926 Site has yielded a total of 42 whole bottles and jars. Of these, just over half (22) are readily identifiable thanks to their embossed lettering:

Color	H (in)	Embossing	Type
Amber	4	Lysol (in cursive) / LYSOL INCORPORATED BLOOMFIELD, N.J.	ABM
Amber	7	FATHER JOHN'S MEDICINE LOWELL, MASS.	BIM
Aqua	4	3-IN-ONE OIL CO. / "THREE IN ONE"	BIM
Aqua	4	3-IN-ONE OIL CO. / "THREE IN ONE"	ABM
Aqua	5	TRADE MARK LIGHTNING REGISTERED U.S. PATENT OFFICE / PUTNAM (on base) w/glass lids	ABM
Aqua	5	TRADE MARK LIGHTNING REGISTERED U.S. PATENT OFFICE / PUTNAM (on base) w/glass lids	ABM
Aqua	6	TRADE MARK LIGHTNING / PUTNAM 757 (base) w/glass lid	ABM
Aqua	7½	THREE IN ONE OIL CO. / "THREE IN ONE" / 6 (on base)	ABM
Clear	2½	JAPANESE GOLD PAINT / CERSTENOORFER BROS. NEW YORK, CHICAGO	BIM
Clear	3	DAGGETT & RAMSDELL'S PERFECT COLD CREAM TRADE MARK CHEMISTS (all on base)	ABM
Clear	5	BAKER'S FLAVORING EXTRACTS BAKER EXTRACT COMPANY / STRENGTH & PURITY / FULL MEASURE	BIM
Clear	5	BAKER'S FLAVORING EXTRACTS BAKER EXTRACT COMPANY / STRENGTH & PURITY / FULL MEASURE	ABM
Clear	5	BAKER'S FLAVORING EXTRACTS BAKER EXTRACT COMPANY / STRENGTH & PURITY / FULL MEASURE	ABM
Clear	5	BERRY'S CANKER CURE / BOSTON / CUTLER BROS & CO.	BIM
Clear	7	LISTERINE LAMBERT PHARMACAL COMPANY	ABM
Clear	7½	THREE IN ONE OIL CO. / "THREE IN ONE" / 6 (on base)	ABM
Clear	7	WARRANTED OVAL	BIM
Milk	1	MUM MFG. CO PHILADELPHIA	ABM
Milk	2¾	MUSTEROLE CLEVELAND (base)	ABM
Milk	2	RESINOL CHEMICAL CO. BALT'O MD (base)	ABM
Milk	3	HARRIET HUBBARD AYER FAMOUS TOILET PREPARATIONS U.S.A. (on lid)	ABM
Milk	3¾	MENTHOLATUM REG TRADE MARK (base)	ABM

With the Automatic Bottle Machine process becoming mainstream in the early 1900s, it is not surprising that, at a site dating to the mid-1920s, most of these bottles were produced in that manner. However, there were about a half-dozen Blown in Mold exceptions. All of these are the "tooled lip" types, meaning that they would date towards the end of this particular method, ca. 1890-1915.

The most commonly found bottles included those for "3-IN-ONE OIL," "BAKER'S FLAVORING EXTRACTS," and "LIGHTNING" canning jars. The latter originally came with disc-shaped glass lids that were secured in place by a wire frame. Many of these wire frames had rusted away, but I recovered at least eight of these very attractive, aqua-colored discs in good (unbroken) condition. Three of them are embossed with the "LIGHTNING" label and "PATD APR 25 [18]82" date.

Twenty other whole bottles were also recovered, but again, their identification remains a bit more challenging since they had little to no embossing on them. Presumably, most of these had paper labels which have long since disintegrated. Here, too, the ABM bottles outnumber the BIMs, but the latter are represented:

Color	H (in)	Unmarked	Type
Amber	5	"E.R.S.&S. (5) N.Y." (on base)	ABM
Amber	5	"W" (on base)	ABM
Amber	5	"W" (on base)	ABM
Aqua	5½	Unmarked bottle (round, slightly cracked)	BIM
Clear	1¾	Unmarked small glass vial	?
Clear	2¼	Unmarked small glass vial	?
Clear	2¼	Unmarked small rounded (perfume?) bottle, screw top	ABM
Clear	2¾	Unmarked small triangular shaped bottle, 11 (on base)	ABM
Clear	3¼	Unmarked sm. rect. bottle, small diamond & 1 on base, screw top	ABM
Clear	4¼	Unmarked small bottle "88 1/2" (on base) slightly cracked	ABM
Clear	4½	Unmarked small rectangular bottle, small triangle on base, screw top	ABM
Clear	5½	Unmarked bottle, flat back, slightly rounded front	ABM
Clear	5½	Unmarked "W.T.CO./K/USA" (on base)	ABM
Clear	5	Unmarked "J.B.W.Co." (base) "5 FL.OZ." chipped	ABM
Clear	6	Unmarked medicine bottle with dosages (3/2/1) and CC	BIM

Chapter 26 – The "1926 Site"

		(90/60/30); moon & star on base, screw top	
Clear	10	Unmarked (ketchup?) bottle	ABM
Clear/Lav	11½	Unmarked wine bottle, small dot on base	BIM
Green	6	Unmarked pint bottle "4" (base)	ABM
Lavender	7½	Unmarked wide-mouthed jar, cracked	ABM
Milk	15/16	Unmarked jar	ABM

I estimate that maybe 65% of the glass artifacts that I encountered here were broken. Fortunately, many were broken *in situ*, so the recovery of their fragments—especially the embossed ones—was relatively simple. The fragments all belong to products that date to the mid-1920s or earlier:

Color	Embossed Glass Fragments
Amber	"...DMAN...MINN" (cursive)
Aqua	"...[D]RUG & CHEMICAL CORPORATION BOSTON, MASS U.S.A." (in 2 pcs.)
Aqua	"LEOTRIC" (canning jar)
Clear	"[CA]LIFORNIA...SYRUP CO. SAN FRANCISCO, CAL. (57)"
Clear	"...AR..."
Clear	"...ONOL...Y AS SOAP""
Clear	"AL...CREAM A.S. HINDS CO PORTLAND MAINE, U.S[.A.]"
Clear	"CREAM A.S. HINDS PORT[LAND]"
Clear	"CUTICURA SYSTEM BLOOD AND SKI[N] PURIFICATION"
Clear	"DUDLY-WEED DRUG CO. [P]ORTLAND, MAINE"
Clear	"FEEN-A...[T]HE CHEWIN[G]...[HEA]LTH PRO[DUCT]...NEW [YORK]"
Clear	"LAVORIS CHEMICAL CO MINNEAPOLIS, MINN" (base)
Clear	"LAVORIS CHEMICAL CO. MINNEAPOLIS" (base) x2
Clear	"QUEEN TRADEMARK WIDE MOUTH ADJUSTABLE" (cursive)
Clear	"S.C.JOHNSON & SON RACINE WIS." (base)
Clear	"SAGADAHO...TABLE...SOUT[H]..."
Clear	"SANFORD'S (7)" (bell jar base)
Clear	"SHEAFFERS SKRIP" (base)
Clear	"SQUIBB" (shoulder)
Clear	"SYLPHO-NATHOL CABOT'S REG.U.S.PAT.OFF BOTTLE MADE IN U.S.A." (in 2 pcs.)
Clear	"THE PURIFICO C[O...]...FOREST...LLE, N..." (in 2 pcs.)
Clear	"WELLCOME CHEM. WORKS (103A)" (base)
Dark Green	"...LEHNER'S..UNYADI..ANOS...RQUELLE" (base)
Light green	"PLUTO WATER...[A]MERICA'S PHYSIC"
Light green	"PLUTO" (base) x3
Light Green	"WM F. KIDDER [NE]W YORK"
Milk glass	"MUSTEROLE CLEVELAND" (base)

Rounding out the glass artifacts are three glass stoppers. The bottles to which they originally belonged have not been located. Each measures about 1½ inches in length, but that's where their similarities end:

Color	L (in)	Glass Stoppers
Aqua	1½	Round, tapering, aqua blue (club-sauce type, missing cork sheath)
Clear	1¾	Crown-shaped, "OL(Y?)" embossed on crown; "DEPOSE" in very small letters below the crown (perfume bottle?)
Opaque	1½	Round, tapering, internally fractured, quartz-like

One other glass object recovered from this site has already been profiled: the "Edison"-style, untipped drawn tungsten lamp bulb.

B. Ceramics

Fragments of both earthenware and stoneware vessels were found at this site. Virtually all of them were unmarked and otherwise nondescript. However, one particular item—a stoneware jug—deserves some recognition. Having unearthed over a dozen or so of its pieces, I set about the task of reconstructing it at home. When I finished, I realized that I had collected *all but one* of its fragments. A three-inch, rhombus-shaped hole was all that needed to be filled for its completion. I immediately returned to the site, hoping to find that elusive, missing piece. It was a bit like trying to find a needle in a haystack, but my search proved successful. That final shard fit like a glove, and the stoneware jug is whole once again:

Chapter 26 – The "1926 Site"

Most of the ceramics recovered from this site are porcelain fragments. The fragments are representative of at least 20 different styles. Of these 20, I have been able to identify 9; the remaining 11 are yet unknown:

Company/ Origin	Pattern	Date (ca.)	Wares/Extent found	Notes
C.C. Thompson E. Liverpool, OH	Plain white?	1868-1938	Saucer – 1 piece, 60%	"FRANCIS" below mark
Cauldon England	H 9120 (Aqua, Souvenir)	1920-1932	13 frags. from at least 3 different wares	3 maker's marks accompanied by "H 9120 F"; "H 9120 W"; "CAULDON" stamp; only traces of original blue remain
Cook Pottery Co. Trenton, NJ	Floral (roses?) pattern	1894-	Saucer – 1 piece 50% Teacup – 2 pieces 50% +4 frags.	"Etruria – Mellor & Co."
Johnson Bros. England	Plain white?	1920s	Saucer – 2 pieces, 80% +1 base to bowl/pitcher	"ROYAL IRONSTONE WARE" & squared off crown
Meissen	Blue		Plate 1 – 6p., 40%	

Germany	Onion		Plate 2 – 4p., 35% +3 frags.	
NIPPON[177] Japan	White w/gold trim	1891-1921	Saucer – 1 piece, 55%	
Ridgway England	Willow (Blue)	1924	Toy plate? – 4 small frags.	Backstamp: Engraved for W Ridgway & Co 1832 England, Semi China (and impressed date for 1924?)
Sarreguemines Lorraine, France	Unknown (Red floral)	1850s	Base + 8 frags.	This has the U & C mark which was the period of Porzellanfabrik Paul Utzschneider & Cie (U & C) and dates to around the 1850s or so. The word Perse in the mark represents Faïence de la Perse – Persian Faïence, named to represent a Persian influence. These are very hard to find today.
Unknown Miscellaneous	At least 5 different patterns			
Unknown	Bluebells		Plate – 5 frags.	
Unknown	Bright red flowers, green leaves, blue swirls		Plate – 8 frags.	
Unknown	Brown floral & leaves		Plate – 1 piece 30%	4 line mark, partial: "…ries"/ "…R"/ "..RAYS."/ "…LEMAN" in tied-log design
Unknown	Gray with simple blue striped trim		3 frags.	

---

[177] "Nippon" first appeared on porcelain objects in response to the US McKinley Tariff Act (1891), which forbade the import of items that weren't "plainly marked, stamped, branded, or labeled in legible English words." Nippon is the Anglicized version of "Japan," but in 1921, the word was ruled Japanese in origin. Henceforth, imported Japanese china was stamped "Japan."

Chapter 26 – The "1926 Site"

Unknown	Navy blue leaves in blue-gray setting		Plate – 7 pieces 70% Teacup? – 11 frags.	Unmarked, "7F" stamped on the bottom
Unknown	Yellow ware	1910s	1 frag.	Small 6" yellow ware mixing bowl with triple brown stripe
W H Grindley & Co. England	IDIS	1891-1925	Saucer 1 - 2 pieces, 90% Saucer 2 - 3 pieces, 90% +7 frags.	All online examples are blue; these are green; maker's mark features a steamer & globe

C. Metal

The samples of metal items recovered from this site (as well as those that were left behind) are a blend of domestic and agriculturally based artifacts. A few of the objects in particular (e.g., the Massachusetts license plate, the shotgun shell, and the tobacco tin) continue to support the dating of this site to ca. 1926. As is generally true, the NFM items tend to be found in better condition than the IB ones:

Item	Size (in)	Comp.	Cond.	Engraving & other notes
Buckle	1½ L	NFM	G	Square
Buckle	1½ L	IB	F/P	Square
Buckle	2¼ L	IB	P	D-shaped
Buckle	2½ L	NFM	G	D-shaped
Buckle	2½ L	IB	P	Rectangular
Button	½ dia.	NFM	G	
Clothes hook	2 L	NFM	G	thumb shaped
Compact	2½ dia.	NFM	G	Round, hinged, decorative lid, fused shut, "L" on side
Fuse	1¼ dia.	IB	F	
Hand rake	9 W	IB	F	
Hinge	15½ L	IB	F	Large, decorative
Hoe	6½ W	IB	F	
Hook & chain	6 L	IB	F	
Horseshoe	4¼ dia.	IB	P	
Horseshoe	6 dia.	IB	G/VG	
Hose nozzle	2 L	NFM	G	
License plate	6½ H x 12½ L	IB	P	"61 446 / 1926 / MASS"
Nails	6 L	IB	F	4, flat heads
Oil lamp burner	2½ dia.	NFM	G	"EAGLE"
Oil lamp burner	2½ dia.	NFM	P	

O-ring	1½ dia.	IB	P	
Ox shoe	4¾ L	IB	F	
Ox shoe	5½ L	IB	F	5 nails still intact
Peg	4¾ L	IB	F	Large, "H" on top
Piping	8 L	NFM	VG	
Plow blade	18 L x 11½ H	IB?	G/VG	"OLIVER 83 C. H. X." (Oliver Chilled Plow, South Bend, IN)
Salt shaker	2 H	NFM	G	shaker holes in a star pattern
Saw/Knife	14½ L	IB	F	Large, serrated
Scissors	3¼ L	IB	F	
Scissors	8 L	IB	F/P	
Screw top lid	1½ dia.	NFM	G	Octagon "C & Co." = Colgate & Co.
Shotgun shell	1 dia.	NFM	G	"REM-UMC No. 12 NEW CLUB" w. star in middle, c. 1911-1925
Spike	3½ L	IB	F	
Spike	3¾ L	IB	P	
Spike	5½ L	IB	G	
Spike	6 L	IB	F	
Stove burner	8¾ dia.	IB	G	
Stove damper?	9 dia.	IB	F	"AMERICAN NO. 2 GRISWOLD MFG. CO ERIE PA"
Stove door	10½ L x 6¾ H	IB	F	"CLEAN OUT"
Stove mantel	20 H	IB	F	"43 MANUFACTURED BY PORTLAND STOVE FOUNDRY CO, PORT..."
Tin	1 dia	IB	F	Round
Tobacco tin	4½ L x 3 H	IB	P	"Velvet Tobacco Liggett & Myers Tobacco Co." c. 1925
Toilet chain	18 L	NFM	G	
Water pump	10 L	IB	G	"FURBER PUMP SACO, ME"
Wheels	4½ dia.	IB	G	2, part of pulley system?
Window weights	7½ to 16 L	IB	F/G	6; etched with Roman numerals

D. Miscellaneous Items

Rounding out this inventory, three more artifacts remain. The first is a whet stone, used for sharpening knives. The second is an amber-colored toothbrush with an embossed manufacturer and patent date. The third, as profiled above, is the Rudolph Valentino newspaper clipping that I discovered tucked away inside of a milk glass jar.

Chapter 26 – The "1926 Site"

Item	Size (in)	Comp.	Cond.	Engraving/Notes
Newspaper Clipping	5½ H x 1½ W	paper	G	Found tucked away inside of a milk glass jar
Toothbrush	6 L	plastic	G	"Sterilized Dr. West's Patented Jan 2, 1923 1,440,785 Weco Products" Missing bristles.
Whet stone	3¼ L	stone	F	

Chapter 27
The "Plateau Site" Report

General Description

This site is the largest and most complex of those 12 known on campus. The house's rectangular foundation is marked by a prominent, elevated rock wall perimeter approximately 90 feet long and 52 feet wide. Such an arrangement results in something resembling a manmade plateau, which gives rise to this site's nickname.

Presumably, the house itself faced southeast. An L shaped channel flanked by fieldstones cuts into the foundation on its southwestern side. Adjacent to all this, to the southwest, is a level area of corresponding size, faintly bordered by submerged stone walls.

This site is literally littered with bricks, broken glass, porcelain, and lots of metal objects—both agricultural and domestic. Consequently, the sheer number of artifacts recovered here is far greater than at the other sites. So, too, is the length of the timetable involved. The dates of these items span a century or so—from the 1840s to the 1940s. Of course, such a chronology suggests multi-generational use. Indeed, this assessment corroborates the information we have about this particular site in the property records.

Inventory of Artifacts

A. Glass
As noted, glass is plentiful at this site. Early hand-blown bottles with blob tops and open-pontiled bottoms are well represented, but (much to my dismay) virtually all are broken. Nevertheless, many of the existing fragments are embossed, and so continue to bear the name, manufacturer, location, and/or patent date of the products they once conveyed:

Chapter 27 – The "Plateau Site"

Color	Embossing/Notes	Date
Amber	"M....PO[RTLAND?]"	
Amber	"1872" "DOYLES" "HOP" "BITTERS " – 7 pcs	1872
Amber	"37 BE..."	
Amber	"PAINE'S / CELERY/ [COMPOUND]" – 4 pcs.	1870
Amber	"PAINE'S [CELERY COMPOUND] (Burlington VT)	1870
Amber	"SCHLOTTERBECK & [F]OSS CO/[M]ANFACTURING CHEMIS[TS]/[P]ORTLAND, MAI[NE]" 2 pcs.	1890
Amber	"WERNER'S SAFE CURE"/ "ROCHESTER" (w/ picture of a safe) – 14 pcs., from 3 bottles	1880-90
Aqua	"[BOST]ON MASS, U.S.A." – side	
Aqua	"[CURTI]S & PERKINS [C]RAMP & [PAIN]KILLER" open pontil	1850-65
Aqua	"[HOOD'S SARSA] PARILLA LOWELL MASS [HOOD & CO APOTHEC]ARIES (38)"	1875-
Aqua	"[LEA & P]ER[RIN'S]/WOR[CHEST]ERSH[IRE]"	1890s
Aqua	"[ME]XICAN/[MUST]AN[G/LINIMENT]"	1850s
Aqua	"[VEGET]ABLE/...ARY/...M"	
Aqua	"...& PERKINS/ ...RUP/...ORS" – 2 pcs.	
Aqua	"....NNAT..." – side	
Aqua	"...[DR]UG & CHEM. COR[P]" – side	
Aqua	"...HEM. CORP." – side	
Aqua	"...ILL'S" – side	
Aqua	"...SN.."	
Aqua	"...UINE SANFORD'S GINGER DELICIOUS COMBINATION OF [GI]NGER, FRENCH BRANDY AND [C]HOICE AROMATICS, REGD. 1876" 2 pcs.	1876-
Aqua	"0144 PATD. 1869" (base)	1869-
Aqua	"ALLEN'S ...[SAR]SAPARILLA"	1880s
Aqua	"APOTHEC[ARY]"	
Aqua	"ATWOOD'S GENUINE BITT[ER]S" (bottom) "N. W[OOD SOLE PROPRIE]TOR" (top) – 2pcs.	1880s
Aqua	"BLO.../...VER..."	
Aqua	"C.I. HU..."	
Aqua	"DAVIS' /[VE]GETABLE"/[PAIN KILLER] – 2 pcs.	1880s
Aqua	"DR. S. PITC[HER'S]/CASTORIA" (a castor oil substitute)	1880-1900
Aqua	"DRS F.E. & J.A. GREENE" / "NEW YORK & BOSTON" (for Nervura, a nerve tonic w/18% alcohol) – 11 pcs. from at least 5 different bottles	1890
Aqua	"DRUGGISTS BOST[ON]" – side	
Aqua	"ESTABLISHED 1843 NATHAN WOOD & SON PORTLAND ME."	1843-
Aqua	"JOHNSON'S AMERICAN ANODYNE LINIMENT" – 12 pcs. from at least 3 bottles	1845-60
Aqua	"L.F. ATWOOD" (bottom)	
Aqua	"L.F.HHH..." (top)	
Aqua	"MASS. U.S.A." – side	
Aqua	"PATD JAN 19 1869" (bottom) (Mason's improved quart fruit jar)	1869-
Aqua	"POTTER DR..."	
Aqua	".R./...WA.../[NE]W Y[ORK]"	
Aqua	"REG.../4../PR." – base – 4 pcs.	
Aqua	"W. (G or C). W." (bottom)	

Aqua	"WOOD'S BLACK. INK PORTLAND" (in 2 pc.)	1840-60
Aqua	Symbol: "CFJ Co" (Consolidated Fruit Jar Company)	
Clear	"[DRS F.]E. & J.[A. GREENE" / "NEW YORK & BOST]ON" 2 pcs.	1890
Clear	"[P.]C. CROWLEY [& CO]/[2]45-247 & 2[49]/[AT]LANTIC AVE/[BOS]TON,[MASS] (whiskey flask)	1890s
Clear	"...N MED. CO." – side	
Clear	"ATLAS E-Z"	
Clear	"BAKER...[F]LAVORING F...ER EXTRA[CT]"	
Clear	"DR. TRUE'S ELIXIR ESTABLISHED 1851 DR. J.F TRUE & CO. INC. AUBURN, ME."	
Clear	"H. W. Huguley Co. [13]4 Canal St. Boston"	
Clear	"HARRIS PURE FLAVORS/ BINGHAMTON N.Y." – 3 pcs. from 2 bottles	
Clear	"July 10 1888 Sept 10 1889 & Oct 7, 1890" Easley's Reamer (juicer)	1890s
Clear	"L.F.HH HAY SOLE ACT" (top)	
Clear	"RAWLEI[GH'S]/[TR]ADE MA[RK]" (cursive script)	1890-1930
Clear	"SIMM[ONS] & HAMMOND PORTLAND. ME." [Pat Jan 24, '88]	1888-
Clear	"TRADE MARK/D&R SPECIAL FLASK" (whiskey)	1900-1909
Clear/ Lavender	"DR. S.B.H. & CO./ REGISTERED 81/PR." (Dr. Samuel B. Hartman & Co., and the "PR." stood for "Peruna", medical product)	1890s
Olive green	"A..../S..."	
Olive green	"U..."	
Lavender	"....LE. KY."	
Lavender	"...[&]SON [R]ACINE WIS."	

Some whole bottles were recovered. Most of them are unmarked, and they usually date from the 1880s on:

Color	H (in)	Description and notes
Clear	2¼	Small, 12-sided (1890s) (BIM)
Clear	2½	Small, round bottle with metal cap inside
Clear	3¾	Black ink-style bottle (BIM?)
Clear	5	Shouldered all the way to the base, cup-bottom mold (BIM) (1880s-90s)
Clear	6	Milk-shaped bottle, wide-mouthed (3 dots triangularly arranged on bottom) (BIM)
Clear	7	Small flask, chipped lip (BIM)
Clear	Various	8 total, mostly later ABM jars

Only three whole embossed bottles and one jar have been found. They are as follows:

Color	H (in)	Embossing, etc.
Aqua	2½	"WOOD'S BLACK. INK PORTLAND" – top slightly broken (1840-60) – open pontiled
Aqua	4¼	"JOHNSON'S AMERICAN ANODYNE LINIMENT" (1845-60) – open pontiled
Clear	4½	"Larkin Co. / BUFFALO" "MACHINE OIL" (1890s) (BIM)
Milk	1¾	"POND'S" (jar)

Two of these, the Wood's Black Ink and the Johnson's Liniment, are particularly early (and relatively rare) specimens. But to complete our Glass inventory, the following artifacts should also be noted:

Item	Color	Size (in)
Canning jar lid, "LIGHTNING PATD APR 25 [18]82"	Aqua	3 dia.
Cup-shaped object; unknown use	Red	2½ dia.
Lid, "MASON'S IMPROVED PATD MAY 10. 1870" w/metal rim	Aqua	2½ dia.
Lightbulb, "SYLVANIA 40 W 120V"	Frosted	4 L
Plate, small stemmed	Pink	2½ H
Plate; depression glass, 5 pcs. (30%) "F" inside shield (Federal Glass Co.)	Lime Green	various
Tubing; 3 pieces; unknown use	Clear	1½-2 L

B. Ceramics

The Plateau Site has yielded more ceramic patterns than any other site. At least 29 different styles are represented here, with some (such as the ubiquitous Blue Onion) appearing on nearly a dozen different wares:

Company/ Origin	Pattern	Date (ca.)	Wares/Extent found	Notes
Alfred Meakin Hanley, England	Plain white with dotted edge	1891-1930	Plate – 1 pc. 30%	Back mark: "Semi Porcelain Alfred Meakin Ltd England" w/ crown
Belgium	Plain white, ribbed		Ramekin – 1 pc. 45%	Back: "[Po]rcelaines a feu" "Made in Belgium"
Doulton Burslem England	Adrian (blue floral)	1891-1902	Plate – 5 pcs. 10%	
James & George	Ironstone	1851-1890	Chamber pot – 5 pcs 90%	White with wheat stalks, grass,

Meakin England (Hanley?)					pine cones and leaves. Back stamp: "Ironstone China J. & G. Meakin" w/ crest & "Droit"
Leedsware				Misc. plates – 12 pcs. <10%	White with slightly impressed blue feather edge
Meissen Germany	Blue Onion	1885-1934		Serving bowl- 6 pcs. 90% Plate 1 – 13 pcs. 80% Plate 2 – 7 pcs. 65% Plate 3 – 10 pcs. 75% Plate 4 – 5 pcs. 50% Plate 5 – 4 pcs. 45% Plate 6 – 3 pcs. 33% Plate 7 – 4 pcs. 30% Plate 8 – 2 pcs. 10% Misc. – 22 pcs.	"Meissen" (in circle) & "Germany." "Germany" & "S/6V" "Meissen" (in circle) over a star "Meissen" star "Germany" "2/3H" "Meissen" star "Germany" "Germany" "Meissen" star
Staffordshire, England	Blue Willow	1890-1920		Plate 1 – 10 pcs. 20%	"England" on back
Staffordshire, England?	Brown transferware			Chamber pot? – 20 pcs. 45%?	Scene w/3 figures, a dog, goats, trees, mountains, a palace, a bridge, and a floral pattern on rim.
Unknown	Cherries & leaves			Plate – 5 pcs. 65% Bowl – 5 pcs. 60% Misc. - 3 pcs.	Back mark reads "TF/121/5."
Unknown	Green gilt border with rose designs			Plate – 1 pc. 30%	Back mark: "Crow..." "1665"
Unknown	Plain white			Plate – 2 pcs. 70%	Unmarked
Unknown	White w/gray floral			Plate – 3 pcs. 65%	Back mark: "...02"
Unknown Misc.	Various			34 pcs.	At least 17 different patterns

In addition to the porcelain finds, several different types of stoneware were also recovered:

Company/Origin	Pattern – Glaze	Wares/Extent
E. Swasey & Co. Portland, ME (c. 1890)	Brown & white exterior, dark brown interior	Pot – 10 pcs. 25%

Chapter 27 – The "Plateau Site"

Unknown	Gray exterior, dark brown interior	Pot – 10 pcs. 30%
Unknown	Tan exterior, dark brown interior	Pot – 14 pcs. 20%
Unknown	Brown exterior, brown interior	Pot – 2 pcs. <10%
Unknown	Misc. glazes – 5	7 pcs.

The only identifiable stoneware here is that from E. Swasey & Co. Although this manufacturer went out of business a long time ago (during the Great Depression), its prominently signed brick factory remains a landmark near Portland's waterfront to this day.

C. Metal

The number of metal artifacts recovered from this site is considerable. Hundreds are listed here; if I were to include each nail as well, the count would approach a thousand. They represent a mixture of domestic and agricultural uses, and should provide good sampling data for sociological or cultural research projects:

Item	Size (in)	Comp	Cond.	Engraving & other notes
Axe heads	6½ L x 4¼ W	IB	F	2 total
Belt buckle	1½ x 1½	NFM	G	Ornate design w/very faint image of woman at window, "SILVER PLATE" inscribed on reverse side
Bike hand pump part	6¼ L	NFM	G	Small tube with cap inscribed "MADE FOR MORGAN AND WRIGHT CHICAGO" (pre-1906)
Bit	3½ L	IB	G	Side piece to a horse bit? Ring portion with attachment
Bits	10½-11½ L	IB	G	3; jointed horse bits with attached rings
Bolt receiver	20 L	IB	G	Very large, wrought iron, hand forged; used to secure barn door?
Bottle cap	1½ dia.	IB	F	"GRAND UNION COMPANY T"
Bowl	8 dia.	IB	P/F	Tin
Brackets	1¼-3½ L	IB	F-G	11; U shaped with sharp points on either end
Brooch?	1¾ dia.	NFM	F	Silver? Round encircled w/8 clover(?)-type leaves, back shank broken

Buckles, D	1-2 L	IB	P-VG	9 total, 6 with toggles
Buckles, fig. 8	2 L	IB	G	Figure 8 shaped, toggle in center
Buckles, long	3 L	IB	G	3 total, all with toggles
Buckles, wide	1-2 W	IB	P-G	10 total, 8 with toggles
Button	1½	IB	F	2 pieced, straight shank, wheeled/floral design, corroded
Button	½	NFM	G	1 piece, straight shank
Button	¾ dia.	NFM	G	Riveted clothing button, "W.H. REED PATENT" (patented 1865)
Can	12 L	IB	P	"PHOSPHORUS WORKS/A&W TRADE MARK/ESTABLISHED AD 1844"
Cap	1 dia.	NFM	VG	"MODJESKA TOOTH POWDER" (1890s)
Catch plates	2½ L	IB	G	4 total, 2 identically shaped; for receiving the bolt of a door lock
Chains, linked	7–24+ L	IB	G	9 total; some hand-wrought
Chamber pot	8 dia.	IB	F/G	Glazed, w/handle
Chisel	8½ L	IB	F	
Clamp (hose)	2 dia.	IB	G	3 total; varying styles
Cleat	7½ L	IB	G	Pi shaped; for flagpole?
Cultivator?	6¼ dia.	IB	G	"PAT OCT 6[or 5?] 1874"
Cup	2¼ H	NFM	P	Silver? Tin? Badly damaged, but ornate, border design around base
Door handles	6¼ - 7 L	IB	P-VG	7; 6 with latches
Drill bit	5½ L	IB	F	Spear-shaped wood bit
Egg beater	8½ H	IB	F-G	Broken crank, "DOVER EGG BEATER...NOV 24th 1891", 2 pcs.
Faucet handle	4½ L	NFM	F-G	
File	7 L	IB	F	3-sided
Filter	4 dia.	NFM	G	Coffee filter (recent?)
Fork	6½ L	IB	F	2-pronged, wooden handle deteriorated, but present
Fork	4¼ L	IB	P	2-pronged, no handle
Fork	7¼ L	IB	F	3-pronged, wooden handle badly deteriorated, but present
Frame	7 L	NFM	F-G	Ornate floral decoration; part of a picture or mirror border?
Garter clip	1½ L	NFM	G	"VELVET GRIP BOSTON GARTER" & illegible pat. dates (1892-95)
Garter clip	1½ L	IB	F	Whole, but very corroded
Garter snap	¾ L	IB	G	Paired component to the garter clip
Gear	1 dia.	NFM	VG	7 teeth; center bar; unknown use
Gear	¾ dia.	NFM	VG	8 teeth; unknown use
Gun, toy	5½ L	IB	F	2 pcs.
Handle	6 W	IB	F	Unknown use
Handles	6-6½ L	IB	F	3 of identical style; straight w/pointed ends
Handles	1-2 L	NFM	F	3 varying; with wooden inserts
Hinges	3½ L	IB	P-F	5; short inner door hinges
Hinges	6½-10½ L	IB	P-F	3; long outer door hinges
Hoe	6½ W	IB	F	With circular eye-hole
Hoe	5 W	IB	F	With attached handle
Hooks	3 L	IB	F-G	4 identical; clothes hooks w/knobby ends

Chapter 27 – The "Plateau Site"

Hooks	3¾ L	IB	P-G	2 identical; clothes hooks w/acorn shaped ends; one w/broken base
Hooks	3½-5 H	IB	F-G	3; wrought iron J-hooks with eyes (for use with rope?)
Hooks	2¾-3½ L	IB	P-G	4 of various shapes and functions
Horseshoe	2¾ dia.	IB	G	Exceptionally small; for pony?
Horseshoe	4½ dia.	IB	G	Therapeutic shoe, connected at the base
Horseshoes	4¼-5 dia.	IB	F-VG	17 total; various condition, 1 twisted
Jack knife	3½ L	IB	F	Blade only
Kettle lid	6¼ dia.	IB	VG	Cast iron, "PAT. APPLIED FOR 1871" "BMF Co." (cursive script)
Key (winding)	3½ L	IB	F	Decorative, unknown use
Knife	6½ L	IB	G	Blade corroded, but bone handle still attached & in good shape
Knife?	6 L	IB	F	Short, triangular blade, bent handle
Knives	4½-5¾ L	IB	F-P	4; all heavily corroded; 2 blades F, other 2 are P
Knob	½ dia.	NFM	F	"THE SOLAR/FM & CO." (fr. 19th cent. Japanese IMARI oil lamp base)
Latches	5½ - 7 L	IB	G	2; with NFM handles
Lock	4L x 2¼W	IB	VG	Cast iron, external housing, ornate design, "NORWICH" (late 1800s)
Lock	3½ L	IB	F	Internal mechanism, missing external housing
Mousetrap	4½ L	IB	P	"THE"-inscribed
Nails	½-8½ L	IB	P-VG	Literally hundreds of various shapes and sizes; mostly hand wrought
Nutmeg grater	5 L	IB	F-G	
Nuts & bolts	2-3½ L	IB	F	13 pcs.
Oil lamp burner	2 dia.	NFM	F	Brass
Oil lamp cover	4 dia.	NFM	F	Brass; slightly bent
Oil lamp cover	4½ dia.	NFM	G	Brass; w/ceramic lid attached
Ox shoes	3½-5 L	IB	P-VG	11 total; 6 right, 5 left
Padlock	3¼ H	IB & NFM	G	Heart-shaped smoke house padlock, brass cover w/eagle & shield "D & M" (Davenport Mallory, mid 1800s)
Padlock	3¼ H	IB & NFM	G	Heart-shaped smoke house padlock, brass cover w/eagle & shield "DM & Co" (Davenport Mallory, mid 1800s)
Padlock	3¼ H	IB & NFM	G	Heart-shaped smoke house padlock, brass cover w/"D.M & Co" (Davenport Mallory, mid 1800s)
Pegs	4½-9 L	IB	F-G	4 total; 2 interconnected
Pipe	4½ L	NFM	VG	Elbow coupling; brass
Pipes	13¾ - 18½ L	NFM	G	4; 1 is threaded; 2 are copper; (other 2 may be lead?)
Pitchforks	11-16 L	IB	F-G	3 total, 2 missing one of the 4 tines
Plough blades	12½ L x 8 H	IB	G-VG	4 total; 3 right-sided, 1 left-sided
Pocket watch casing (back)	2¼ dia.	NFM	VG	Silver? Inscribed with gradients between "S.....F" (for "slow" and "fast"?), includes nob and top ring
Pulley	4¼ L	IB	F	

Rings	1½-3 dia.	IB	P-G	10 total, simple, various sizes
Rings	1-2½ dia.	IB & NFM	F-G	11 total; various washers, brackets, couplings
Robe fastener	3½ L	IB	G	Also known as "stays," metal strips sewn into robes
Safety pin	1½ L	NFM	G	
Salt shaker	1½ dia.	IB	F	Holed cap
Saw blade	14½ L	IB	F	Hacksaw
Saw blades	18½ - 22 L	IB	F	2 wood saws
Shell, bullet	¼ dia.	NFM	G	Head stamp: "U" (Remington, 1885 on)
Shell, shotgun	¾ dia.	NFM	G	Head stamp: "NITRO 10 GA EXPRESS" (1926 on)
Shovel heads	7-14 L	IB	F	3; 2 square, one rounded; missing handles
Sickle	16 L	IB	G	Handsome tool w/handle
Slag	3 L	NFM	G	Rolled sheet metal (lead?)
Spoon	6 L	IB	VP	Straight-handled spoon, highly corroded, broken bowl
Spoon	14 L	IB	F	Very large stirring spoon
Spoon	6¼ L	NFM	G	Silver plated, crown (upper handle) 2 stars (back) "BRISTOL PLATED"
Spoon	8¼ L	NFM	G	Silver plated, w/lily pad design on handle (front & back)
Spoon	3½ L	NFM	F	Silver plated, broken handle
Spoons	7½ L	IB	P	3 identically-styled (heart-shaped handles), 1 broken
Spoons	7¼ L	NFM	G	2 identically-styled, silver plated, "C.H.H. CO" + 3 maker marks
Spoons	5¾ L	NFM	G	2 identically-styled, beaded, "CROWN SILVER PLATE CO." (NY, 1890s)
Spring	1¼ H	IB	F	Egg-shaped
Stakes/spikes	2½-10 L	IB	F-G	13 total
Stirrup?	4¼ dia.	IB	G	
Suspender clips	1- 2¼ W	IB	P-F	6 total; 1 with NFM inner clasp
Thimble	¾ dia.	IB	P	topless & very corroded
Thimble	½ dia.	NFM	G	Decorated with 7 circular flowers around base
Thimble	1 dia.	NFM	F	Plain, flattened
Tins	Various	IB	P-F	2 boxes, 6 canisters, 5 lids, 2 handles; fairly corroded
Tobacco tin	4¼ H x 3 W	IB	P	"HI-PLANE SMOOTH CUT TOBACCO FOR PIPE AND CIGARETTES" with twin engine plane
Tobacco tin	3½ H x 6¼ L	IB	F	"SENSATION CUT PLUG P. LORILLARD & Co" (1910s)
Tongs	3 L	NFM	VG	"Shaw's" inscribed in cursive; ornate design; included w/chocolate?
Trough or planter?	17 L x 7 W	NFM	P	Made entirely of copper, without ornamentation
Unidentified	Various	Var.	Var.	Over 4 dozen miscellaneous pieces.
Vegetable peeler	5 L	IB	F	Gear-shaft piece; "R. H. CO. READING, PA" (1868)
Wedges	2-4½ L	IB	F-G	5

Chapter 27 – The "Plateau Site"

Wheel	1¾ dia.	IB	F	Furniture roller, w/stem
Wire	Various	NFM	G	6; various lengths and thicknesses
Wire	3 dia.	IB	F	Bracelet-shaped with 2 holed tabs
Wire	3¼ dia.	IB	G	Bracelet-shaped, wrought iron
Wrench	3¼ L	IB	P	"SAMSON"
Wrench	5½ L	IB	F	Screw-threaded handle base
Yoke bar	21 L	IB	G	With harness attachment
Zipper pull?	1 L	NFM	G	

D. Miscellaneous

Completing our inventory is the miscellaneous category. Nearly all of these are domestic items:

Item	Size (in)	Comp.	Cond.	Engraving/Notes
Belt	6 L	Leather?	P	
Bones	Various	Animal	G	8 total, including one cow?
Button	½ dia.	?	G	4-holed, white, radiating design
Button	½ dia.	Stone	G	4-holed, gray, plain
Button	¾ dia.	?	G	Faceted, unknown black material (onyx, obsidian?), hairline fracture across face, straight shank
Button	¾ dia.	?	G	4-holed, white, plain
Door nobs	2 dia.	Wood	G	2, burled wood (ca 1885-1910)
Insulator	1¾ dia.	Porcelain	G	
Pipe bowl	2 H, 1 dia.	Clay	G	"T D" w/spur, broken off stem
Pipe bowl	1½ H, 1 dia.	Clay	VG	Brown, complete; reed stem trade pipe, ringed elbow type (1860-90s)
Pipe stem	2 L	Clay	F	With metal mouthpiece, "1" on spur, broken off bowl
Pipe stems	1-1¾ L	Clay	F	5 total, all broken pieces
Shoe	1 L	Porcelain	F	Child's toy? Painted red
Shoe – heel	2½ dia.	Rubber?	P	Man's heel, with nails
Shoe – upper	4 L	Leather	F	Stitch work still evident
Siding	9 L x 4½ W	Wood	F	Painted white
Whetstones	2½-4 L	Stone	G	4 total

Chapter 28
The "Methuselah Site" Report

General Description

This site consists of a relatively small and unassuming house foundation. It appears as a U-shaped berm opening to the southwest. Large, heavy fieldstones still line the edges; others have collapsed into the central depression. The footprint measures approximately 30 feet wide and 32 feet long. The house—now gone—was probably of wooded construction with some brickwork (perhaps a chimney?), as both nails and bricks are ubiquitous. Most artifacts recovered here are among the oldest on campus. (That's why I've nicknamed it "Methuselah," after the oldest character in the Bible.) Most date to the mid-1800s, but some go back to the late 1700s. While these objects constitute some of the most fascinating items unearthed, they also tend to be among the most deteriorated and fragmentary. Such is the nature of this locale.

Inventory of Artifacts

A. Glass
As of yet, not a single whole bottle has been recovered from this site. However, two specimens have come close. Both are mostly (85-95%) complete, except for being broken at the top:

Color	H (in)	Nearly whole, Unmarked	Type
Aqua	3½	Small rectangular aqua-colored bottle (non-pontiled)	BIM
Olive green	3¼	Small cylindrical bottle – (pontiled) - 2pcs	HB

Even glass fragments are relatively scarce. However, they include hand-blown pieces with pontiled bases and applied lips. Only a few of the fragments feature any embossing. These include the following:

Color	Embossed Glass Fragments
Aqua	"[...]WELL/[POR]TLAND/...E
Aqua	"....D/...OC" (HB, pontiled)
Aqua	"AYER'S [CHER]RY [PECTO]RAL/[L]OWELL MASS" (BIM, non-pontiled) (1860-90) – 7 pcs.
Clear	"HINDS HONEY AND ALMOND CREAM " "[...HI]NDS CO " (1890-1930) (BIM)

B. Ceramics

The porcelain fragments recovered from this site mostly date from the early 1800s. They are generally small and in poor condition. Nevertheless, they represent an interesting variety of primarily British-based types and patterns.

Company/ Origin	Pattern	Wares/Extent found
China?	Imperial Chinese design in cobalt and light blue	Unknown – 25 pcs. <10%
Leedsware	White w/slightly impressed feather edge	Plate 1 – 8 pcs. <10%
Leedsware	White with slightly impressed blue feather edge	Plates? 39 pcs <10% Unknown. 13 pcs <10%
Staffordshire, England	Blue transferware	Unknown – 3 pcs. <10%
Staffordshire, England	Blue transferware; backmark: "[CH]INE[SE] PAGODA AND BRIDGE"	Soup Plate – 40 pcs. 30%
Staffordshire, England?	Black transferware; female in front of stag (Artemis?), drums & trumpets?	Unknown – 17 pcs. <10%
Staffordshire, England?	Black transferware; lute serenade, buildings, trees, and mountains Backmark: lion & "PANO..."(?)	Bowl – 18 pcs. 10%
Staffordshire, England?	Brown transferware; trees, and Capitol building?	Bowl – 8 pcs. <10%
Unknown Misc.	At least 7 different patterns	Various - 18 pcs.
Unknown	Blue mocha ware w/black stripes	Unknown – 5 pcs. <10%
Unknown	Blue mocha ware w/white stripes	Unknown – 3 pcs. <10%
Unknown	Gilded blue leaf & green border	Plate 1 - 4 pcs 30% Plate 2 - 5 pcs 15% 9 pieces – misc.

Unknown	Tiny blue & red dotted flowers w/green leaves	Unknown - 14 pcs <10%
Unknown	White mocha ware w/red striped board & floral center	Unknown – 5 pcs. 10%
Unknown	Yellow mocha w/brown dendrites	Pot/bowl – 7 pcs. <10%
Unknown	Yellow mocha ware w/blue dendrites	Pot/bowl – 11 pcs. 10%
Unknown	Yellow mocha ware w/double white & brown striped border	Unknown – 7 pcs. <10%

Earthenware pottery is far more prevalent here than at many of the other sites. The fragments are generally much larger than the porcelain shards. Although most of their original glazing has worn away, the residue that did survive bears witness to a variety of once-colorful objects:

Glaze	Wares/Extent found
Dark brown exterior	Pot – 5 pcs. 50%
Dark brown interior, tan exterior	Unknown – 4 pcs. <10%
Gray interior	Unknown –16 pcs. <10%
Light brown interior	Unknown – 3pcs. <10%
Red interior	Unknown—3 pcs. < 10%
Unglazed	Unknown— 6 pcs. <10%
Yellow interior	Unknown – 7 pcs. < 10%

Stoneware

The glazing on the stoneware pieces has proven to be much more durable than that on the earthenware. In addition to the many pieces that were recovered, one circular lid measuring about 5½ inches in diameter was unearthed nearly whole (80% extant) and in good condition:

Glaze	Wares/Extent found
Gray exterior w/ cobalt blue designs; dark brown interior	Unknown – 21 pcs. 10%
Gray exterior	Lid – 2 pcs. 80%

C. Metal

This site has yielded a balanced mixture of domestic and agricultural items. As a rule, the IB objects consistently demonstrate a more advanced state of rusting and corrosion than those recovered from the other sites. This is to be expected because of their age; however, soil chemistry and saturation levels also play a role.

Item	Size (in)	Comp.	Cond.	Engraving & other notes
Axe head	4 x 4	IB	P	Broken
Bed nob	2¼ H	NFM	VG	Brass?
Bowl	6½ dia.	Tin	G/F	
Buckle	1 W	IB	F	Hat or knee?
Buckle	1 w x 1¼ H	IB	P	
Buckle	1½ x 1½	IB	F	
Buckle	3½ L x 2¼ H	IB	G	Saddle buckle?
Button	½ dia.	IB	P	4-holed
Button	½ dia.	NFM	G	Flat, 1 piece, straight shank
Button	½ dia.	NFM	G	Octagonal cross design, gilt, straight shank
Button	½ dia.	NFM	F	Flat, 1 piece, no shank, back mark "BEST QUALITY" w/eagle & 5 stars over laurel leaves (1800-20)
Button	¾ dia.	NFM	G/F	Flat, 1 piece, "IMPERIAL EXTRA STAN" on reverse, bent shank
Button	1 ½ dia.	NFM	VG	1 pieced, straight shank, engraved (1789)
Button	1 ½ dia.	NFM	G	1 pieced, straight shank, not engraved
Button	1 dia.	NFM	F	Flat, 1 piece, broken shank
Buttons	½ dia.	NFM	F	2, 1 piece, w/ 6 oak leaves and sunburst on front and "ORANGE COLOUR" on reverse, bent shanks
Buttons	1 dia.	NFM	G	3 plain, 1 pieced, straight shanks
Coffee Pot	5 H 4½ dia.	Tin	G	Tin, with lid (detached), but missing spout (1860s)
Cup	6 dia. 3 H	Tin	F/P	w/handle; flattened on one side, strainer holes in the base
Fork	4¾	NFM	G	2-pronged, no handle
Forks	5-5½	IB	P	3 total; 2-pronged, no handles
Forks	7 L	IB	P	2 total; w/ wooden handles
Gear, toothed	1½ dia.	NFM	G	Perhaps to a pocket watch?
Hoe blade	6 W	IB	F	Heart-shaped w/rounded handle hole
Hoe blade	7 W	IB	P	Square-shaped w/rounded handle hole
Horseshoe	4½ dia.	IB	F	
Horseshoe	5¼ dia.	IB	F/P	
Key (door)	3½ L	IB	F/G	Broken handle

Key (winding)	5½ L	IB	G	
Knife, table	5½ L	IB	P	Broken; missing handle
Knife, table	7 L	IB	F/P	Bone handle with diagonal stripe design
Knife, table	8¾ L	IB	G/F	Bone handle with diagonal stripe design
Lid/ring	4¼ dia.	Tin	P	Star-punch design around rim, oil lamp part?
Nails	Various	IB	G-P	Hundreds, mostly hand-wrought
Oil lamp	4½ H	Tin	F-G	tin petticoat whale oil lamp
Oil lamp burner	2½ dia.	NFM	VG	Brass?
Oil lamp?	4½ dia.	NFM	P	Brass casing?
Ox shoe?	4½ L	IB	F	Thicker and more curved?
Ox Shoes	4½ L	IB	F	3 total, 1 left, 2 right
Penny	¾ dia.	NFM	P	1864 Indian Head
Rake?	8½ L	IB	G/F	Broken at one end
Ring	1½ dia.	IB	F	Non-ornamental; pipe coupling?
Ringed handle	1¼ H	IB	F	Small part to unknown item
Saddle clip?	3½ H	IB	F	
Scissor (half)	4¾ L	IB	F	
Sickle blade	14 L	IB	G	Missing handle
Slag?	1¼ dia.	NFM	P	coin-like object (round, metal, size of a shilling),
Spoon	5¼ L	NFM	G	silver plated teaspoon w/4 maker's marks (flower, cross, leaf, thistle) George Richmond Collis & Co. (ca. 1840-1893)
Spoon (head)	1½ L	IB	F	Broken stem
Spoons	8-9 L	IB	F	5 total; unmarked
Suspender clip	1½ W	IB	F	
Suspender clip	2¾ W	IB	F	Wire-construction
Thimble	¾ H	NFM	G	Topless
Trowel	9 L	IB	G	Bent, missing handle
Unknown	3 L	NFM	F	Flattened copper-based object
Wedge	9 L	IB	F	

A couple of these items have been verified to be 230 years old—and some perhaps even older. That is fairly remarkable by US history standards.

D. Miscellaneous Items

Rounding out our inventory are the miscellaneous items below. Clay tobacco pipes comprise much of this category. However, this site also produced a surprisingly large number and variety of animal bones. Most of these have yet to be properly identified, but a preliminary dental analysis has confirmed the remains of both pig and deer.

Chapter 28 – The "Methuselah Site"

Item	Size (in)	Comp.	Cond.	Engraving/Notes
Bones	various	Animals	G	41 total; wide variety, including pig jaw and deer tooth (3rd premolar)
Oyster shells	various	Shell	F	2
Pipe bowl	2 H x 1 dia.	Clay	F/G	Ornate heart-shaped design
Pipe bowl	2 H x 1 dia.	Clay	G/VG	"43" encircled on bowl and "252" on stem
Pipe frags.	various	Clay	P	9 fragments of bowls and stems; "T. D." on bowl
Pipe stem	3¼ L	Clay	G	"HENDERSON/MONTREAL" (1847-76)
Pipe stem	1¼ L	Clay	F	"W. WH…/…SGOW " (=W. WHITE/GLASGOW, 1805-91)
Pipe stem	1¼ L	Clay	F	"W. WHIT…/.LASGOW" (=W. WHITE/GLASGOW, 1805-91)
Shoe heel	3 dia.	Unknown	P	

Introduction to the Campus Lots

With the completion of the Site Reports, we now turn to this book's final set of chapters—those dedicated to tracing the chains of ownership of each of the campus's properties. In this respect, this project has come full circle, for we are finally on the brink of answering the relatively simple question Mike Russell posed to me at the onset: Who was here before us? As it turns out, this simple question requires a very complicated answer!

To begin, it is first necessary to define what we mean by "here." In other words, what land does the College actually own? Where exactly are the campus's boundaries? With a bit of sleuthing, I found three maps that assisted me in this regard. The first, obtained from our Facilities Department, is a Google Earth satellite-view of our campus, outlining our current real estate holdings:

Over this map, I superimposed the original Second Division boundaries using the Proprietor's Map found in Chapter 2. This resulted in the following:

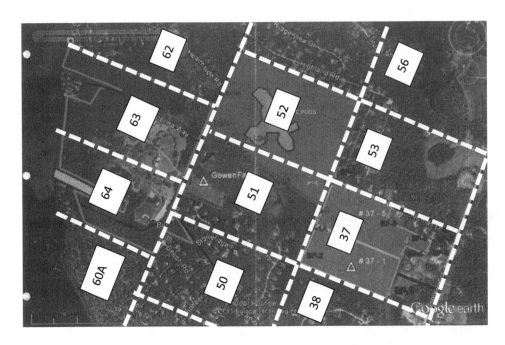

With this image, we can see that the College owns either all, or large portions of, five of the original 100-acre Second Division lots. Two of these lots—64 and 63—lie on the northwestern (or lake) side of Whites Bridge Road. Two others—51 and 52—lie on the southeastern (or farm) side. (It's helpful to remember that as it divides the Saint Joseph's College campus, Whites Bridge Road runs northeast to southwest, as shown by the compass icon on the previous map.) The fifth lot—37—lies to the southeast of all of these, and is primarily accessible from Nicholas Drive or Shannon's Way off Route 35/Chadbourne Trail.

Reconstructing the chains of ownership for these lots was not always an easy or straightforward task. A number of variables complicated the matter. First of all, properties in the Registry cannot be searched by lot number. Rather, they must be located either by volume and page, or by name—either of the grantor (seller) or grantee (buyer). Given the Proprietors' failure to record the names of the original owners of the Second Division Lots, there was no definitive place to start. Here's where a third map—an 1871 residential map of Standish—proved to be invaluable.[178] By overlaying it with the Proprietors' map, I could more or less work my way backwards and forwards from the names that it contained:

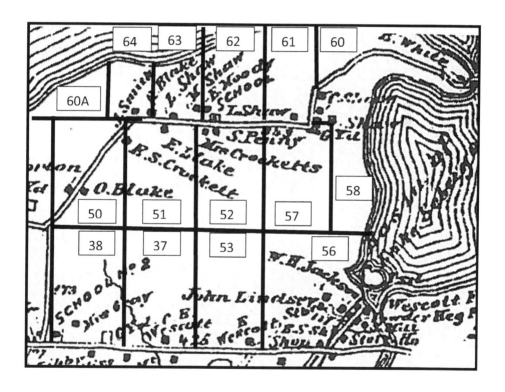

---

[178] The one I used was taken from the *Atlas of Cumberland Co, Maine* (New York: F. W. Beers & Co., 1871), p. 19. Since then, I have also become acquainted with Sidney Baker's even earlier residential *Map of Cumberland County* (Portland, Maine: J. Chase, Jr., 1857). I have found Baker's map, which is 14 years older, to be similarly useful.

Every grantee will eventually become a grantor, so the chains of ownership should—theoretically—be easy to trace. But this was not always the case. Sometimes landowners died, and the willing of their property wasn't always filed with the Registry. These situations are especially difficult to track if the new recipient had a different last name or was unrelated altogether.

Other complications arose as well. For instance, the dating of contracts could present certain challenges. In some cases, the parties involved made an agreement (oral or written) at one point in time, but the official filing of their contract took place years—or even decades—later. So when, exactly, should these transactions "count?" A similar issue is raised by private mortgages, a practice common in the 18th and 19th centuries. If the property is bought by one party, but mortgaged to another, which party should appear as its rightful owner?

There were also a host of issues involved with the deeds themselves. Some of these titles—especially the earlier hand-written ones—can be difficult to decipher. Some are rambling and verbose, which can make the process time-consuming—even more so when multiple properties are involved in a single transaction. At the other end of the spectrum, some deeds are so nondescript that even basic identification becomes a challenge. In some cases, especially early on, property descriptions include the original lot number and the names of the owners of neighboring lots, which is tremendously helpful. But as time went on, lot numbers tended to disappear, and properties were often described relative to objects (rocks, trees, stone walls, etc.) that may or may not have survived. And then there are all varieties of errors within the deeds and/or the Registry itself. The most common is the misspelling (or alternative spelling) of names. Acreage is occasionally misestimated, and in one instance, an incorrect lot number was assigned to a property, and then reassigned over (and over and over) again.[179]

But far and away the most difficult challenge of this undertaking arose when landowners decided to subdivide their lots. In light of this practice, one chain of ownership could quickly splinter into two, three, four, or even more lines that all have to be traced independently of each other. As time passed, these parcels of land could be further subdivided, or, on occasion, merged back together again. Often, such dynamics complicated the process immensely.

In the end, however, persistence was rewarded. What follows is, in effect, our campus's "pedigree" or "genealogy." These are our terrestrial predecessors, a nearly complete listing of all those who held this land before us. Over the next few chapters, I will present the chains of ownership for all five of our lots. Included in each entry will be a description of the lot, its history of transmission, and any peculiarities that I discovered while examining the deeds. Procedurally, I have included the names of the property owners, the years they had the lots (or portions thereof), the references to their deeds (volumes and page numbers) as they appear in the Cumberland County Registry, and the amount of acreage that they owned. I have also put asterisks next to those individuals whose names appear on the 1871 map of Standish, and italicized those individuals whose profiles have appeared in the Part I of this book.

It seems natural to me to work our way through these properties in the order that the College obtained them (more

---

[179] This involved a half-dozen deeds relating to Lot 62, which erroneously cited the property as Lot 64.

or less). We will begin, therefore, with the region that Saint Joseph's College first purchased from the Verrills in the mid-1950s. This is the area that typically comes to mind when "the campus" is referred to: Lots 64 and 63. The subsequent chapters will examine the property across the road, or what many simply refer to as "the farm": Lots 51 and 52. Finally, we'll round out our survey with an examination of the College's least known and most recent acquisition, Lot 37.

One last thing. When working with legal contracts involving unfamiliar strangers devoid of context, there's not much of an emotional payoff. However, some of these contracts contain some fairly unique, peculiar, and downright charming details. Where possible, I've made every effort to include them.

Chapter 29
Lot 64 and its Previous Owners

Lot 64 consists of a 100-acre rectangle that comprises the western corner of the current campus. Together, Lots 64 and 63 make up the most developed area of the College. Indeed, they are what most people most readily identify as "Saint Joseph's College." Lot 64 runs parallel to Burke Road (which it includes) and is bounded by Whites Bridge Road to the southeast and Sebago Lake to the northwest. The northeast border of Lot 64 runs roughly through the heart of the campus. Today, Lot 64 includes the Larry Mahaney Baseball Diamond, the Ward Park Softball Field, and their adjacent parking lots. It also encompasses the Service Building, the trio of Cassidy, Cuneen, and Gingras Halls, Saint George Hall, Clark's Court, Saint Joseph's Hall, the Heffernan Center, Mercy Hall, the Stone Chapel, and the Field Hockey Field. The most westerly section of Lot 64 does not belong to the College, but rather to the half-dozen or so waterfront residences clustered together at the end of Burke Road.

The earliest deed I could find for Lot 64 is its sale from Theophilus and Sarah Bradbury to John Quinby in 1795 (23:19). How the Bradburys first came to acquire this land is unclear. Theophilus did own at least one First Division property (30 acre Lot 6) in Standish as early as 1769 (5:204), so it is possible that he drew Lot 64 at the original disbursement of Second Division lots. If that's the case, he would have retained this land for 20 years.

John Quinby had this property only seven months before selling it to Benjamin and Thomas Skillings in 1796 (23:457). The Skillings brothers held it for a few years before relinquishing it to Jedediah Lombard, Jr., in 1800 (33:590). Upon purchasing this lot, Lombard immediately mortgaged it to John Harding, Jr. (33:591). However, this mortgage agreement was fairly short-lived. Within a year, Lombard began to sell the property, 50 acres at a time, to Philip Cannell, Jr. (35:462/38:11). Cannell owned Lot 64 until 1809; following him, it would literally never be the same.

Cannell sold this lot to John Butterfield in 1809 (57:536). That same day, Butterfield resold most of it to James Hasty (57:539). However, Butterfield set aside a portion of land—specifically, the section that abutted Lot 63—and sold it to Benoni Wood (58:76). According to Butterfield's deed to Hasty, the portion set aside was 30 acres, but Butterfield's eventual deed to Wood establishes it as 20. For his part, Wood had previously orchestrated the same deal with Samuel Shaw, then-owner of neighboring Lot 63 (68:548). In doing so, Wood effectually created a new, 40-acre lot sandwiched between Lots 64 and 63. And from that point forward, this newborn lot was bought and sold independently of its parents. We'll return to this hybrid lot momentarily.

James Hasty owned the bulk of Lot 64 for ten years, from 1809 to 1819. I say "bulk," since, as I mentioned, his original deed with Butterfield suggests that his property comprised 70 acres. However, James' deed to his son Joseph puts the acreage at 91 (82:469). Given that Wood took 20 acres from Lot 64, the correct number should be 80 acres, as the later deeds involving this parcel correctly have it. Joseph Hasty retained this property for the next 45 years (1819-1864). He is the individual perhaps most associated with it, the "Joseph Hasty farm" being frequently mentioned in subsequent deeds. Hasty left the property to his daughter (in-law?), Sarah (Jackson) Hasty, who eventually sold it to Lemuel Rich III in 1869 (368:465). Altogether, then, the Hastys occupied this particular piece of real estate for 60 years. By measure of longevity, no family—not even the

Verrills—has a greater claim to the legacy of Lot 64 than the Hastys.

In less than a year, Lemuel Rich III sold Lot 64 to John F. Smith (379:108).[180] Although Smith held the property for only five years, it is his name that appears on the 1871 map of Standish. Eliab Blake, who (as we shall see) owned land across the street, purchased this lot from Smith in 1875 (414:361). He held it for 20 years before selling it to Leander Clements in 1895 (632:149). Clements had it for a decade, and then sold it to Harry M. Verrill in 1905 (764:65). Including Verrill, then, this portion of campus had at least 15 owners since 1795:

Names	Year(s)	Volume: Page	Acres
Theophilus & Sarah Bradbury	-1795	23:19	100
John Quinby	1795-96	23:457	100
Benjamin & Thomas Skillings	1796-1800	33:590	100
Jedediah Lombard, Jr.	1800-1801/2	35:462/38:11	100
(Mortgaged to John Harding, Jr.)	1800	33:591	100
Philip Cannell, Jr.	1801/2-1809	57:536	100
John Butterfield	1809	57:539	70 (error)
James Hasty	1809-19	82:469	91 (error)
Joseph Hasty	1819-64	Willed	82

---

[180] The deed listed (379:108) is technically a mortgage document between these two men. However, it references a prior deed of sale—one that I was unable to locate. Nevertheless, the sale must have occurred, since Smith is listed as the owner of the property in the sale to Eliab Blake (414:361).

Sarah M. (Hasty) Jackson	1864-69	368:465	82
Lemuel Rich III	1869-70	379:108	82
*John F. Smith	1870-75	414:361	82
Eliab Blake	1875-95	632:149	82
Leander Clements	1895-1905	764:65	82
Harry M. Verrill	1905-		82

These 15 owners don't include those associated with the aforementioned 40-acre combo Lot 64/63, to which we now turn.

Chapter 30
Combo Lot 64/63 and its Previous Owners

This lot was created out of—and is literally sandwiched in between—Lots 64 and 63. It lies northeast of the former and southwest of the latter. It is bordered by Whites Bridge Road to the southeast and Sebago Lake to the northwest. Today, the boundary line between Lots 64 and 63 is demarcated by the remnants of two parallel stone walls—located just to the southwest of the small pond at the College's Main Entrance—which run in a northwesterly direction, perpendicular to Whites Bridge Road and towards the lake.

This hybrid lot originated when John Butterfield and Samuel Shaw each sold 20 acres of Lots 64 and 63, respectively, to Benoni Wood. The original agreement between Shaw and Wood (68:548) was likely a good-faith one that occurred around 1804. The written deed governing this transaction wasn't filed until much later (1813), and was done so retroactively. No doubt the subsequent purchase and sale of this property necessitated the clarification and legitimization of its status. Wood never lived on the entire 40 acres. He appears to have occupied the 20 acres of Lot 63 for at least five years, but upon purchasing the adjoining 20 acres of Lot 64 from Butterfield (58:76), he immediately sold the bundled lot to William Tompson.

From what I can tell, William Tompson sold the property to Benjamin March in 1810 (59:529). Shortly thereafter, March mortgaged the land back to Tompson (61:170). In 1822, March sold the land to Simon Plaisted, but assigned the mortgage to Abraham Anderson (93:129). Later that year, Plaisted sold it back to March (94:259), and then March resold it back to Plaisted (98:160). Presumably, this last transaction was done so that Simon Plaisted could sell it to his son, John (98:159).

John Plaisted owned this combination lot from 1824 until 1832, when he sold it to his brother, Samuel (128:168), who lived there for seven years. In March of 1839, Samuel gave his lawyer, Joseph Jerritt, power of attorney over this property in order "to settle an action now pending in the Court of Common Pleas for the Country of Cumberland commenced by Jonathan M. Plaisted against Simon Plaisted for my benefit...." (165:193). I don't know the precise nature or outcome of this lawsuit, but Samuel wound up selling this land eight months later to Priscilla Harmon (167:19).

Evidently, Harmon lived here for five years and then mortgaged the property to Leonard Shaw in 1845 (192:520). The next year, Shaw bought this lot outright (194:504), and shortly thereafter mortgaged it to Ephraim Crockett (203:414). According to the terms of their agreement, Shaw was responsible for the maintenance and support of Ephraim and his wife, Martha, as well as their sons, Andrew and James, so long as Ephraim and Martha survived. Leonard held the property for nine years before selling it to Samuel Plummer in 1854 (259:90). It should be noted that Shaw's deed to Plummer puts the size of this lot at 50 acres, not 40. This must be a mistake (rather than an expansion), since Shaw's deed describes the property as the very same that Harmon originally sold to him. Nevertheless, this error continues to be replicated in all of this parcel's deeds hereafter.

Plummer did not retain this property for long. He passed away, and in 1856, his son David sold it to Alfred (also spelled Alford) Libby (265:462). That same year, Libby sold it to Joseph Parker (269:58). However, Libby most likely continued to live here until 1864, since the eventual sale of this land to Reuben Blake names both Parker and Libby as grantors (324:244).

Of all the previously named owners of the blended Lot 64/63, Reuben Blake kept it the longest: nearly 40 years, from 1864 until 1903. Appropriately enough, it is Reuben Blake's name that appears on the 1871 map of Standish. After Blake's death, Harry Verrill acquired this property from Blake's children and grandchildren (737:181). Including Verrill, then, this Lot has seen 15 different owners—or more, depending on how one counts them:

Names	Year(s)	Vol: Page	Acres
Samuel Shaw	1804	68:548	20 acres from Lot 63
John Butterfield	1809	58:76	20 acres from Lot 64
Benoni Wood	1804-09	58:77	40 acres
William Tompson	1809-10	59:529	40
Benjamin March	1810-22	93:129	40
(mortgaged to William Tompson)	1810	61:170	40
Simon Plaisted	1822	94:259	40
(assigned to Abraham Anderson)	1822	93:129	40
Benjamin March	1822	98:160	40
Simon Plaisted	1822-24	98:159	40
John Plaisted	1824-32	128:168	40
Samuel Plaisted	1832-39	167:19	40
(Joseph Jerrett, power of attorney)	1839	165:193	40
Priscilla Harmon	1839-46	194:504	40
(mortgaged to *Leonard Shaw*)	1845	192:520	40
Leonard Shaw	1846-54	259:90	40
(mortgaged to Ephraim Crockett)	1847	203:414	40
Samuel Plummer	1854-56	265:462	50 (error)

Alfred Libby	1856	269:58	50 (error)
Joseph Parker & Alfred Libby	1856-64	324:244	50 (error)
*Reuben Blake	1864-1903	737:181	50 (error)
Harry Verrill	1903-		50 (error)

Chapter 31
Lot 63 and its Previous Owners

Lot 63 is a 100-acre rectangle that lies just to the northeast of Lot 64. It is bounded by Whites Bridge Road to the southeast and Sebago Lake to the northwest. It runs parallel to Westerlea Way, which it encompasses. Today, Lot 63 includes the most recently developed and soon-to-be-developed areas of the campus. It contains the Main Entrance to the College, Alfond Hall, Scully and Putnam Halls, Xavier Hall, O'Connor, Currier, Feeney, Carmel, and Standish Halls, Alfond Center, and the improved waterfront area. (At present, it also includes the soon-to-be-constructed sports complex.) The College owns nearly all of Lot 63, except for the half-dozen or so lakeside residences at the terminus of Westerlea Way.

Lot 63 was originally drawn to none other than Moses Pearson. On June 7, 1773, Pearson deeded this particular lot—along with two others—to his daughter, Eunice, and his son-in-law, Samuel Deane. Pearson did so "in consideration of the love and affection" that he bore towards them (12:249). However, Pearson's deed wasn't filed with the Registry until ten years later, so it's a little unclear as to when this property exchange actually occurred.

Samuel and Eunice (Pearson) Deane held Lot 63 for approximately 25 years. Between 1796 and 1798, they parted it out in thirds, and sold the three shares to Thomas Bangs (23:458), Stephen Harris (28:331), and Peter Crockett (29:24), respectively. What transpired next is not clear. I suspect that Bangs and Harris turned their shares over to Crockett, who in turn willed the entire 100 acres to his son, Enoch. The next reference to this property that I could find was Enoch's sale of the entire lot (minus the timber he had cut on it) to Samuel Shaw in 1813 (68:280).

Chapter 31 – Lot 63

It was Samuel Shaw who took 20 acres out of this lot and sold it to Benoni Wood (68:548) as part of the aforementioned 40-acre Lot 64/63. Samuel and his wife, Mary, lived on the remaining 80 acres for the next 22 years. They would be first of many Shaws to own this lot. Samuel sold the 80-acre lot to his son, Ebenezer Shaw, in 1835 (140:518).[181] In 1839, Ebenezer passed this property along to his brother, Leonard Shaw (163:28). The following year, Leonard deeded 25 acres back to Ebenezer, together with "one cow, three sheep, one plough, and one chain" (170:168). From that point forward, the property remained further subdivided, with the 55-acre southwestern parcel being bought and sold separately from the 25-acre northeastern one.

Fortunately, the 55-acre section is easily traced. This is primarily because Leonard and his wife, Betsy, resided there for more than 53 years. He eventually turned this property over to his son, Albert S. Shaw, in 1892. But even then, Leonard and Betsy retained "the full and unrestricted use of the premises herein conveyed during their joint and separate lives, to manage and control the same as they shall desire and choose to do" (590:175). Leonard Shaw died in 1892, but Betsy survived until 1907. In 1910, Albert sold these 55 acres to Ernest E. Noble (861:485), who

---

[181] Why the son of Samuel Shaw is referred to in the deeds as Ebenezer, *Jr.* is not entirely clear. Perhaps it somehow distinguished him from his uncle, Ebenezer Shaw III? To further complicate the matter, this particular deed (mistakenly) lists the grantee as Ebenezer 3rd. This would seem to suggest that Samuel Shaw actually sold his property to his *brother* rather than to his *son*. But a number of clues seem to indicate that this was not the case: 1) when Ebenezer, Jr. later sells this property (163:28), he describes the place as "being the same on which I now live"; 2) his wife, Lucinda H. Shaw, also signs off on the sale; and 3) when his brother, Leonard, sells some of this property back to him (170:168), it is eventually willed to his son, Mahlon.

immediately resold this land to Harry M. Verrill (865:137). It should be noted that these last two deeds both mention a "small cemetery lot in the rear of the house on said place." "The house" mentioned is that of Leonard Shaw, which the 1871 map of Standish places just to the southwest of Westerlea Way. Remnants of a foundation can be found there today, and the Leonard Shaw Cemetery is located in the woods just behind it, across from Feeney Hall.[182]

Names	Year(s)	Vol: Pg	Acres
Moses Pearson	-1773	12:249	100
Eunice (Pearson) & Samuel Deane	1773-98		100
Thomas Bangs	1796-	23:458	1/3rd lot
Stephen Harris	1798-	28:331	1/3rd lot
Peter Crockett	1798-	29:24	1/3rd lot
Enoch Crockett	-1813	willed?	100
Samuel & Mary Shaw	1813-35	68:280	100
Benoni Wood (cf. 40-Acre Lot 64/63)	1804/1813	68:548	20
Ebenezer Shaw	1835-39	140:518	80
*Leonard (& Betsy) Shaw	1839-92	163:28	80
...Ebenezer Shaw (see below)	1840-	170:168	25
Albert S. Shaw	1892-1910	590:175	55
Ernest E. Noble	1910	861:485	55
Harry M. Verrill	1910-	865:137	55

As for the remaining 25 acres of Lot 63, that history is a bit more complicated. When Ebenezer died, he willed two-thirds of this property to his son, Mahlon H. Shaw. Mahlon sold that parcel back to his mother, Lucinda Shaw, in June of 1865 (331:527). Within three months, Lucinda passed

---

[182] For a listing of those individuals buried here, see Appendix A.

away, having entrusted the property back to Mahlon. Mahlon then sold it to his sister, Rebecca Y. Shaw, that September (337:111). Seven years later, in 1872, Rebecca sold this property back to Mahlon (395:341). Despite the fact that this sale occurred in October of 1872, it is Mahlon's name—not Rebecca's—that appears on the 1871 map of Standish. Two years after that, in 1874, Mahlon sold it back to Rebecca (408:132).

In 1875, a third Shaw sibling, Nancy H. (Shaw) Smith, and her husband, William W. Smith, became involved with this parcel as well. Together, the Shaw trio mortgaged the land to Joseph M. Merchant with a remarkably complicated and lengthy deed (416:415). However, this mortgage proved to be short-lived, and was discharged the very next year (434:292). Three years later, in 1879, the Shaw siblings sold this 25-acre tract to their uncle, Leonard Shaw (460:191). Five years later, in 1884, Leonard Shaw sold it to his son, Charles H. Shaw (688:284). Charles would then retain it for the next 25 years.

In 1909, Charles sold this section of Lot 63 to his brother, Albert S. Shaw. Why there are two deeds recording this same transaction (849:239//863:305), I do not know. At any rate, Mary L. Gilman bought this property from Albert in 1911 (874:409), and resided there for the next 43 years. She sold it to James and Shirley Marshall in 1954 (2171:445), the same couple from whom the College would eventually purchase it.

Names	Year(s)	Vol:Page	Acres
Ebenezer Shaw	1840-64	170:168	25
Mahlon H. Shaw	1864-65	Willed	25
Lucinda Shaw	1865	331:527	2/3rds
Mahlon H. Shaw	1865	Willed	25

Rebecca Y. Shaw	1865-72	337:111	25
*Mahlon H. Shaw	1872-74	395:341	25
Rebecca Y. Shaw	1874-79	408:132	25
Nancy H. (Shaw) & William W. Smith	1875-79	Willed	25
(mortgaged to Joseph M. Merchant)	1875	416:415	"about 30"
(mortgage discharged)	1876	434:292	"about 30"
Leonard Shaw	1879-84	460:191	25
Charles H. Shaw	1884-1909	688:284	25
Albert S. Shaw	1909-11	849:239 863:305	25
Mary L. Gilman	1911-54	874:409	25
James R. & Shirley E. Marshall	1954-	2171:445	25

It should be recognized that the bulk of Lot 63 (the 100-acre, 80-acre, and 55-acre parcels) was continuously owned by five members of the Shaw family for 97 years (1813-1910), with Leonard Shaw owning it the longest, for 53 years. The smaller, 25-acre parcel was also continuously owned by the Shaw family (although in this case, by 10 different family members) during a nearly identical time period (98 years, from 1813 to 1911). Clearly, the Shaw legacy is strongly tied to this lot. It is only fitting, then, that some of them continue to "Rest in Peace" here even unto this day.

Crossing the Road...

Now that we've covered one side of the campus, it's time to cross the street and examine the other side. Making one's way through the histories of Lots 64 and 63 is good training for the rigors of Lots 51 and 52. It's sort of like running a 10K road race in preparation for a marathon. The good news is that, comparatively speaking, the remaining Lot 37 will feel like a well-deserved cool-down, something along the lines of an easy 5K.

Chapter 32
Lot 51 and its Previous Owners

Lot 51 is located on the southeasterly (farm) side of Whites Bridge Road. It is bounded by Whites Bridge Road to the northwest, Lot 52 to the northeast, Lot 37 to the southeast, and Lot 50 to the southwest. It lies across the street from the majority of Lot 63 (the southwestern part), but overlaps with some of the northeastern section of Lot 64 as well. Today, the large southeast/central section of this lot is unbuildable wetlands. What the College does own of this lot consists of the grazing fields for Pearson Town Farm's livestock, the Stone Barn, and the cultivated, agricultural croplands. The College recently constructed a lighted pathway through the northwest region of this property. The pathway passes behind two stone-walled graveyards that are close to the road and also occupy this lot. The cemetery to the southwest contains the remains of R. Harold Gowen, and that to the northeast includes several members of the Blake family.[183]

The earliest reference I can find to Lot 51 is a tax sale dated 1787 (16:201). In it, Sargent Shaw, acting as Tax Collector for the Commonwealth of Massachusetts, explains that the owner (who, unfortunately, is not named) failed to pay the requisite levies due on this lot for the year 1786. By law, the owner was advised, and the property was put up for sale at public auction in 1787. Daniel Cram was the highest bidder (at exactly "one pound, one shilling and eight pence"[184]), and so Lot 51 was conveyed to him. But no explanation is given as to why only 97 acres of this land was included. Fortunately, the remaining three acres eventually surfaced. Daniel Cram managed to purchase them from Timothy Pike in 1792 (22:528), just shortly before Cram

---

[183] For the full list, see Appendix B.
[184] According to one on-line calculator, such a sum today would be worth approximately $178.00.

unloaded the entire lot. How Pike originally came to acquire this bit of property remains unknown. However, Pike was married to Elizabeth Jones, the daughter of Ephraim Jones and Mary Pearson. Mary was the daughter of Moses Pearson, so the property may well have come to Pike through his family connections.

Beginning in 1792, a game of real-estate "hot potato" ensued. Daniel Cram sold all 100 acres to brothers[185] Nathaniel and Christopher Dunn (23:315). That same year, Nathaniel sold his half share to the trio of Isaac Elder, Elijah Elder, and Daniel Gammon (25:21); shortly thereafter, Christopher did the same (31:414). From 1792 to 1798, then, all 100 acres of Lot 51 were co-owned by Isaac Elder, Elijah Elder, and Daniel Gammon. In 1798, Elijah and Daniel sold their two-third shares to Isaac (30:377). In turn, Isaac immediately set one third of this lot aside for his son, Isaac Elder, Jr. (30:379).

What happened next is difficult to reconstruct. On February 16, 1799, Isaac Elder sold 50 acres of this lot to John Green, Jr. (32:166). That same day, John Harding, Jr. also sold 50 acres of this lot to John Green, Jr. (32:167). How and when John Harding, Jr. came to acquire half of this lot, and from whom (Isaac Elder or Isaac Elder, Jr.) is not clear. But from this point forward, the 50-acre parcels were bought and sold independently of one another. Before moving on, then, let's summarize what we have so far:

---

[185] I am assuming that the Nathaniel and Christopher Dunn named in the deed are brothers, as there was a Dunn family with those names living in Gorham at the time. However, their father's name was also Nathaniel, so it could have been the father/son combination as well.

Names	Year(s)	Vol.:Pg.	Acres
Town of Standish (unpaid taxes)	-1787	16:201	97
Timothy Pike	-1792	22:528	3
Daniel Cram	1787-92	23:315	100
Nathaniel & Christopher Dunn	1792		100
Nathaniel to Isaac Elder, Elijah Elder, Daniel Gammon	1792	25:21	50
Christopher to Isaac Elder, Elijah Elder, Daniel Gammon	1792	31:414	50
Elijah Elder & Daniel Gammon to Isaac Elder	1798	30:377	100
1/3 from Isaac Elder to Isaac Elder, Jr.	1799	30:379	33
Isaac Elder to John Green, Jr.	1799	32:166	50
John Harding, Jr. to John Green, Jr.	1799	32:167	50

In 1801, John Green, Jr. sold the northeast half of Lot 51 to Philip Cannell, Jr. (35:408). Green retained the southwest half until 1805, when he sold it to James Hawkins (46:372). From here, the history of both of these parcels gets fairly complicated. To make things a little easier, we'll begin with Cannell's northeast half first, and return to Hawkins' southwest half below.

At some point between 1801 and 1806, Philip Cannell, Jr. must have transferred his 50-acre lot to Nathan Penfield. Unfortunately, I have been unable to find any record of this transaction, but in 1806, Penfield sold this same property to Ebenezer Shaw, Jr. (48:552). How long Ebenezer Shaw, Jr. actually owned this lot is subject to debate. He sold it to Ithiel Blake with a deed that was filed with the Registry on October 19, 1835 (145:306). However, that same deed indicates that the sale between these two men actually took place much earlier—on August 25, 1810. If the latter is correct, then the eventual time span that the Blake family owned the northeast half of Lot 51 is 85 years (1810-95).

While the Blake family may have owned this 50-acre parcel for a while, they were not its only residents. In 1819,[186] Ithiel Blake cordoned off a 15-acre, parallelogram-shaped section at the southeast end of the lot (i.e., the back end, furthest from the road) and sold it to Benjamin Haskell, Jr. (177:92). Haskell mortgaged this property to Horatio Swasey in 1842 (178:293), and then sold it to him outright in 1847 (207:74). In 1847, Swasey sold this little sub-lot to William H. Hasty (252:191). These 15 acres finally made their way back to the Blake family when Enoch Blake (Ithiel's son) purchased them from Hasty in 1854 (254:377). So here's the tentative summary of the 50-acre northeastern parcel:

Names	Year(s)	Vol.:Pg.	Acres
John Green, Jr.	1799-1801	35:408	50 acres of NE parcel
Philip Cannell, Jr.	1801-	missing	50 acres of NE parcel
Nathan Penfield	-1806	48:552	50 acres of NE parcel
Ebenezer Shaw, Jr.	1806-10	145:306	50 acres of NE parcel
Ithiel Blake	1810-57		50 acres of NE parcel
(Benjamin Haskell, Jr.	1819-42	177:92	SE end, 15 acres)
(Horatio Swasey	1842-47	178:293 207:74	SE end, 15 acres)

---

[186] This deed was not filed with the Registry until 1842.

(William H. Hasty	1847-54	252:191	SE end, 15 acres)
(Enoch Blake	1854-60	254:377	SE end, 15 acres)

Meanwhile, the 50-acre southwestern parcel of Lot 51 was undergoing its own complicated series of exchanges. As mentioned, John Green, Jr. sold this half of the lot to James Hawkins in 1805 (46:372). Hawkins resold it back to Green two years later (51:266). Just three months after his purchase, Green sold this property (including "the dwelling house and barn standing thereon") to Edward Tompson (52:207). Tompson retained it for four years, and then sold it to James Newbegin in 1811 (64:75). So far, so good. But then things get a little more convoluted....

James Newbegin decided to divide the southwest 50-acre half of Lot 51 in half, yet again. He sold 25 (unspecified) acres of this land to Solomon Newbegin in 1813 (66:567), and the remaining 25 acres to Solomon in 1814 (70:356). So Solomon possessed all 50 acres of this lot, but only for a few months (May to October). That fall, Solomon sold 25 acres to John Newbegin (74:294). Unfortunately for John, this property was about to be confiscated from him.

It's at this point in the lot's history that things get a bit scandalous. In June of 1814, Edward T[h]ompson won a lawsuit in the Circuit Court of Common Pleas at Portland against Thomas Cummings and James Newbegin. (The Registry paperwork offers no details regarding the nature of this suit.) Including legal fees, the judgment awarded to Tompson was a sum of $570.80—or in today's dollars, somewhere in the neighborhood of $7,580. The court order calls upon the acting Sheriff of Cumberland County to seize "the goods, chattels, or lands of the said Thomas and James within your precinct," and "cause to be paid and satisfied unto the said Edward at the value thereof in money...." The order further stipulates that

> for want of goods, chattels, or lands of the said Thomas & James to be by them shewn unto you, or found within your precinct, to the acceptance of the said Edward to satisfy the sums aforesaid, we command you to take the bodies of the said Thomas & James and them commit unto our gaol in Portland in our county of Cumberland aforesaid and detain in your custody within our said gaol until they pay the full sums above mentioned with your fees, or that they be discharged by the said Edward the creditor, or otherwise by order of law....

Pursuant to this judgment, William Hasty, Daniel Moulton, and William Tompson were chosen to appraise the land belonging to James Newbegin.[187] They assessed the southwesterly half (26 acres) of this lot "at the sum of one hundred and fifty-six dollars and no more."[188] This land was subsequently turned over to Tompson, and the sum of the judgement awarded to him was reduced accordingly. The entire matter appears to have been settled by December 21, 1814 (71:150).

In 1816, Edward Tompson sold this 26-acre section of the southwestern half of Lot 51 to Ithiel Blake. There are

---

[187] Technically, James Newbegin had already sold this property to Solomon Newbegin, who, in turn, had sold it to John Newbegin. Nevertheless, it was apparently repossessed for the sake of James Newbegin's debt.

[188] I can't help but question the integrity of this $156 assessment. James Newbegin had previously sold the two 25 acre parcels of this lot to Solomon Newbegin for $250 each; Solomon then resold this particular parcel to John Newbegin for $300. Edward Tompson himself would later sell this property to Ithiel Blake for $200 up front, plus another $200 to be paid within the next four years (= a total of $400). In light of all of this, $156 appears to be a low-ball appraisal. The fact that William Tompson, Esq.—Edward's uncle—was chosen as one of the "impartial" assessors makes this matter all the more questionable.

actually two deeds pertaining to this transaction. In the first, Tompson appears to sell the property outright to Blake for $200 (143:272). But in an usual second deed, it appears that Blake is given the option of selling the property back to Tompson for the same sum, or retaining the property if (another?) $200 is paid to Tompson within the next four years (120:445). Both deeds were originally drawn up on the same day in 1816, although they were filed with the Registry much later (1830 and 1835). Ithiel Blake evidently came through with the money, because the property continued to remain in his name.

As you may recall, Ithiel Blake was also the owner of the 50-acre northeastern half of Lot 51 (see above). So with this purchase of the southwestern quarter, Blake now owned three-quarters of Lot 51 (or 76 acres). This was the case from 1816 until 1819, when (as mentioned above), Blake sold off a 15-acre section at the southeast end of the northeastern lot. This action reduced Blake's holdings of Lot 51 to around 61 acres, approximately the amount of land that Ithiel and his wife, Eunice, handed over to their sons, Eliab and Enoch Blake, in 1857 (278:471).

The contractual obligations put upon the Blake sons are worth relating (especially because they sound so foreign to us today). Eliab and Enoch are given the land ("consisting of sixty three acres more or less") in consideration of

> the maintenance of me, the said Eunice Blake, and Ithiel Blake my husband during our natural life and shall well and faithfully find and provide for the said Eunice and Ithiel Blake good and sufficient meat, drink, clothing, and lodging and all other necessaries fit and convenient for persons their age and condition during the whole of their natural life and also provide meat, drink, clothing, and lodging for Eunice Blake, daughter of said Eunice and Ithiel Blake during her natural life, or until she should marry, and in case she should marry to have a fixing out

of household good and money to the value of two hundred and fifty dollars paid by Eliab and Enoch Blake....(278:471).[189]

Evidently, the Blake boys upheld their end of this agreement. They retained this property together for the next 12 years. In 1869, Enoch sold his share of this lot—plus the 15-acre section of the northeastern parcel he had purchased back in 1854 (see above)—to Eliab (368:172). The deed of sale puts the total at 86 acres.[190] Eliab Blake resided here for another 26 years; consequently, it is his name that appears on the 1871 map of Standish. Eliab eventually sold this property to Leander Clements in 1895 (632:149). This transaction marks the end of the Blake family's 85-year-long association with Lot 51. Actually, that's not entirely true. Given their close connection to this particular piece of real estate, is it only fitting that we should find some of them there (in their family cemetery) even to this day.

From this point forward, the 86-acre parcel of Lot 51 is fairly easy to trace. Leander Clements owned it for 10 years and then sold it (while retaining its cemetery rights) to Harry Verrill in 1905 (776:253). In 1928, Verrill transferred all of his real estate holdings to his personal company, Woldbrook, Inc. (1275:359). Woldbrook sold this property to Percival and Virginia Jackson in 1950 (2015:453). Six years later, the Jacksons sold it to R. Harold Gowen (2287:395).

R. Harold Gowen loved this land. In fact, he loved it so much that in 1989 he carved out a small plot next to the

---

[189] Although it seems as though this contract was authored by Eunice, she must have had someone write it up for her. Her illiteracy is indicated by the "X" that she supplied in the space for her signature.

[190] I'm at a loss as to how this number is derived. According to my calculations, the 63 acres inherited from their parents plus the 15 acres that Enoch bought should come out to somewhere around 78 acres. Where the additional eight acres came from, I haven't a clue.

Blake Cemetery to serve as his own final resting place (8923:217). When he died in 1996, he willed this property to his son, Richard H. Gowen (12539:258/20843:224). The College purchased it from Richard H. Gowen in 2004 (21491:195).

Names	Year(s)	Vol.:Pg.	Acres
John Green, Jr.	1799-1805	46:372	50 acres of SW
James Hawkins	1805-07	51:266	50 acres of SW
John Green	1807	52:207	50 acres of SW
Edward Tompson	1807-11	64:75	50 acres of SW
James Newbegin	1811-1813/14	66:567 70:356	50 acres of SW
Solomon Newbegin	1813-14	74:294 to John N.	25 SW + 25 SW 50 acres of SW
John Newbegin	1814	71:150	25 acres of SW
Edward Tompson	1814-16	143:272	26 acres of SW
(back to Edward Tompson unless $200 paid by 1820)	(1816-20)	120:445	26 acres of SW)
Ithiel Blake	1816-57	278:471	26 acres of SW
Eliab & Enoch Blake	1857-69	368:172	26 SW + 35 NE = approx. 63 acres NE/SW
*Eliab Blake	1869-95	632:149	63 NE/SW + 15 NE = 86 acres NE/SW
Leander Clements	1895-1905	776:253	86 acres NE/SW
Harry Verrill	1905-28	1275:359	86 acres NE/SW
Woldbrook, Inc.	1928-50	2015:453	86 acres NE/SW

Percival & Virginia Jackson	1950-56	2287:395	86 acres NE/SW
R. Harold Gowen	1956-96	12539:258 20843:224	86 acres NE/SW
Richard H. Gowen	1996-2004	21491:195	86 acres NW/SW

Before we can move on from Lot 51, one little "loose thread" remains. As mentioned, James Newbegin had sold all 50 acres of the southwest lot (in two 25-acre parcels) to Solomon Newbegin in 1813 and 1814. Solomon sold one of those 25-acre parcels to John Newbegin. That section was subsequently confiscated by the court and awarded to Edward Tompson. The history of that sub-lot, and its eventual merge with the northeastern section of Lot 51, is outlined above. However, what we have not yet accounted for is the other 25-acre parcel of the southwest half of Lot 51— the one that was last in the hands of Solomon Newbegin. It is to that remaining parcel that we now turn.

Once the dust settled on Edward Tompson's lawsuit, Solomon Newbegin sold the remaining 25 acres of the southwest half of Lot 51 to Thomas Beck (74:189). The deed notes that the transaction includes "all the buildings thereon standing...excepting what has since been set off to the said Tompson by Execution." In 1818, Beck passed this property along to Henry Crockett (81:33). Crockett's purchase of this land began what would prove to be a long family association with this particular piece of real estate.

Henry Crockett held this property for 28 years. In 1846, he sold this parcel (along with two others, 75 acres in all) to his son, Elias Crockett (197:352). Elias retained this land for another 58 years. When he passed away in 1904, a curious dynamic appears to have taken place in light of (and contrary to) his will.

As a conscientious spouse, Elias endeavored to make all the necessary arrangements to provide for his surviving wife, Rebecca, after his death. In his will, he leaves to Rebecca

> all my personal property; and I also give, devise and bequeath to my said wife a comfortable support, so long as she shall survive me on my homestead farm, or at such other place as she and my neice [sic], Harriet D. Shaw, may agree upon to be furnished her by my said neice [sic].

It seems reasonable that Elias would entrust his wife to the care of his niece. But Elias takes it a step further:

> My homestead farm I give and devise to the said Harriet D. Shaw, subject to the payment of my lawful debts and all due charges of my death and burial and a gravestone to my grave, and also subject to the maintainance [sic] of my said wife as aforesaid and the expenses of the death and burial and a gravestone at the grave of my said wife (742:8).

Turning the family farm over to his niece is a plan that Elias may not have previously discussed with his wife...or his niece. Or if he did, then this plan may have looked better on paper than in reality. Just two months later, Harriet Shaw relinquished her right to the homestead farm back to Rebecca Crockett. In her deed, Harriet acknowledges that her aunt, for her part,

> has released me from all further obligations under said will for her support and otherwise and has paid me for what I have expended for carrying on the place up to the date that I left there, and for the undertakers [sic] bill and my notes against said Elias S. Crockett. I have made no charge for my own services to her

and for her care and she assumes whatever outstanding charges upon the property now remain (761:207).

At least their parting of ways appears to have been cordial!

Rebecca Crockett did not retain the property for long. In less than a month, she sold it to Albert S. Shaw (764:157). This sale marked the end of the Crockett family's association with this 25-acre parcel, an association that spanned a total of 87 years (1818-1905).

In 1910, Albert Shaw transferred the entire "Crockett bundle" to Ernest Noble (861:485). Noble immediately passed it along to Harry Verrill (865:137). So our chain of ownership for this last, 25-acre section of the southwestern half of Lot 51 looks like this:

Name	Year(s)	Vol.:Pg.	Acres
Solomon Newbegin	1813-15	74:189	25 acres of SW half
Thomas Beck	1815-18	81:33	25 acres of SW half
Henry Crockett	1818-46	197:352	25 acres of SW half (+ other parcels)
Elias Crockett	1846-1904	742:8	25 acres of SW half (+ other parcels)
Rebecca Crockett & Harriet D. Shaw	1904-05	761:207	25 acres of SW half (+ other parcels)
Rebecca Crockett	1905	764:157	25 acres of SW half (+ other parcels)
Albert S. Shaw	1905-10	861:485	25 acres of SW half (+ other parcels)
Ernest Noble	1910	865:137	25 acres of SW half (+ other parcels)
Harry Verrill	1910		25 acres of SW half (+ other parcels)

Chapter 33
Lot 52 and its Previous Owners

Before proceeding to Lot 52, fair warning is in order. This lot is easily the most complicated and convoluted property history that I've encountered. It starts off simple enough, but it's like going down the proverbial rabbit hole...once you begin, it's easy to get lost. You just keep hoping that eventually you'll make it back out again. Or, to revisit our marathon analogy, this upcoming stretch is the part where you're really going to feel the burn. The course is long, winding, difficult, and confusing. But then again, no pain, no gain....

****

Lot 52 shares its southwest border with Lot 51, and is bounded by Whites Bridge Road to the northwest. To the northeast, it extends nearly to Highland Road, and to the southeast, it reaches nearly as far as Cedar Drive. Probably at least half of the students, faculty, and staff at Saint Joseph's are unaware that Lot 52 belongs to the College. That's because, like Lot 37, little operational activity transpires there. Today, Lot 52 encompasses the septic pods, the Honoratus Residence, newly constructed Marian Hall, and the surrounding woodlands. Given the passive role it plays for the campus, one would expect its history of ownership to be equally mundane. But nothing could be further from the truth.

Lot 52 was originally drawn to Captain Moses Pearson. On June 7, 1773 (the same day he gave Lot 63 to the Deane's), Pearson turned three Second Division lots over to his daughter, Elizabeth (Pearson) Wise (9:182). Among them was Lot 52. Elizabeth possessed this property until 1791, when she sold it to her sister and brother-in-law, Lois (Pearson) and Samuel Deane (18:68).

The next deed involving Lot 52 is its sale from the Town of Standish to George Bradbury in 1818 (81:165). According to the deed, this lot had been in the possession of Samuel Deane, but in 1815 it was committed to Caleb Philbrick, the appointed Tax Collector for the Town of Standish, to collect the back taxes owed on it—a whopping sum of 98 cents! Since no one appeared to discharge the said taxes (Samuel and Eunice had no children, so when he passed in 1814, no heirs would have seen to this), Philbrick advertised and posted the property as the law required. In 1818, this lot was auctioned off to the highest bidder in a public sale held at Edward Tompson's inn. George Bradbury proved to be the highest (and probably only) bidder. He purchased all 100 acres of this lot for a grand total of one dollar and 98 cents—equivalent, according to one online calculator, to around $38 today.

Bradbury certainly snagged himself a bargain. In fact, many of the early owners of this lot profited handsomely from it—but none more than Bradbury. Three years after he acquired it, he sold Lot 52 to Ephraim Blake for the sum of $200 (112:155)—a 10,000% gain! Blake retained the land for 14 years, and sold it, in 1835, for $1,000 (a 400% profit) to Alden Pierce and Ezra Carter, Jr. (142:337). Pierce and Carter, Jr, both "traders," unloaded this lot just three months later to Elisha North for $1,300 (145:243)—a "mere" 30% profit. Of course, the real estate bubble couldn't have lasted forever. In 1840, the first recorded loss was taken on this property when North sold it to Charles Davis for only $1,000 (168:224).

Thus far, the history of Lot 52 has been easy to trace. That trend changes dramatically beginning with Charles

Davis. So before proceeding any further, let's summarize what we have so far:

Name	Year(s)	Vol.:Pg.	Acres
Moses Pearson	-1773	9:182	100
Elizabeth (Pearson) Wise	1773-91	18:68	100
Samuel Deane	1791-1815	Forfeited	100
Town of Standish	1815-18	81:165	100
George Bradbury	1818-21	112:155	100
Ephraim Blake	1821-35	142:337	100
Alden Pierce & Ezra Carter, Jr.	1835	145:243	100
Elisha North	1835-40	168:224	100
Charles Davis	1840-		

Evidently, Charles Davis was not content with keeping Lot 52 intact. In 1840, he sold 30 acres of the northeast section to Ephraim Brown (170:537), and another 10-acre parcel to Henry Crockett (174:206). But then it appears that Davis changed his mind, and decided to simply divide the entire lot in half. This he did. In 1841, Davis sold one half to Edward Bolton (175:3), and the other half to Daniel Libby (175:7). Of course, in order to do this, Ephraim Brown first had to relinquish to Bolton and Libby the 30 acres he had purchased from Davis. That is exactly what Brown did (174:90). But Crockett did not. Instead, he sold his 10-acre lot to Hannah and Joseph P. Shaw, and this parcel became their residence (182:108). So from 1842 onward, Lot 52 had a tri-part division. Edward Bolton and Daniel Libby each held about 45 acres, and Hannah and Joseph P. Shaw owned the remaining 10. Of these three, the 10-acre parcel is the easiest to trace. Let's tackle that one first, and then we'll return to the 45-acre parcels below.

10 Acre Sub-lot

As mentioned, Charles Davis sold a 10-acre parcel of Lot 52 to Henry Crockett in 1840 (174:206), and Crockett sold it to Hannah and Joseph P. Shaw in 1843 (182:108). That same year, the Shaws mortgaged this property to Benjamin Chadborne (182:486), but retained ownership of it. The Shaws resided there until the death of Joseph, when the land was entrusted to his daughter, Zilpah A. Shaw. Zilpah sold the homestead to Lydia B. Shaw in 1857 (283:131). Three months later, Lydia also purchased from Edward Boulton a small tract of land (< 1 acre) within Lot 52 that adjoined the 10-acre parcel which she already owned (283:280). This may have functioned as an alternative right of way to her property. Whatever the case, Lydia did not hold on to her land for long. Somehow it made its way into Henry S. Shaw's hands—Henry was the son of Joseph P. Shaw, and the brother of Zilpah. The next deed that I could find pertaining to this parcel was Henry's sale of it to Lydia B. and Eben(ezer) Moody in 1861 (306:322). In 1862, the Moodys sold it to Anna Crockett (310:480). Actually, the Moodys sold their three-fourths share of this property to Crockett. Leonard Shaw evidently held the other one-fourth share (though how he came to acquire it is not clear). At any rate, Leonard also sold his portion to Crockett at the same time as the Moodys (310:479).

Anna Crockett owned the 10-acre parcel of Lot 52 for 18 years, from 1862 until 1880. Consequently, it is her name that appears on the 1871 map of Standish. When she passed, she left her estate to Sumner P. Shaw (605:479), who sold it one year later to Mary C. Plummer (478:373).

Plummer retained this land for 12 years. In 1893, she sold it to Rozilla Shaw (604:33). Rozilla kept it for 24 years, from 1893 to 1917. However, she mortgaged the property to Charles F. Mabry beginning in 1894 (611:410). Eventually, Rozilla sold it to Mary L. Gillman (1002:12). Rozilla's sale of this property marked the official end of the Shaw family's association with it. Collectively, eight different members owned this parcel for a total of 45 years. But Mary L. Gillman nearly outdid them all, singlehandedly maintaining the property for the next 37 years (1917-54).

Gillman died in 1954. In her will, she bequeathed this property (and another 25-acre lot) to James R. and Shirley E. Marshall (2171:445). The Marshalls had it for fifteen years, and in 1969, they sold their 10-acre parcel of Lot 52 to Harold Gowen (3111:250). It is from his family that the College eventually purchased this land.

Name	Year(s)	Vol.:Pg.	Acres
Charles Davis	1840	174:206	10
Henry Crockett	1840-43	182:108	10
Hannah & Joseph P. Shaw	1843-57	Willed	10
(Benjamin Chadbourne mortgage)	1843	182:486	10
Zilpah Shaw	1857	283:131	10
Lydia B. Shaw	1857-	missing?	10
(Edward Bolton to Lydia B. Shaw)	1858	283:280	<1 acre
Henry S. Shaw	-1861	306:322	10
Lydia B. & Eben(ezer) Moody	1861-62	310:480	¾ of 10
& *Leonard Shaw*	1862	310:479	¼ of 10
*Anna Crockett (Burbank)	1862-80	605:479	10

Chapter 33 – Lot 52

Sumner P. Shaw	1880-81	478:373	10
Mary C. Plummer	1881-93	604:33	10
Rozilla Shaw	1893-1917	1002:12	10
(Charles F. Mabry mortgage)	1894	611:410	10
Mary L. Gilman	1917-54	2171:445	10
James & Shirley Marshall	1954-69	3111:250	10
Harold Gowen	1969-		10

So we've made it this far into Lot 52. Here's where things get really, really complicated. Seriously, it's pretty ridiculous. But rather than trying to convince you of that, let me just show you instead:

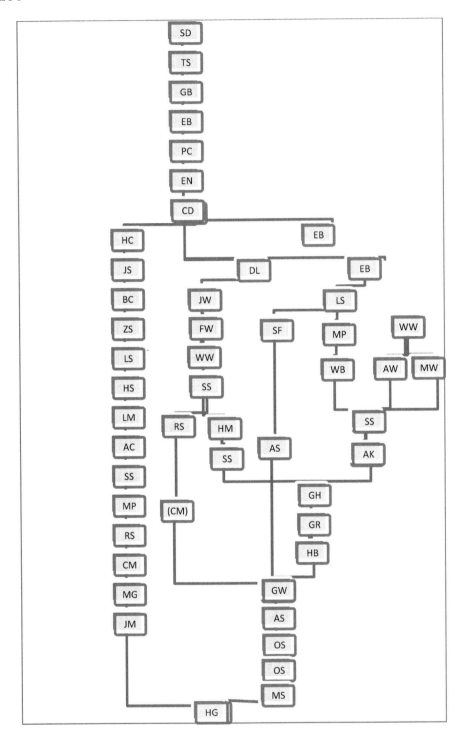

Chapter 33 – Lot 52

Each lettered box in the chart above contains the initials of a landowner of Lot 52. The neat series of boxes at the top are the aforementioned owners of the 100-acre parcel. The orderly chain of boxes on the left represent those who owned the 10-acre subdivision, which we just discussed above. The chaotic jumble in the middle? Well, that's what happened to the two remaining halves of this land—that which Charles Davis parceled out to Daniel Libby and to Edward Bolton. What makes this property history so remarkable is not that it became so fractured, but that all of those subdivisions were eventually reunited. In fact, over the span of 129 years (from 1840 to 1969), Lot 52 went from being a one-owner, 100-acre plot, to being splintered into seven different parcels. Amazingly, those seven different parcels then merged, slowly but surely, back together again into a one-owner, 100-acre plot. I find this dynamic astounding...but also exceptionally challenging to try to trace and reconstruct. What follows is my best endeavor to do so. References back to the illustration above may help the reader better comprehend this process. But fair warning: proceed at your own risk!

To briefly review...Charles Davis had acquired the entire 100-acre lot from Elisha North (168:224). Davis sold 10 acres of it to Henry Crockett (174:206), leaving him with 90 acres left to play with. He sold 30 to Ephraim Brown (170:537), but then changed his mind. He divided the 90 acres in half, more or less, and sold those halves to Edward Bolton (175:3) and Daniel Libby (175:7). It is to these two men that Ephraim Brown also relinquished his rights (174:90). That's where we left off. I should add that while these transactions were taking place (1842), both Libby and Bolton redistributed their properties. Bolton granted certain rights to Libby (174:150), and Libby granted certain rights to

Bolton (178:13). Libby resided with Bolton and Bolton's wife, Mary. Accordingly, Libby was granted

> ...that part of the dwelling house embracing the porch, kitchen, and two bed rooms, with a privilege to go up chamber and down cellar; with one half of the chamber and one half of the cellar; and also a privilege of using the road to his field (174:150).

Such stipulations seem aimed at facilitating a peaceful co-existence between these parties, especially given their close boundaries and shared quarters. Let us proceed, then, one half at a time, beginning with Libby's property.

Daniel Libby's Half

Daniel Libby retained ownership of his parcel until 1849, when he sold it to John Whitmore (218:26). However, Whitmore immediately mortgaged it right back to Libby (217:326). Inexplicably, Whitmore then mortgaged the same property to Catherine Gillman just five days later (217:353). John Whitmore held these 50 acres for 20 years, until he died in 1869. A year later, his wife, Fanny Whitmore, sold them to William Wescott, Jr. (377:304). Wescott sold them in 1873 to Sumner P. Shaw (414:127).

There are a number of individuals who have an unusual relationship with Lot 52. Sumner Shaw is one of them. Of the seven different subdivisions of this lot, Sumner Shaw owned, at one point or another, six of them. (Every "SS" in the chart above refers to him.) He seemed both eager to collect and to sell these parcels. At any rate, Sumner Shaw held this 50-acre parcel for a while (21 years), before divvying it up.

In 1894, Sumner sold the larger, northwest section of this half-lot to his sister, Rozilla Shaw (610:364). (The portion isn't specified, but it must have been around 40 acres). In turn, Rozilla (and her husband, Alvin C. Shaw) mortgaged it to Charles F. Mabry (611:410). Nevertheless, Rozilla maintained ownership of this parcel for 22 years. She sold it, in 1916, to George A. Woodbury (979:333). Like Sumner Shaw, George Woodbury also had a knack for acquiring pieces of Lot 52. He, too, would eventually own six of the seven different fragments of this lot.

In the meantime, Sumner Shaw sold the smaller (specifically, 10-acre), remaining section of his half-lot to Henry W. Manchester in 1901 (703:152). Following Manchester's death, his wife, Cora, sold it back to Sumner Shaw in 1913 (913:171). That same year, Shaw sold it to the trio of George H. Hanscomb, Gardner R. Freeman, and Howard S. Freeman (916:299). Like Sumner Shaw and George Woodbury, this group also had a propensity for obtaining Lot 52 properties. They would go on to procure four of the seven parcels.

In 1916, Hanscomb, Freeman and Freeman sold this 10-acre parcel (along with others from Bolton's side, as discussed below) to another trio: George W. Roberts, Lewis L. Files, and H. Greeley Parker (973:120). Since they bought this land in the spring and sold it in the fall just four months later, this trio may primarily have wanted it for its timber. Indeed, their deed of sale to Howard H. Boody specifically "reserves the right to remove the sawed lumber now seasoning on the premises" (979:59). Boody held this property (within the larger bundle) for a few years, and then sold all of it, in 1919, to George A. Woodbury (1027:7).

Given the consolidations that are involved with Lot 52, it is probably best to move over to Edward Bolton's half now, and examine the history of that property. However, before doing so, we can summarize what we have covered so far as it pertains to Daniel Libby's half. Note that the subdivisions to this half that begin with Sumner P. Shaw end, in both cases, with George A. Woodbury.

Name	Year(s)	Vol.:Pg.	Acres
Charles Davis	1840-42		100
Ephraim Brown	1840-41	170:537	30
Daniel Libby (from Brown)	1841	174:90	quitclaim
Daniel Libby (from Davis)	1842	175:7	50
Daniel Libby (from Bolton)	1842-49	174:150	reconfigured
John Whitmore	1849-69	218:26	50
(Daniel Libby mortgage)	1849	217:326	50
(Catherine Gilman mortgage)	1849	217:353	50
Fanny Whitmore	1869-70	willed	50
William Wescott, Jr.	1870-73	377:304	50
Sumner P. Shaw (& see below)	1873-94	414:127	50
Rozilla (& Alvin C.) Shaw	1894-1916	610:364	40
(Charles F. Mabry mortgage)	1894	611:410	40
George A. Woodbury	1916-25	979:333	40

Name	Year(s)	Vol.:Pg.	Acres
Sumner P. Shaw	1873-1901	414:127	50
Henry Manchester	1901-12	703:152	10
Cora (Manchester) Libby	1912-13	willed	10
Sumner P. Shaw	1913	913:171	10
George H. Hanscomb, Gardner R. Freeman & Howard S. Freeman	1913-16	916:299	10

George W. Roberts, Lewis L. Files & H. Greeley Parker	1916	973:120	10+
Howard H. Boody	1916-19	979:59	10+
George A. Woodbury	1919-25	1027:7	10+

Edward Bolton's Half

Like Libby, Bolton came to his half of Lot 52 through a combination of factors, including the quitclaim from Ephraim Brown (174:90), the purchase from Charles Davis (157:7), and the property exchange with Libby (178:13). But Bolton held his parcel much longer than Libby. He retained it from 1842 until his death in 1876. The property and residence passed to his son, Charles F. Bolton, a minor whose legal guardian was George Libby. The Bolton/Libby team subsequently sold the 50 acres to Leonard Shaw (419:163).

Under Leonard Shaw's ownership, some real estate dealings are clear. However, others are a bit murkier. It is evident, for instance, that Leonard Shaw parceled out 10 acres of this property and sold it to Morris Parker in 1878 (451:133). Eight months later, Parker sold it to William Buxton (454:352). Buxton held those 10 acres for five years before they were purchased by Sumner Shaw in 1883 (498:480). Twenty years later, in 1903, Sumner Shaw would sell them, plus another 40-acre bundle, to Augustus F. Kemp (731:4). But let us return to that transaction momentarily.

Meanwhile, Leonard Shaw divided out another section of land, about 11½ acres, and sold it in 1880 to Sarah Freeman (467:110). Freeman held it for only a year or so before selling it to Ann E. Shaw (671:351). Shaw retained this property—the former residence of Edward Bolton—for over 40 years. Following her death, her husband, Winthrop M. Shaw, sold it in 1922 to George A. Woodbury (1106:192).

The deeds above are those that I could successfully identify as having come from Leonard Shaw's ownership of Bolton's half of Lot 52. But what I have not been able to ascertain is what happened to the remaining 30 acres of this property. Registry searches involving Leonard Shaw (and his direct descendants) have turned up nothing, so I find myself at a bit of a loss here. One partial explanation is that over time, some of this acreage leeched into the surrounding properties. So, for example, Leonard Shaw's original sale to Sarah Freeman was for 11½ acres (467:110). This is what she sold to Ann E. Shaw (671:351). Supposedly, that very same property was also sold to George A. Woodbury, but Woodbury's deed puts it at 16¾ acres (1106:192). That five extra acres must have come from somewhere, and given its location, it most likely came from Leonard Shaw's parcel.

A similar dynamic can be seen with a transaction involving Sumner Shaw. The year after Leonard Shaw received Bolton's half, William Wescott, the owner of the neighboring Lot 57, passed away. In his will, he gave to his two daughters, Abbie A. Wescott and Mary C. Wescott, "a good home out of my Estate up to the time of their marriage" (447:22). Five years later, in 1883, these same two women sold to Sumner Shaw (498:479/499:349) a 30-acre parcel that adjoined the other 10 acres that Sumner had purchased from William Buxton out of Leonard Shaw's parcel (498:480). Sumner bundled these 30 acres together with his 10 and sold the whole package to the aforementioned Augustus Kemp in 1903 (731:4). Shaw's deed to Kemp lists the bundle as "fifty acres more or less," but the previous figures establish a total of 40. Again, given its location, if Sumner truly sold 50 acres to Kemp, then at least some of that land

(10 acres or so) must have been taken from Leonard Shaw's parcel.[191]

Augustus Kemp retained Sumner Shaw's 50-acre bundle for ten years. In 1913, he sold it to the previously encountered trio of George H. Hanscomb, Gardner R. Freeman, and Howard S. Freeman (916:169). As you may recall, this partnership also purchased from Sumner Shaw the 10-acre parcel from Libby's half (619:299). These two sales increased their total holdings from Lot 52 to around 60 acres. That is what was subsequently passed along to George W. Roberts, Lewis L. Files and H. Greeley Parker (973:120), what they passed to Howard H. Boody (979:59), and what Boody passed to George A. Woodbury (1027:7).

By the time George A. Woodbury received the 60-acre parcel from Bolton's half in 1919, he had already held the 40-acre parcel from Libby's half, which (as noted above) he had received from Rozilla Shaw in 1916 (979:333). And as previously mentioned, he purchased the 16¾-acre parcel from Ann E. Shaw in 1922 (1106:192). Collectively, these transactions gave Woodbury a total of 117 acres, including the 30 from Lot 57. If we factor out those 30, Woodbury would have held a total of 87 acres of Lot 52.

At this point, let's recap what we've covered with respect to Edward Bolton's half:

Name	Year(s)	Vol.:Pg.	Acres
Charles Davis	1840-42		100
Ephraim Brown	1840-41	170:537	30
Edward Bolton (from	1841	174:90	quitclaim

---

[191] It should be noted that from this point forward, the 30 acres from Lot 57 were more or less merged into Lot 52 property, and bought and sold inseparably. Consequently, these acres need to be accounted for in Lot 52 totals.

Brown)			
Edward Bolton (from Davis)	1842	175:3	50
Edward Bolton (from Libby)	1842-76	178:13	reconfigured
Charles F. Bolton/George Libby	1876	willed	50
Leonard Shaw (& see below)	1876-80	419:163	50
Sarah Freeman	1880-81	467:110	11.5
Ann E. & Winthrop M. Shaw	1881-1922	671:351	11.5
George A. Woodbury	1922-26	1106:192	16¾ (17)

Name	Year(s)	Vol.:Pg.	Acres
Leonard Shaw	1876-78	419:163	50
Morris Parker	1878	451:133	10
William Buxton	1878-83	454:352	10
Sumner Shaw	1883-1903	498:480	10
Abbie A. Wescott and Mary Wescott to Sumner Shaw	1883	498:479 499:394	+30 (from Lot 57)
Augustus F. Kemp	1903-13	731:4	50
George H. Hanscomb, Gardner R. Freeman & Howard S. Freeman	1913-16	916:169	50 + 10 from Libby half, above
George W. Roberts, Lewis L. Files & H. Greeley Parker	1916	973:120	60
Howard H. Boody	1916-19	979:59	60
George A. Woodbury	1919-25	1027:7	60 (+ 40 fr Libby & 17 fr Bolton, above) = 117

Chapter 33 – Lot 52

If you're still with me on this, congratulations are in order. Seriously, you may want to consider organizing an Everest expedition, launching a career in nuclear physics, or undertaking a *real* marathon. I suspect any of these endeavors would be far easier to accomplish! The good news is that we're now in the relatively straightforward final stretch of this elaborate property history.

So as we have seen, a number of parcels converged with George Woodbury. Woodbury must have been exceptionally fond of real estate. At the time of his death in 1925, he had acquired no fewer than 63 properties throughout Gorham, Standish, and Windham. All of his holdings, including the 87 acres from Lot 52, were bequeathed to Philip E. Abbott and Horace A. Sheesley (1240:355). Abbott and Sheesley might have felt somewhat overwhelmed by Woodbury's sizable real estate portfolio. Nevertheless, they unloaded this property relatively soon.

Owen P. Smith purchased this land in 1927 (1253:428) and retained it until his death in 1943. Following his passing, the property was willed to his two surviving children, Owen M. and Margaret Smith (1679:419). They maintained joint ownership over it until 1963, when Owen M. relinquished his share to Margaret (3092:280). Following Margaret's death in 1969, the property was sold to R. Harold Gowen (3105:509). Two months later, Gowen also purchased the 10-acre section of Lot 52 from the Marshalls (3111:250). This transaction brought Gowen's total holdings of Lot 52 to 97 acres and effectually restored this once hopelessly fragmented property back to its original, one-owner state.

The College would go on to purchase most of Lot 52 from R. Harold Gowen in 1986 (7116:282). However, Gowen sold what is today known as the Honoratus Residence to David Driscoll and Dorothy Regan in 1987 (7964:232). The

College eventually acquired it from this couple in 1995 (11901:141).

Name	Year(s)	Vol.:Pg.	Acres
George A. Woodbury	1919-25	1027:7	117/87 acres
Philip E. Abbott & Horace A. Sheesley	1926-27	1240:355	117/87 acres
Owen P. Smith	1927-43	1253:428	117/87 acres
Margaret & Owen M. Smith	1943-63	1679:419	117/87 acres
Margaret Smith	1963-69	3092:280	117/87 acres
R. Harold Gowen	1969-87	3105:509	117/87 acres
R. Harold Gowen	1969-87	3111:250	10 (=127/97 total)
Saint Joseph's College	1986-	7116:282	122 acres
David Driscoll & Dorothy Regan	1987-95	7964:232	5 acres
Saint Joseph's College	1995-	11901:141	5 (=127/97 total)

Before closing the book on Lot 52, there is one more mystery worth mentioning. The 1871 map of Standish indicates two residences on this property: a "Mrs. Crocketts" and an "S. Penny." We've already identified Anna Crockett (Burbank) as the owner of one of these residences. But none of the property deeds associated with Lot 52 mention an "S. Penny." In fact, only one listing in the entire Registry exists for an S. Penny: that of a tax sale of Stephen Penny's property along the Androscoggin River in 1817 (78:35). Given the dates, it seems highly improbable that these are the same individuals.

The 1871 map of Standish also reveals that a school once stood across the street from the residence in question. According to my research, this was Standish School #1, located in what was (appropriately enough) known as the "Shaw District." The School Committee Report lists a "Mr. Penn**e**y" as its agent for 1871 only. (In the preceding and following years, this job fell to Leonard Shaw.) I cross-referenced the 1870 Standish Census Records, and discovered four individuals with the surname of "Penney," none of whose first names begin with an "S": Augustus (30), Rapeney (61), Anna (18), and Leonard (56). They are all listed within the same household, but its location is not given. According to the Registry, none of them ever owned land in Standish (although Leonard did sell some in Portland in 1859). Nor do any of them reappear in the town's 1880 Census Record.

So who was this "S. Penny" that appears on the 1871 map of Standish? My guess is that it was Leonard Penney. In the handwritten, cursive deeds of the time, capital *L*'s look awfully similar to capital *S*'s, and the misspelling of that last name would have been an easy mistake to make. If so, he and his family certainly didn't stick around long. But how they wound up passing through this area and what sort of living arrangements they made here are questions that remain yet unanswered.

Chapter 34
Lot 37 and its Previous Owners

If you've managed to make it through the gauntlet of Lots 64, 63, 51, and 52, then you can think of Lot 37 as your reward. Comparatively speaking, its property history is much more straightforward. It's a good one to end on, as we round out the real estate holdings of the College.

****

Of all the lots that Saint Joseph's College owns, Lot 37 is unquestionably the least familiar to the campus community. That's because it's a) the College's most recent acquisition, b) the furthest away from the operational hub of the campus, and c) the least accessible of all the properties. Lot 37 lies between Lot 51 to the northwest and Route 35 (Chadbourne Trail) to the southeast. It is bounded by Nicholas Drive to the northeast, and extends just beyond Shannon's Way, to Harding Cemetery, in the southwest. Today, the College owns about three fourths of this lot, most of it in the northwest sector. Its southeast zone (specifically, that which lies along Route 35, both sides of Shannon's Way, and up Nicholas Drive) consists of private residences. At present, the College's portion of this lot is composed entirely of undeveloped woodlands.

On the very same day (June 7, 1773), that Moses Pearson handed Lot 63 over to Eunice and Samuel Deane and Lot 52 to Elizabeth Wise, he also bestowed several lots, including Lot 37, upon his daughter, Lois, and her husband, Joshua Freeman, Jr (8:331). The Freemans would retain this gift of his for the next 29 years. Following Joshua's death, Lois sold the property in 1802 to Benjamin Haskell, Jr (52:404).

Benjamin Haskell held onto Lot 37 for even longer than the Freemans—a remarkable 52 years! He sold it in 1854, just prior to his own death, to Ivory Lord (262:195). It appears that Haskell's wife, Eleanor (variously spelled "Eloner," "Eleaner," and "Elanor" in the deeds), may not have been in total agreement with this deal, because shortly after Benjamin's passing, she bought this property back from Lord (262:194). As noted in the Registry, her purchase received the full backing of Benjamin's remaining heirs (262:196). It should be noted that a minor discrepancy exists between these three deeds. Benjamin Haskell's sale to Lord puts the total acreage at 115. Lord's deed to Eleanor Haskell repeats this same number. But the quitclaim from Benjamin's survivors indicates that 100 acres were involved. This latter figure is technically correct if Lot 37 is the only property included. (Since no other lots are specifically mentioned, I'd say that's a safe assumption.)

Under Eleanor's ownership, Lot 37 underwent a few changes. On the same day that she purchased it (June 7, 1855), Eleanor sold five acres back to Ivory Lord (277:448). From that point forward, this five-acre parcel would be traded separately from the rest of the lot. We'll return to its chain of ownership below. Also on that day, Eleanor cordoned off 20 acres from this lot and sold it to Rebecca P. Haskell (264:374), the daughter of Benjamin's first wife, Nancy (Pride) Haskell. However, that division was relatively short-lived. Three years later, Rebecca—who had since married Joseph H. Haggett—sold this same parcel (but claims only 10 acres were involved) back to Eleanor (287:41).

Eleanor retained ownership of the remaining 95 acres of Lot 37 until 1873, when she sold them to Charles E. Wescott "in consideration of the maintainance [sic] of me Eleanor Haskell and Esther Jordan my sister during all of our natural live [sic]..." (401:174).[192] Wescott may well have already been serving in this capacity, since the 1871 map of Standish lists his name, rather than Haskell's, at this site. Eleanor's sale to Wescott didn't quite mark the official end of her relationship with this lot. She continued to live here until the ripe old age of 96, finally passing away in 1892. But just nine months prior to her death, she and Charles Wescott mortgaged this property to Isaac Rogers (576:205). That deed attests to the 89-year-long association between the Haskell family and Lot 37 (1802-91).

When Charles Wescott passed away in 1900, this property was willed to his brother, James B. Wescott (663:478). The latter Wescott retained it until 1906, when Wilbert A. Libby purchased it (791:27). According to Libby's deed, the premises contained "100 acres, more or less," but that wasn't all he received. James Wescott also granted to Libby

> one pair of black horses, one double dump rigging, one single rigging, one mowing machine, one Concord wagon, one road cart, one rack, one chamber set, one dining room set, and all live stock, farming tools, machinery, and utensils and all furniture, glass, silverware, and crockery, kitchen utensils, and all personal property of every name, nature and description whatsoever now on, in, or about the premises and buildings on said farm.

This transaction apparently encompassed even the kitchen sink!

In 1911, Wilbert A. Libby passed Lot 37 to his son, Willie M. Libby (885:371), who held it for the next 20 years. During that time, Willie M. entered into a three-year contract, beginning in 1915, with the Standish Land &

---

[192] Previously, in 1863, Eleanor had sold to Wescott a small tract from this lot (about two-tenths of an acre), most likely as a right of way to Wescott's neighboring property (321:373).

Lumber Co. for the property's timber (953:416). In 1922, he also granted a small section of this land to the Harding Cemetery Association for the burial grounds that can be found there to this day (1104:11). In 1931, Willie M. Libby sold Lot 37 (still listed at 95 acres) to his sister, Kate M. Gage (1376:304). Gage held it for another 10 years. When she sold it in 1941 to Violet K. and Farnsworth F. Jewett (1644:379), that transaction marked the end of a 35-year-long association between the Libbys and Lot 37 (1906-41).

Since its origins, Lot 37 hadn't been compromised too much. The vast majority of it (around 95 acres) had, up to the Jewetts, remained together. But that streak was about to come to a dramatic end. To be fair, Violet and Farnsworth maintained the integrity of the property for 37 years (1941-78). In 1978, they sold a portion of it to their son and daughter-in-law, Wilbert S. and Judith R. Jewett (4329:206). But the real splintering of this lot took place following Farnsworth's death in 1999. On May 14 of that year, Violet Jewett sold parcels of Lot 37 to Philip Valente (14756:243), Stephen L. Goodine (14756:252) and Peter Busque (14756:265). On that same day, Wilbert and Judith Jewett sold parcels of their share of Lot 37 to Michelle Busque (14756:271), Kevin Tibbitts (14756:277), and Linda Griffin (14756:286). While each of these deeds describes the boundaries of the given parcel, they fail to specify the acreage involved. Since most were subsequently developed for residential purposes, they were relatively small sub-lots. At any rate, we shall not continue to trace these parcels, since they are not included in the College's holdings. The College eventually purchased most of the remaining, undeveloped sections of Lot 37 from Gorham Savings Bank in 2013 (30799:145).

So the history of Lot 37, minus the five acres that Eleanor Haskell sold back to Ivory Lord in 1855, looks something like this:

Name	Year(s)	Vol.:Pg.	Acres
Moses Pearson	-1773	8:331	100
Lois (Pearson) and Joshua Freeman, Jr.	1773-1802	52:404	100
Benjamin Haskell, Jr.	1802-54	262:195	115 (error)
Ivory Lord	1854-55	262:194	115 (error)
Eleanor Haskell (and see below)	1855-73	262:196	100
Rebecca Haskell	1855-58	264:374	10 or 20 acres
Rebecca (Haskell) Haggett back to Eleanor	1858-73	287:41	10 or 20 acres
Eleanor to Charles E. Wescott (ROW)	1863-1900	321:373	0.2 acres
*Charles E. Wescott	1873-1900	401:174	95
(Isaac Rogers mortgage)	1891	576:205	95
James B. Wescott	1900-06	663:478	95
Wilbert A. Libby	1906-11	791:27	95
Willie M. Libby	1911-31	885:371	95
(Standish Land & Lumber Co.)	1915-18	953:416	timber rights
(Harding Cemetery Association)	1922-present	1104:11	1 acre
Kate M. Gage	1931-41	1376:304	95
Farnsworth F. & Violet K. Jewett	1941-99	1644:379	95
Judith R. & Wilbert S. Jewett	1978-99	4329:206	unspecified

Philip Valente (from Violet Jewett)	1999-	14756:243	unspecified
Stephen L. Goodine (from Violet Jewett)	1999-	14756:252	unspecified
Peter Busque (from Violet Jewett)	1999-	14756:265	unspecified
Linda Griffin (from Wilbert Jewett)	1999-	14756:286	unspecified
Michelle Busque (from Wilbert Jewett)	1999-	14756:271	unspecified
Kevin Tibbitts (from Wilbert Jewett)	1999-	14756:277	unspecified
Saint Joseph's College	2013-present	30799:145	Remainder

Given some of the peculiarities involved with the 95-acre portion of Lot 37, readers will be relieved to know that the chain of ownership for its remaining five-acre parcel is relatively simple and straightforward. As mentioned above, it originated with Eleanor Haskell's resale of this small parcel back to Ivory Lord in 1855 and included "the privilege of using my other land in the Winter to haul wood" (277:448). Lord retained this property for 32 years before selling it to Isaac R. Rogers in 1887 (544:219).

When Isaac Rogers passed away in 1904, this five-acre parcel was bequeathed to his son, Wilbur F. Rogers (742:91). The younger Rogers sold the property three years later, in 1907, to Clement P. Wescott (798:352). Wescott retained it for four years. He then sold it, in 1911, to Daniel W. Fogg (888:187).

Daniel W. Fogg's acquisition marked the beginning of an 88-year-long family association with this little lot. Daniel held the property in his own name for 15 years. In 1926, he transferred the deed of ownership to his wife, Mary P. (also known as Polly) Fogg (1233:141). Together, Mary and Daniel W. retained it for another 22 years. In 1948, they sold it to their son and daughter-in-law, Daniel P. and Elizabeth S. Fogg (1918:33). This latter couple managed to maintain possession of these five acres for another 51 years. It wasn't until 1999 that they finally sold them to Peter J. Busque (14750:163). Following Busque's death in 2011, the College purchased this lot from his estate in 2013 (30850:76). Thus, the entire history of this five-acre parcel of Lot 37 can be summarized accordingly:

Name	Year(s)	Vol.:Pg.	Acres
Eleanor Haskell	1855	277:448	5
Ivory Lord	1855-87	544:219	5
Isaac R. Rogers	1887-1904	742:91	5
Wilbur F. Rogers	1904-07	798:352	5
Clement P. Wescott	1907-11	888:187	5
Daniel W. Fogg	1911-26	1233:141	5
Mary P. Fogg	1926-48	1918:33	5
Daniel P. & Elizabeth S. Fogg	1948-99	14750:163	5
Peter J. Busque	1999-2013	30850:76	5
Saint Joseph's College	2013-present		5

Conclusion to Part II

Our comprehensive survey of the campus's previous property owners is now complete. Our review of the deeds has generated a list of around 160 names. (For the sake of convenience, they can all be found listed in alphabetical order in Appendix C.) Keep in mind, however, that these 160 names really only represent the tip of the iceberg when it comes to the question of who was here before us. They are the property owners only—they do not include any non-contracted affiliates (spouses, children, siblings, parents, other relatives and/or acquaintances) who were here with them as well. To identify these individuals, one would have to cross-reference the residential owners with the available census data listing other household occupants (as we did, for example, in Leonard Shaw's profile). Such an undertaking falls well beyond the capacity of this volume. Nevertheless, it is one that I hope might be accomplished in the future.

****

And so it is that we've finally reached the conclusion of this book—but not the end of this project. My hope is that this work represents only the beginning of a much more comprehensive study of the campus's history. So where do we go from here? Allow me to suggest a few areas to pursue.

First, of the thousands of artifacts I have recovered, and of the 160 previous owners I have identified, I've managed to profile just a handful. Far more are deserving of such treatment. Researching these objects and predecessors and learning their back stories is the only way to truly appraise the richness of our material heritage. So clearly, much more work remains to be done in this regard.

Certainly, this first task is considerable unto itself. Nevertheless, there is ample opportunity for further expansion. As noted, I have located at least 12 artifact-bearing sites on the College's property, and my research on those has only been preliminary. All of these sites deserve to be more thoroughly investigated (and this is certainly my intention). At the same time, this project would also benefit from a more systematic canvassing of our nearly 500 acres. Who knows how many more sites are out there? Or what additional surprises lie within them?

Likewise, with just a couple of exceptions, most of the chains of ownership have been completed. Unless the College enlarges its campus, that work is largely accomplished. However, as I indicated, the 160 or so former property owners are just the beginning when it comes to the question of who was here before us. A thorough cross-referencing of the census registers would provide us with a far more extensive record of our terrestrial ancestry, and would undoubtedly yield additional remarkable predecessors among them.

The foregoing tasks pertain mostly to the continued collection of physical evidence, research data, and background information. At the next levels, considerations arise of conservation and preservation, and of education and the dissemination of information. Along with this book, my hope is that we might develop other platforms by which we can educate others about the history of this place. I would love to see Saint Joseph's College establish some sort of Heritage Center or Museum dedicated to the campus's past—one in which visitors could learn all about our remarkable predecessors and encounter for themselves some of its storied artifacts. For those unable to make it to campus, perhaps a corresponding virtual site could be developed as well. We'll see....

Finally, a few questions remain regarding the broader impact of this project. In this respect, this book now comes full circle, back to some of the observations made in its opening pages. As President Dlugos recognized in his Foreword, I have sought to address the questions of who was here before us and what they may have left behind. (I hope I have answered those questions to some satisfaction for my readers!) But his subsequent question—Why should we care?—still lingers. What does this past have to do with the Saint Joseph's College of the present—the vibrant community who lives and works right here, right now? What does it mean to us on a philosophical level? And how does it (or should it) affect us pragmatically? What relationship does this history have to our institutional identity? And how does it (or should it) affect our Mission? These questions, of course, are both open-ended and ongoing. I'm sure some answers will gradually emerge over the next few months or years, but some could be decades away. Nevertheless, I, for one, am a firm believer that the richness of this heritage will ultimately prove beneficial for our institutional well-being. By emphasizing those connections that Professor Connolly alluded to in his Preface, I think our campus's storied past can play a positive and powerful role in shaping and promoting of our College's future.

Appendix A
Occupants of the Leonard Shaw Cemetery

Leonard Shaw
    Died: 9 Jan 1891   76 yrs.

Betsy Shaw, wife of Leonard Shaw
    Died: 7 Aug 1907   87 yrs. 5 mo. 29 days

Lydia C. Shaw, daughter of Leonard & Betsy Shaw
    Died: 1 Feb 1860   4 yrs.

Frank P. Shaw, son of Leonard & Betsy Shaw
    Died: 12 May 1855   3 yrs.

Sarah C. Shaw, wife of Mahlon H. Shaw, WSRC Corp. 16 (1869)
    B: 1836   D: 1904

A field stone next to it

Hannah P. Shaw, daughter of Samuel & Mary Shaw
    Died: 16 Aug 1843   23 yrs. 6 mo.
        "Her days and night of distress
        And weeks of affliction are o'er
        She met with a happy release
        And has gone to be troubled no more."

Several other stones unable to read[193]

---

[193] Notes from the Standish Historical Society, Map #21, pp. 141-42.

Appendix B
Occupants of the Blake Cemetery

Eliab Blake   Died: 12 Mar 1902   77 yrs. 3 mos.

Eunice Blake   Died: 30 Aug 1880   72 yrs. 5 mos.

Eunice, wife of Ithiel Blake
         Died: 15 Aug 1868   84 yrs. 10 mos.

Patience Blake   Died: 20 Apr. 1846   27 yrs.

Ithiel Blake   Died: 28 July 1862   82 yrs. 3 mos.

Ellen, daughter of Clement & Lydia L. Blake
         Died: 9 Apr. 1848   1 yr. 8 mos.[194]

---

[194] Notes from the Standish Historical Society, Map #22, p. 75.

Appendix C
An Alphabetical Listing of All Lot Owners

Last name	First name	Lot(s)
Abbott	Philip E.	52
Anderson	Abraham	64/63
Bangs	Thomas	63
Beck	Thomas	51
Blake	Eliab	51, 64
Blake	Enoch	51
Blake	Ephraim	52
Blake	Ithiel	51
Blake	Reuben	64/63
Bolton	Charles F.	52
Bolton	Edward	52
Boody	Howard H.	52
Bradbury	George	52
Bradbury	Theophilus	64
Brown	Ephraim	52
Busque	Peter J.	37
Butterfield	John	64
Buxton	William	52
Cannell	Philip, Jr.	51, 64
Carter	Ezra, Jr.	52
Chadbourne	Benjamin	52
Clements	Leander	51, 64
Cram	Daniel	51
Crockett	Anna	52
Crockett	Elias	51
Crockett	Enoch	63
Crockett	Ephraim	64/63
Crockett	Henry	51, 52
Crockett	Peter	63
Crockett	Rebecca	51
Davis	Charles	52
Deane	Samuel	63, 52
Driscoll	David	52
Dunn	Christopher	51
Dunn	Nathaniel	51

Elder	Elijah	51
Elder	Isaac	51
Files	Lewis L.	52
Fogg	Daniel P.	37
Fogg	Daniel W.	37
Fogg	Elizabeth S.	37
Fogg	Mary P.	37
Freeman	Gardner R.	52
Freeman	Howard S.	52
Freeman	Joshua, Jr.	37
Freeman	Sarah	52
Gage	Kate M.	37
Gammon	Daniel	51
Gilman	Catherine	52
Gilman	Mary L.	63, 52
Gowen	R. Harold	51, 52
Green	John, Jr.	51
Hanscomb	George H.	52
Harding	John, Jr.	64
Harmon	Priscilla	64/63
Harris	Stephen	63
Haskell	Benjamin, Jr.	51, 37
Haskell	Eleanor	37
Haskell	Rebecca	37
Hasty	James	64
Hasty	Joseph	64
Hasty	Sarah M.	64
Hasty	William H.	51
Hawkins	James	51
Jackson	Percival	51
Jackson	Sarah M.	64
Jackson	Virginia	51
Jerrett	Joseph	64/63
Jewett	Farnsworth F.	37
Jewett	Judith	37
Jewett	Violet K.	37

Jewett	Wilbert S.	37
Jones	Sarah	64
Kemp	Augustus	52
Libby	Alfred/Alford	64/63
Libby	Daniel	52
Libby	George	52
Libby	Wilbert A.	37
Libby	Willie M.	37
Lombard	Jedediah, Jr.	64
Lord	Ivory	37
Mabry	Charles F.	52
Manchester	Cora	52
Manchester	Henry	52
March	Benjamin	64/63
Marshall	James R.	63, 52
Marshall	Shirley E.	63, 52
Merchant	Joseph M.	63
Moody	Eben(ezer)	52
Moody	Lydia B.	52
Newbegin	James	51
Newbegin	John	51
Newbegin	Solomon	51
Noble	Ernest E.	51, 63
North	Elisha	52
Parker	H. Greeley	52
Parker	Joseph	64/63
Parker	Morris	52
Pearson	Eunice	63
Pearson	Lois	37
Pearson	Moses	63, 37
Penfield	Nathan	51
Pierce	Alden	52
Pike	Timothy	51
Plaisted	John	64/63
Plaisted	Samuel	64/63
Plaisted	Simon	64/63
Plummer	Mary C.	52

Appendix C: All Lot Owners

Plummer	Samuel	64/63
Quinby	John	64
Regan	Dorothy	52
Rich	Lemuel 3rd	64
Roberts	George W.	52
Rogers	Isaac	37
Rogers	Wilbur F.	37
Shaw	Albert S.	51, 63
Shaw	Alvin C.	52
Shaw	Ann E.	52
Shaw	Betsy/Elizabeth	63
Shaw	Charles H.	63
Shaw	Eben, Jr.	63
Shaw	Ebenezer, Jr.	51
Shaw	Hannah	52
Shaw	Harriett D.	51
Shaw	Henry S.	52
Shaw	Joseph P.	52
Shaw	Leonard	64/63, 63, 52
Shaw	Lucinda	63
Shaw	Lydia B.	52
Shaw	Mahlon H.	63
Shaw	Nancy H.	63
Shaw	Rebecca Y.	63
Shaw	Rozilla	52
Shaw	Samuel	63
Shaw	Sumner P.	52
Shaw	Winthrop M.	52
Shaw	Zilpah	52
Sheesley	Horace A.	52
Skillings	Benjamin	64
Skillings	Thomas	64
Smith	John F.	64
Smith	Margaret	52
Smith	Owen M.	52
Smith	Owen P.	52

Smith	William W.	63
Swasey	Horatio	51
Tompson	Edward	51
Tompson	William	64/63
Verrill	Harry M.	51, 64
Wescott	Abbie A.	52
Wescott	Charles E.	37
Wescott	Clement P.	37
Wescott	James B.	37
Wescott	Mary	52
Wescott	William, Jr.	52
Whitmore	Fanny	52
Whitmore	John	52
Wood	Benoni	64/63
Woodbury	George A.	52

Index

A

Acker, Jean, 65
Adams, John, 115, 134, 143, 144, 202, 203
Adams, John Quincy, 115, 117, 123, 132, 144, 149, 150
Adams, Samuel, 115, 120, 160, 202
American Academy of Arts and Sciences, 115, 142

B

Baxter, Percival, 3
Blake, Ithiel, 185, 272, 273, 275, 276, 278, 313, 314
Booth, John Wilkes, 191
Bowdoin College, 116, 149, 150, 190, 196, 198
Bowdoin, James, 115, 160
Bradbury, Francis, 122, 131, 132, 143, 144, 148, 150
Bradbury, George, 122, 123, 131, 132, 135, 147, 148, 149, 283, 284, 314
Bradbury, Sarah Jones, 122, 123, 124, 125, 126, 128, 129, 130, 131, 132, 134, 147, 152, 153, 157, 256
Bradbury, Theophilus, 122, 125, 126, 128, 130, 131, 132, 134, 135, 136, 137, 139, 140, 141, 142, 143, 144, 147, 149, 155, 158, 201, 202, 203, 256, 258, 314
Bridge, Camilla Fecteau, xvii, 26, 323
Brown University, 116, 202

C

Cobb, J. Harold, 90, 91, 97, 98
Coca-Cola, 30, 31, 32, 33, 34, 36, 37
Connolly, Michael, xiv, xvii, 310
Coolidge, William D., 58, 60, 61
Cumberland Country, creation of, 134
Cumberland County, creation of, 103, 156

D

Deane, Eunice Pearson, 102, 112, 264, 266, 283, 300, 316
Deane, Samuel, xviii, 14, 102, 110, 111, 112, 113, 114, 115, 116, 117, 118, 119, 120, 121, 133, 146, 157, 158, 201, 202, 264, 266, 282, 283, 284, 300, 314
DeMille, Cecil B., 3
Dlugos, Jim, xi, xvii, 310

E

Edison, Thomas, 56, 57, 58, 59, 60, 61, 226
Edwina, Mother M., 8

F

Falmouth, Burning of, 107, 111, 119, 122, 136, 158
Ferland, Durward, xvi, 3, 21
Franklin, Benjamin, 70, 71, 78

H

Hancock, John, 115, 202
Harvard University, 110, 111, 117, 120, 121, 134, 135, 145, 147, 150, 153, 191
Higgins, Sr. Mary Raymond, xvi, 2, 3, 20
Hobbs, Humphrey, 15, 16, 17

Index

House, David, 3

J

Jesus, 84, 85, 86, 87, 118

L

Lincoln, Abraham, 45, 191, 195
Lombard, Jedediah Jr., 164, 168, 169, 201, 202, 256, 258, 316
Lombard, Jedediah Sr., 164, 165, 168, 201, 202
Louisbourg, 14, 15, 103, 108, 109, 163

M

Madison, James, 115, 149, 202
Maine Historical Society, 105, 108, 119, 120, 121, 132, 136, 152, 162, 163, 173, 191, 192, 197
Maine, Statehood, 15, 117
Mathis, June, 65, 66, 68
Mayflower, 18, 152
McAuley, Catherine, 4, 5, 290, 292, 315
McHugh, Fr. John, 52
McLellan, Cary, 164, 165, 166, 167, 168
McLellan, Hugh, 16, 109, 164, 169
Melville, Herman, 75
Moby Dick, 75, 76, 78
Montauk, USS, 190, 191, 197
Mowatt, Henry, 136, 137, 138, 139, 164

O

O'Brien, Fr. John, 52, 53, 54
O'Brien, Fr. Timothy, 53, 54
O'Toole, Sr. Mary George, xvii, 1, 2, 3, 5, 6, 9, 11, 20

P

Parsons, Theophilus, 132, 135, 136, 144, 150, 158
Pearson, Moses, 13, 14, 15, 18, 19, 102, 103, 104, 105, 106, 107, 108, 112, 122, 134, 153, 155, 156, 158, 161, 163, 170, 171, 175, 264, 266, 271, 282, 284, 300, 304, 316
Pepperell, William, 14, 103

Q

Quinby, John, 108, 155, 158, 159, 160, 161, 162, 163, 256, 258, 317

R

Rambova, Natasha, 66, 67
Rielly, Edward, xii, xvii
Ruppert, Jacob, 38, 39, 40, 41, 42
Russell, Mike, 11, 13, 20, 21, 23
Ruth, George Herman "Babe", 40, 41

S

Sears, Albert, xvi, 13, 14, 15, 16, 18, 19, 20, 104, 106, 107, 109, 152, 157, 169, 173, 174, 177
Shaw, Ebenezer, 18, 102, 170, 171, 172, 175
Shaw, Ebenezer III, 173, 174, 175, 265
Shaw, Ebenezer Jr., 172, 173, 174, 179, 187, 265, 266, 267, 272, 273, 317
Shaw, Leonard, 173, 174, 177, 179, 180, 181, 182, 183, 184, 185, 186, 187, 188, 261, 262, 265, 266, 267, 268, 285, 286, 293, 294, 295, 296, 299, 312, 317

Sheridan, Daniel, xii, xvii
Shirley, William, 14, 15, 103
Silverstein, Robert, 92, 93, 94, 95, 96, 97, 98
Smith, Owen M., 191, 297, 298, 317
Smith, Owen P., 190, 191, 192, 193, 194, 195, 196, 197, 198, 199, 297, 298, 317
Standish Historical Society, 13, 21, 312, 313
Standish, Myles, 18
Strout, Charles, 195, 196
Strout, Sewall, 195

T

Taft, Howard, 3
Tokaz, Fr. John, 52
Toohey, Sr. Mary Xaveria, 2

V

Valentino, Rudolph, 63, 64, 65, 66, 67, 68
Verrill, Harry M., 3, 6, 7, 8, 9, 254, 258, 259, 262, 263, 266, 277, 278, 281, 318

W

Ward, Mother M. Evangelist, 8
Warde, Sr. Frances Xavier, 5
Washington, George, 89, 90, 91, 92, 93, 98, 116, 140, 168, 201, 202
White House, 45

Y

Yankees, New York, 40, 41

About the Author

Steven L. Bridge is a Professor at Saint Joseph's College, where he teaches historical-critical courses on the Hebrew Scriptures, the Christian Gospels, and the Pauline Epistles, among others. He has authored over a hundred articles and several critically-acclaimed books, including *Getting the Gospels*, which was awarded a Starred Review in *Publishers Weekly*. Bridge's research has taken him around the world, including stints in Israel, Jordan, Turkey, Greece, Italy, and Malta. He also oversees the College's International Service Trips to Haiti (since 2004) and Guatemala (since 2006). The College's teams have worked on construction projects, staffed medical and dental clinics, organized children's programs, initiated small business ventures, and distributed thousands of pounds of humanitarian supplies. An amateur geologist and gem cutter, Bridge is a member of the Maine Mineralogical and Geological Society, and has chaired its Annual Gem and Mineral Show at Saint Joseph's College since 2012. In his spare time, Bridge enjoys a wide variety of sports and outdoor activities, and regularly competes in local road races and triathlons. He lives in Maine with his wife, Camilla, and his three daughters.

Made in the USA
Middletown, DE
14 December 2016